LOSS OF INNOCENCE

LOSS OF INNOCENCE

AMERICA'S SCANDALS IN THE POST-WAR YEARS

Melvin E. Matthews Jr.

Algora Publishing
New York

Library of Congress Cataloging in Publication Control Number: —

Names: Matthews, Melvin E., author.
Title: Loss of innocence: the U-2 incident, the quiz show scandal, and the
    beginning of the credibility gap / Melvin E. Matthews, Jr.
Description: New York: Algora Publishing, [2019] | Includes bibliographical
    references and index.
Identifiers: LCCN 2018061462 (print) | LCCN 2019014477 (ebook) | ISBN
    9781628943566 (pdf) | ISBN 9781628943504 (pbk: alk. paper)
Subjects: LCSH: Social values—United States—20th century. | Truthfulness
    and falsehood—United States. | United States—Politics and
    government—20th century. | Trust—United States. | Political
    corruption—United States. | U-2 Incident, 1960—Public opinion. |
    Television quiz shows—United States—20th century—Public opinion. |
    Fraud—United States.
Classification: LCC HN90.M6 (ebook) | LCC HN90.M6 M38 2019 (print) | DDC
    303.3/720973—dc23
LC record available at https://lccn.loc.gov/2018061462

Printed in the United States

Acknowledgement

The author wishes to thank those who helped make this book possible: Julie Abernethy and Chuck Flynn, who helped with technical challenges; Gene Marrano, who edited the manuscript; Robyn Schon, who reviewed the publishing contract; and Fr. George and Miranda Tsahakis who provided financial support.

Table of Contents

INTRODUCTION

On two separate occasions during a six-month interval from November 1959 to May 1960, the American people became aware of what was, for that time, a shocking reality: to their disbelief, they learned that their institutions didn't always tell them the truth.

In the first instance, they discovered that the contestants on the big-money quiz shows, a wildly successful format of '50s television, had been coached; not only had they been supplied the answers to the questions they were asked on-air, they had been coached as to how they were to conduct themselves during their broadcast appearances. The quiz show champs, who had become popular folk heroes, turned out to be fakes.

Shortly thereafter the United States government was caught in a lie regarding the activities of the CIA's U-2 reconnaissance planes overflying the Soviet Union on intelligence-gathering missions. On May 1, 1960, just weeks before a major big-power summit conference was scheduled to convene in Paris, a U-2 was downed over Soviet territory. Initially the U.S. government denied the U-2 was engaged in an espionage mission. But when Soviet Premier Nikita Khrushchev produced indisputable evidence, including the revelation that the U-2's pilot, Francis Gary Powers, was alive and in Soviet custody, President Dwight D. Eisenhower was forced to admit that the U.S. had in fact lied about the U-2's true purpose and that he himself had authorized the overflights. The resulting furor scuttled the scheduled Paris summit and Eisenhower's state visit to the Soviet Union and any chance of improving Soviet–America relations during a tense time in the Cold War.

Both the quiz show scandal and the U-2 incident were played out against the backdrop of the Cold War. Their immediate impact was to call into question some black-and-white assumptions: that Americans told the truth and trusted their government to always do the right thing. The television programming of the era reinforced such notions, as one baby-boomer testified when reminiscing:

> Watching television, drinking delicious hot cocoa, and getting a decoder badge to boot? What boomer doesn't have fond memories of Captain Midnight and his goofy sidekick Icky? Or Buffalo Bob and his honking compadre Clarabelle? Boomers sat in pajamas, mesmerized by a parade of guys in space suits and white hats, spouting truth, justice, and the American way, while in the "real world" Joe McCarthy was busy blacklisting many of the actors who played them.[1]

The Western, which enjoyed the same level of popularity on Fifties television as the quiz show, was especially suited to conveying the simplistic Cold War themes of the time. As one contemporary analyst of this philosophy phrased it: "Though we are a peaceful people at heart, we let no one push us around, and find a warm kinship in reading of the Westerners who wouldn't be pushed either, or who so colorfully retaliated with six-guns, fists, or lariat." The first television Westerns, 1930s B films and serials, followed by productions expressly made for television, were targeted mainly at the juvenile audience and stressed both idealized adult role models the young viewers should emulate and patriotic values.

If Westerns carried subtle Cold War messages, it should come as no surprise then that the era's big-money quiz shows did the same, albeit quite differently. The quizzes arose because one of the sponsors, a cosmetics firm, wanted to best the lipstick sales of a competitor. What made this important was that consumption of capitalist-produced consumer items, a system the United States championed as the superior alternative to the Soviets' economic system, had its perfect outlet via the television medium. Quiz show contestants were "the stars of a consumer society devoted to the marketing of still more lavish goods."[2] Additionally, they were heroes not only with the public but heroes in the Cold War. The quiz shows elevated the intellectual, who, until recently, had been vilified during the McCarthy era, to a stellar place of honor in the United States, a position he had never before held.[3] That standing would become crucial in the midst of the crisis arising from the Soviet Union's successful launching of *Sputnik:* America's number one enemy had made the first foray in space. "The appeal of the programs, with the ris-

---

[1] Richard Croker, *The Boomer Century, 1946-2046. How America's Most Influential Generation Changed Everything* (New York: Springboard Press, 2007), 19-20.

[2] Stephen J. Whitfield, *The Culture of the Cold War* (Baltimore: The Johns Hopkins University Press, 1991), 173.

[3] *The American Experience:* "The Quiz Show Scandal," www.pbs.org/wgbh/amex/quizshow/filmmore/transcript/index.html. 5 January 2007.

ing challenge of Soviet brain power as a backdrop, was ultimately patriotic," theorized novelist John Updike. When the quiz shows were unmasked as fraudulent, it threw the purity of the American system into disrepute.[4]

America's honor was besmirched even more by the U-2 affair. When the United States admitted the fact that Francis Gary Powers' overflight that May day in 1960 was an espionage mission, it shattered the "spirit of Camp David" that had blossomed with Khrushchev's visit to the U.S. the preceding September. Eisenhower appreciated the risks entailed in sending U-2s soaring over the Soviet Union. Ike declared that had the Russians done the same to the United States, he would request a declaration of war from Congress. Urged to employ the U-2 over Russia "to the maximum degree possible" while meeting with advisers in February 1960, Eisenhower declined, arguing that when he journeyed to the Paris summit that spring, he would possess "one tremendous asset": his reputation for truthfulness. In what proved to be prophetic words, he said, "If one of these aircraft were lost when we were engaged in apparently sincere deliberations, it could be put on display in Moscow and ruin my effectiveness."[5]

Until the May Day incident, Americans had viewed spies as operatives working on behalf of America's adversaries.[6] Just as shocking was the discovery that Dwight Eisenhower, a man who frequently asserted the genuine wellspring of America's might was the nation's "moral" and "spiritual" power, had become the first President to publicly concede that this same United States he had praised as so virtuous had indeed lied, not only to the world, but to its own people as well.[7] "That man," commented a journalist early in the Eisenhower presidency, "has an absolutely unique ability to convince people that he has no talent for duplicity."[8] Just the same, Eisenhower's government lied, not only about the U-2, but about its role in toppling foreign governments—though in the latter, the public continued to be misled without knowing it. Eisenhower himself would say, "Our policy is one of careful neutrality and proper deportment all the way through so as not to be taking sides where it is none of our business."[9]

The CIA's activities, moreover, weren't strictly limited to foreign interventions and spy flights. Though legally prohibited from conducting domes-

[4] Whitfield, *The Culture of the Cold War*, 177-78.

[5] Michael R. Beschloss, *Mayday: Eisenhower, Khrushchev and the U-2 Affair* (New York: Harper & Row, Publishers, 1986), 364, 233-234.

[6] *CIA: Hollywood Spyteck*, Discovery Communications, Inc., 2000.

[7] David Wise, *The Politics of Lying: Government Deception, Secrecy, and Power* (New York: Random House, 1973), 33.

[8] Walter LaFeber, *The American Age: United States Foreign Policy at Home and Abroad since 1750* (New York: W. W. Norton & Company, 1989), 520.

[9] Wise, *The Politics of Lying*, 35-36.

tic "security functions," the agency, beginning in the 1950s, opened letters Americans mailed abroad (some 13,000 missives yearly by 1959) and eavesdropped on journalists and other private citizens.[10]

Despite the outcome of the U-2 affair, Eisenhower remained in good standing with the American people who, for the moment, maintained their unquestioning trust in the government.[11] When the true repercussions of government deception finally struck as a consequence of Vietnam and Watergate, Americans would take a second look at their government and become inclined to lend credence to every sort of conspiracy theory, however bizarre, creating what became known as the Credibility Gap. This skepticism, combined with the turmoil and unrest occasioned by the anti-war, youth, and civil rights movements of the '60s, produced a nostalgic yearning for what popular memory saw as the less chaotic Eisenhower years—overlooking the reality that, in those seemingly tranquil times, the quiz show scandal and the U-2 incident laid the foundation for the Credibility Gap.

---

[10] LaFeber, *The American Age*, 520.
[11] Beschloss, *Mayday*, 395.

1. The $64,000 Question and the Beginning of Quiz Mania (1955–1956)

1955 was a memorable year in television history.[12] On January 4, the "Father of the Atomic Bomb," Dr. J. Robert Oppenheimer, who had recently lost his security clearance due to his opposition to the development of the hydrogen bomb, was the subject of the weekly CBS News series *See It Now*. Despite negative outcries from the likes of Hearst columnist George Sokolsky, the broadcast was well received, with *New Yorker* critic Philip Hamburger calling it "a true story of genius."[13]

Among 1955's new programs were the *Johnny Carson Show* and *The Millionaire*. The debut that fall of *Gunsmoke* (CBS), *Frontier* (NBC), and *Cheyenne* and *The Life and Legend of Wyatt Earp* (the latter pair both on ABC) heralded the arrival of the Adult Western. Of this foursome, *Gunsmoke* would be a hardy survivor—airing until 1975.[14]

Significant as these events were, none of them rivaled the excitement and impact of *the $64,000 Question*. Unveiled by CBS on June 7, 1955, and originally intended to be a summer replacement show, it quickly became the hottest, most popular program on television and inaugurated the era of the big-money quiz shows. The appeal of *the $64,000 Question* lay in the fact that it featured "regular" people playing for big bucks by answering questions in categories

---

[12] Gordon F. Sander, *Serling: The Rise and Twilight of Television's Last Angry Man* (New York: Dutton, 1992), 98.

[13] Erik Barnouw, *The Image Empire: A History of Broadcasting in the United States from 1953* (New York: Oxford University Press, 1970), 53-54.

[14] J. Fred McDonald, *Who Shot the Sheriff? The Rise and Fall of the Television Western* (New York: Praeger Publishers, 1987) 52; Robert Metz, *CBS: Reflections in a Bloodshot Eye* (Chicago: Playboy Press, 1975), 203.

they were well acquainted with. These "average Joes" became heroes to the viewing audience, who identified with the quiz players.[15]

From Radio to Television

The quiz show's transition from radio to television signified two changes: one could now see the action and could now win enormous sums of money.[16] The latter notion that big cash prizes originated on the TV quizzes of the 1950s is a bit inaccurate.

Quiz shows first became popular radio fare during the Great Depression. As the 1940s began, 50 quiz shows were on the air. By decade's end, that number had swelled to 200. *Information, Please* invited its audience to submit questions to a panel of experts, the object of the game being to see if the audience could confound the panel. Hosted by Clifton Fadiman, *Information, Please* was not so much a contest but a forum for the personalities of its panel members such as *New York Times* sports columnist John Kieran and humorist Oscar Levant.[17]

ABC radio's *Stop the Music* was noteworthy: while program host Bert Parks telephoned a contestant chosen at random from across the nation, the show's musical cast would begin performing a popular song. When the contestant answered the call, Parks would exclaim "Stop the music!", then ask the contestant to name the song. Should the listener correctly identify the song, he or she would be given the opportunity to name a more difficult "mystery melody" worth as much as $30,000.

For a time, however, it seemed that such giveaway quizzes would become an endangered species. On August 19, 1949, the Federal Communications Commission (FCC) decreed such broadcasts violated the U.S. Criminal Code on lotteries; moreover, stations airing such programs after October 1 would be denied license renewal. Fighting back in court, the networks contended that the FCC lacked the authority to render judgments in the realm of programming decisions. The networks succeeded in court in thwarting the FCC's October 1 decree, but it took years to achieve a final resolution. By the time the issue was finally settled, the lion's share of giveaway shows had faded from the small screen.

---

[15] Harry Castleman and Water J. Podrazik, *Watching TV: Four Decades of American Television* (New York: McGraw-Hill Book Company, 1982), 99.

[16] Kent Anderson, *Television Fraud: The History and Implications of the Quiz Show Scandals* (Westport, Connecticut: Greenwood Press, 1978), 3-4.

[17] *The American Experience:* "The Quiz Show Scandal"/www.pbs.org/wgbh/amex/quizshow/peopleevents/pande05.html 5 November 2007; Lawrence Bergreen, *Look Now, Pay Later: The Rise of Network Broadcasting* (Garden City, New York: Doubleday & Company, Inc., 1980), 178, 181.

Concentrating on less controversial formats, producers now presented shows featuring guest celebrities (*What's My Line?*), humorous antics (*Beat the Clock, Pantomime Quiz*), and revamped parlor games (*Twenty Questions*).

In reality TV game shows were about to enter a new, even more successful era, lavishing astronomical cash prizes on winning contestants—and all because of one man's vision.[18]

Enter Louis Cowan

That man was Louis George Cowan. Born in Chicago, a 1931 graduate of the University of Chicago, where he earned a bachelor's degree in philosophy, Cowan stayed on in the Windy City, where he began working as a publicity agent. He then became a Big Band press agent. It was while working with Kay Kyser that Cowan discovered his true calling: creating quiz shows. With Kyser, he came up with *The College of Musical Knowledge*, which made Kyser's band a long-running fixture on radio. After taking up the radio programmer trade and enjoying some success at it in the Chicago area, Cowan had his first network success with *Quiz Kids*, which featured a panel of uncommonly brainy children who astounded the radio audience with their skills at answering questions.

As the calendar turned onto 1955, Cowan occupied the summit of his profession. As proof of that, he resided in an immense apartment on New York's Park Avenue as well as a huge Connecticut dwelling, and had four shows airing on radio and television—among them radio's award-winning *Conversation*, hosted by *Information, Please* veteran Clifton Fadiman.

One January morning as 1955 got underway, Cowan just happened to be thinking of two seemingly unrelated subjects: Mount Everest and quiz shows. An inspiration occurred to him: merge the two and, from that mixture, create the definitive quiz show.[19]

Cowan modeled his new program after a popular 1940s radio quiz show, *Take It Or Leave It*, where the contestants, in their quest for an increasingly valuable cash prize, had to face a succession of ever more difficult questions. Each player chose a category of questions from a prepared list and could decide at any time to stop the game and take home the money they'd already won or continue playing—taking the risk of losing every dollar they'd previously won. As the game progressed, the monetary value of the questions multiplied, stopping at what was, for that day, the grand prize—$64. Adding three zeroes to the $64 amount, Cowan created *The $64,000 Question*.[20]

---

[18] Castleman and Podrazik, *Watching TV*, 99.

[19] Anderson, *Television Fraud*, 4-5.

[20] Anderson, *Television Fraud*, 6.

Sixty-four thousand dollars was a stupendous amount of money for 1955. The contestant who correctly answered the $64,000 question on Cowan's show would become instantly wealthy. The key to the success of Cowan's idea would be the existence of those apparently mundane people who truly possessed exceptional knowledge. Lou Cowan viewed his proposed show "as emblematic of the American dream," in that it offered people two opportunities—the chance to acquire instant wealth and to win the respect of their fellow citizens. "It reflected, one of his sons said years later, a 'White Christmas' vision of America, in which the immediate descendants of the immigrants, caught up in their optimism about the new world and the nobility of the American experiment, romanticized America and saw it as they wanted it to be."[21]

Once the format of the show had been conceived, it became necessary to find a sponsor for it. Revlon Products Corporation and Nash-Kelvinator Corporation, were in the market for a new program. Cowan offered them half of the sponsorship; Revlon was the only one to accept. Convincing CBS to come aboard was the next hurdle. Being an independent producer unconnected with the network, Cowan collaborated with Walter Craig of William H. Weintraub and Company to accomplish this.[22]

The $64,000 Question debuted at 10:00 P.M., Tuesday, June 7, 1955. An attractive girl escorted contestants to the stage where they were quizzed by emcee Hal March. The starting point for the game was $64. From there the contestant could continue playing and winning more money so long as he gave the right answers to harder questions—or he could choose to leave the game, taking whatever winnings he had already amassed. In the interval between the $32,000 and $64,000 questions, the contestant was given reference books in his category to study in preparation for the final contest and, in the event he decided to answer the grand prize question, could bring an expert with him for help.

There was an IBM sorting machine that shuffled the question envelopes—but only for the initial questions. When the quiz reached the $1,000 mark, the questions became the responsibility of Ben Feit, a bank officer with the firm that had Revlon's banking account. Seated behind a desk, two uniformed security guards on either side, Feit handed March the big-money questions. In the event a contestant wanted to answer the questions valued at $8,000 and beyond, he then entered a soundproof isolation booth. At this stage of the game, should the contestant fail to correctly answer a question, he received a consolation prize: a Cadillac convertible.

---

[21] David Halberstam, *The Fifties* (New York: Villard Books, 1993), 644.
[22] Anderson, *Television Fraud*, 6.

All of the superstars *the $64,000 Question* sired experienced instant celebrity. During the course of his appearances on the show, Gino Prato had to close his shoe repair shop when multitudes of fans and bunco artists descended upon the establishment. He accepted a $10,000-a-year job as a traveling "good will ambassador" for the American Biltrite Rubber Company, maker of rubber heels.

In addition to being the guest of honor at four Shakespeare festivals, Redmond O'Hanlon received a job offer from a university as lecturer on his literary pastime. Myrtle Power, another $32,000 winner (her specialty was baseball), covered the World Series for the Hearst International News Service and served a one-week stint as CBS *Morning Show* sports analyst.

Adding to *The $64,000 Question* phenomenon was the role of the press. The attention the latter accorded the quiz was, for a television show at the time, unprecedented, and extended beyond America's shores. The show came in for varying degrees of severe rebuke, mainly that it was appealing to the public's "covetous instincts" and materialistic qualities. On the other hand, *New York Times* television critic Jack Gould haled the quiz for elevating the status of the common man: "Television complains continually that it doesn't know where its material will come from next. . . . Yet, meanwhile it overlooks the bottomless reservoir of intelligent people."[23]

When it came to overseeing the questions asked contestants on *The $64,000 Question,* that task was the responsibility of Bergen Evans, the same Bergen Evans who had presided over *Down You Go,* which had also been created by Louis Cowan. In carrying out his duties on *The $64,000 Question,* Evans collaborated with associate producer Merton Koplin and a trio of unnamed authorities in sports, music, and science. Occasionally Evans went to New York City, where he and Carlin went over the questions.

Contestant selection was done through three avenues, letter writing being the most common approach. Each week the show received thousands of letters from would-be contestants; from that mountain of letters, the show's staff mail sorters chose roughly 10%, or they hoped, no more than 500. The letter-writing process yielded roughly two contestants a week.

Naturally, the phenomenal success of *The $64,000 Question* inspired parodies on other shows—both comedic and dramatic.[24] In addition to revitalizing the big-money quiz show, Cowan's mega-hit creation, along with other developments, were changing the nature of American television in the mid-1950s.

---

[23] Anderson, *Television Fraud,* 20-22.
[24] Castleman and Podrazik, *Watching TV,* 101.

Ringing Down the Golden Age

One man who witnessed first-hand the direction television was taking as a consequence of these changes had his first inkling of what the future held the very evening first *The $64,000 Question* broadcast aired. Edward R. Murrow, the host of *See It Now*, was in the control room, preparing for that week's installment of the weekly CBS News documentary series immediately after the new quiz show. Also present in the control room that evening was *See It Now* producer Fred Friendly: "Murrow, who seldom watched any show preceding ours, was riveted and horrified by what he saw," Friendly was later to write of the occasion. "His instincts, accurate as usual, made him realize before the half-hour was over that the carny, midway atmosphere heralded by the big-money quizzes would soon be dominating the airwaves." Leaning over to Friendly, Murrow asked, "Any bets on how long we'll keep this time period now?"[25]

If one wanted to choose a specific date that marked the end of television's Golden Age of the 1950s (which *See It Now* was so much a part of), it could well be June 7, 1955, when *The $64,000 Question* debuted, followed by the beginning of *See It Now*'s slow fade to black.

The success of *The $64,000 Question* showered onto many of those connected with the show. Louis Cowan was elevated to the presidency of CBS, while the bank official responsible for the handling of the questions on the quiz became a vice-president at Manufacturers Trust. The greatest beneficiary of all was the show's sponsor, Revlon. When Revlon began sponsoring Cowan's quiz show, sales took a breathtaking leap forward. In the initial six-month season, Revlon boosted its sale from $33.6 million to $51.6—a rise of 54%. The company stock rose from 12 to 20. The following year's sales figures were even more staggering—$85.7 million. By 1958 Revlon was the undisputed leader in its field. When questioned as to whether its sponsorship of *The $64,000 Question* played a role in helping Revlon become number one, Martin Revson merely stated, "It helped. It helped."[26]

When Revlon agreed to sponsor *The $64,000 Question*, the latter was, to all appearances, an above-the-board quiz show. Such purity didn't last long. Entertainment Productions, Incorporated (EPI) took over production and, unknown to the public, exercised control over both the questions and the contestants. The objectives of this control wee threefold: to find those contestants who would attract and sustain the interest and devotion of the audience; to keep these contestants on air as long as possible; and banish

---

[25] Fred W. Friendly, *Due to Circumstances Beyond Our Control* (New York: Random House, 1967), 77.

[26] Halberstam, *The Fifties*, 646-647.

contestants who failed to win the public's favor. To accomplish this, Merton Koplin would meet with each contestant, discuss the player's area of expertise, gleaning something of an idea of what the contestant knew, then tailor the questions asked of them in such a way as to ensure their continued presence or expulsion from the show. Reportedly some of the contestants had no idea they were being manipulated.

In the wake of the success of *The $64,000 Question*, others sought to secure a piece of the action with big-money quizzes of their own. NBC's *The Big Surprise* was created by Steve Carlin just after Lou Cowan's departure for CBS.

Carlin viewed *The Big Surprise* as a "novelty show with human interest as a major factor." Contestant selection depended on some atypical action they had done, such as "either a small act of kindness or a heroic deed." The show's initial $100,000 winner, Ethel Park Richardson, scored by answering a series of questions on the subject of American folklore submitted by Governor Goodwin Knight of California. *The Big Surprise*, though successful, never equaled the popularity of *The $64,000 Question*.

In April 1956, the sister show of *The $64,000 Question* made its debut. *The $64,000 Challenge* was intended to exploit both the success and the contestants of the original $64,000 quiz.[27] As *Challenge*'s original host Sonny Fox explained: "Here *Question* had spent all this time making these people stars and then . . . there was nothing to be done with them and that didn't sit right. So they said, '. . . If we bring them back and have them challenged, then we have a second crack at them . . . It was a way of merchandising . . . and profiting from what happened on *Question*."[28]

Its shortcomings notwithstanding, by the conclusion of the 1955-1956 season, *The $64,000 Challenge* had occasionally topped *Question* in the ratings wars. Like EPI's other shows, *Challenge* was secretly controlled. The fact that the producers had to ride herd on two competitors and their winnings made *Challenge* most likely the most tightly regulated quiz of its day.

Despite occasionally falling out of the top spot in the ratings, *The $64,000 Question* remained the most popular show aired regularly on the small screen during the 1955-1956 seasons. When it came to explaining both the television industry and the general public's fascination with quiz shows during the 1950s, historian Kent Anderson said the explanation was quite simple: economics. Despite the gigantic sums of prize money, the quizzes numbered among the least costly shows to produce—primarily because they utilized inexpensive sets, required no actors to pay, and were live telecasts. The weekly cost of producing *The $64,000 Question* at the point when the show stood at

[27] Anderson, *Television Fraud*, 29-33.
[28] www.pbs.org/wgbh/amex/quizshow/filmmore/transcript/index.html 5 January 2007.

the pinnacle of its first summer's triumph was approximately $25,000—a sum that included prize money. On the other hand, a filmed program, such as *I Love Lucy*, cost at best $35,000 weekly. "In spite of the rapid inflation in the cost of television time as the 1950s wore on, the quizzes remained inexpensive relative to the industry."[29]

When it came to the public at large, Anderson noted that the big-money quiz show mania occurred during an interval preceded by the McCarthy era in the early to mid-'50s and followed by the launching of the Soviets' *Sputnik* in October 1957.[30] The term "intellectual" had fallen into disrepute during the McCarthy years, when it acquired an ominous, un-American coloring.[31] Intellectuals, according to this negative image, were New Dealers and internationalists who had pursued policies harmful to the United States and which had allowed the Soviets to make gains after World War II. Joe McCarthy personified this resentment at a basic, crude level: that of the less fortunate kid who battled his way from humble beginnings to the top and who would teach the elitists a lesson. "It is not the less fortunate . . . who have been selling this nation out," he thundered, "but rather those who have had all the benefits—the finest homes, the finest college educations, and the finest jobs in government. The bright young men who are born with silver spoons in their mouths are the worst."[32]

This anti-intellectual backlash found expression in popular culture. In the 1952 Paramount film *My Son John*, a small-town Irish-Catholic mother turns her son in to the FBI when she learns he has a key to an apartment occupied by a suspected espionage agent. In contrast to his brothers, big blond football players who loyally support their country by serving in the Korean War, John, a State Department employee, is a dark, sensitive intellectual type with a deferment. His father, a Legionnaire, believes John is in league with "scummies"—the elder's appellation for Communists. A college student, John hob-knobbed with the literati, used "two-dollar" words, didn't play football, and, most grievously, ridiculed his parish priest. Added to these sins, John may also be homosexual and a junkie. To calm his mother's suspicions about him, John goes so far as to swear on the family Bible that he is not now nor has he ever been a member of the Communist Party."

---

[29]Anderson, *Television Fraud*, 36-38.

[30]*Ibid*, 38.

[31] Eric F. Goldman, *The Crucial Decade—And After. America, 1945-1960*. (New York: Vintage Books, 1956, 1960), 123.

[32] Louis Bromfield, The Editors of Time-Life Books, *This Fabulous Century: Volume VI. 1950-1960* (New York: Time Inc., 1970), 50.

John's last-minute realization of the error of his ways cannot redeem him: His erstwhile comrades murder him on the steps of the Lincoln Memorial.[33]

The anti-intellectualism of the era focused primarily on Illinois Governor Adlai Stevenson, the 1952 Democratic presidential candidate. An Eisenhower partisan characterized the average Stevenson supporter as having "a large oval head, faceless, unemotional, but a little bit haughty and condescending." The characterization gave rise to a new term for intellectuals: *egghead*. Presently, novelist Louis Bromfield observed that:

> There has come a wonderful new expression to define a certain shady element of our population. Who conceived the expression, I do not know. . . . It seems to have arisen spontaneously from the people themselves. . . . [It means] a person of intellectual pretensions, often a professor or the protégé of a professor . . . superficial in approach to any problem . . . feminine . . . supercilious . . . surfeited with conceit . . . A doctrinaire supporter of middle-European socialism . . . a self-conscious prig . . . a bleeding heart.[34]

Bromfield offered a dire warning: should Stevenson triumph on Election Day: "The eggheads will come back into power and off again we will go on the scenic railway of muddled economics, Socialism, Communism, crookedness and psychopathic instability."[35] Stevenson was the darling of those later characterized as "the new G.I. Bill intellectuals."

Eisenhower, by contrast, was the idol of traditional well-to-do Republicans and upright, small-town dwellers. If Stevenson's appeal lay with those who read *The New Yorker*, *Harper's*, and the *Atlantic*, Eisenhower, as writer Michael Arlen noted, was the candidate of the *Saturday Evening Post* and *Reader's Digest*.[36]

By 1955, when *The $64,000 Question* debuted both the Korean War and McCarthy were now history, thus the ugly tensions both precipitated had ended. The quiz shows presented a new diversion. Yet, as Kent Anderson observed, the notion that such broadcast fare played a critical role in rehabilitating intellectualism just in time for the *Sputnik* crisis "is probably extreme," yet, he continues, the same Americans who trembled when the Soviet satellite successfully orbited had only recently been enraptured by the college instructor-quiz contestant who became the most renowned of the quiz champs. Such erudition on the part of the quiz show contestants

---

[33] *My Son John*, Douglas T. Miller and Marion Nowak, *The Fifties: The Way We Really Were* (Garden City, New York: Doubleday & Company, Inc., 1975, 1977), 317-318.

[34] *This Fabulous Century. Volume VI*, 50; Goldman, *The Crucial Decade–And After*, 224.

[35] Goldman, The Crucial Decade—And After, 224.

[36] Halberstam, *The Fifties*, 234.

may not have been of the very sophisticated variety, "but the appearance of such television fare gave the populace an interest in knowledge, perhaps even an appreciation for the time when knowledge and its public support would turn serious after it was thrust into the renewed context of the cold war."[37] Post-*Sputnik*, American scientists and intellectuals were in demand in Washington. Away from the halls of power, this new appreciation for *egg-heads* could be seen in colleges and universities, where enrollments in science programs rose by more than a third—the largest increases in math and physics. High school geeks were now more popular than athletes. New Jersey, Tennessee, and Texas high school officials announced that those students excelling academically would be honored, like football heroes, with letters for their sweaters.[38]

The fact that many of these new "average Joe" idols weren't, in fact, all that average, that some of them were highly educated, was kept under wraps. The true reason for the quiz shows' popularity may well have been that through the successes of the contestants, the television audiences found validation for their own sense of celebrity and nobility. Quiz shows additionally mirrored the American notion that one could rise above modest circumstances to achieve material affluence, which, in the quiz shows' case, could happen immediately without having to invest prolonged effort to achieve material affluence. The greatest attraction the quiz shows held for people was money.[39]

Whichever theory one subscribed to, what was certain was that the reign of the big-money television quiz shows was far from over—nor was the behind-the-scenes deception they perpetrated on the public.

---

[37] Anderson, *Television Fraud*, 38-39.
[38] Michael D'Antonio, *A Ball, A Dog, and A Monkey. 1957–The Space Race Begins* (New York: Simon & Schuster, 2007), 209-210.
[39] Anderson, *Television Fraud*, 39-40.

2. Open Skies and the Beginning of the U-2 Program (1954–1957)

Over a month after the debut of *The $64,000 Question*, on July 14, 1955, President Dwight D. Eisenhower departed the United States aboard the presidential plane *Columbine III* for Geneva, where the first summit meeting of American and Russian leaders since 1945 was set to convene the following Monday.

"Eleven years ago, I came to Europe with an army, a navy and an air force," Eisenhower said in his opening statement after arriving at Geneva Airport. "This time, I come with something more powerful . . . the aspirations of Americans for peace." Under a heavy security screen, Eisenhower was then driven to the eighteen-century villa on Lake Geneva that was to serve as the presidential residence for the duration of the conference. After the arrival of the Soviet delegation, headed by Nikita Khrushchev and Nikolai Bulganin, the conference got underway at the Palais des Nations.[40]

The high point of the summit came at the afternoon session the following Thursday, when Eisenhower presented a bold, dramatic proposal for disarmament:

> I have been searching my heart and mind for something that I could say here that could convince everyone of the great sincerity of the United States in approaching this problem of disarmament.
>
> I should address myself for a moment principally to the delegates from the Soviet Union, because our two great countries admittedly possess new and terrible weapons in quantities which do give rise in

---

[40] Beschloss, *Mayday*, 100-101.

other parts of the world, or reciprocally, to the fears and dangers of surprise attack.

I propose, therefore, that we take a practical step, that we begin an arrangement, very quickly, as between ourselves—immediately. These steps would include:

To give each other a complete blueprint of our military establishments, from beginning to end, from one end of our countries to the other; lay out the establishments and provide the blueprints to each other.

Next, to provide within our countries facilities for aerial photography to the other county—we to provide the facilities within our country, ample facilities for aerial reconnaissance, where you can make all the pictures you choose and take them to your own country to study; you to provide exactly the same facilities for us and we to make these examinations, and by this step to convince the world that we are providing as between ourselves against the possibility of great surprise attack, thus lessening danger and relaxing tension.

Likewise we will make more easily attainable a comprehensive and effective system of inspection and disarmament, because what I propose, I assure you, would be but a beginning. . . .

The United States is ready to proceed in the study and testing of a reliable system of inspections and reporting, and when that system is proved, then to reduce armaments with all others to the extent that the system will provide assured results.[41]

Before presenting his proposal, Eisenhower had declared, "I'll give it one shot. Then if they don't accept it, we'll fly the U-2."[42] The U-2 Eisenhower referred to was a newly developed plane designed to penetrate the airspace of the Soviet Union for the purpose of taking high-level photographs of Soviet military installations and other items of interest to the United States Government. The Soviet rejection of Eisenhower's invitation to allow aerial inspection of each other's countries to lessen fears of a surprise attack made U-2 flights over Soviet territory inevitable. The results of these overflights ultimately precipitated a Cold War incident that dashed Ike's hopes for a disarmament treaty between the United States and the USSR before the end of his presidency.

---

[41] Dwight D. Eisenhower, *The White House Years. Mandate for Change, 1953-1956* (Garden City, New York: Doubleday & Company, Inc., 1963), 520; William Manchester, *The Glory and the Dream: A Narrative History of America, 1932-1972* (New York: Bantam Press, 1975), 750.
[42] Beschloss, *Mayday*, 105.

Eisenhower's Fears

Surprise attack was only one of the motivations prompting Eisenhower to seek a disarmament agreement with the Soviets. The other was his concern that the costs of maintaining an enormous military machine in time of peace would prove ruinous to the American economy. .

At the conclusion of a triumphal postwar visit to Moscow in 1945, then General Eisenhower told American journalists, "I see nothing in the future that would prevent Russia and the United States from being the closest possible friends." Unlike General Patton and Field Marshal Montgomery, he did not give time to the notion of rearming the German Army in the event war broke out between Russia and the West. He heatedly brushed aside a reporter's query on the subject and told the U.S. House Military Affairs Committee that "Russia has not the slightest thing to gain by a struggle with the United States. There is no thing, I believe, that guides the policy of Russia more today than to keep friendship with the United States."

Eisenhower also held the conviction that those soldiers who had sacrificed their lives following his wartime commands had to have done so for something more than a mere restoration of the old world order that Americans abhorred. Working together, East and West could devise a better order—one free of hostile confederations; one where the United Nations would regulate nuclear weapons. The establishment of mutual trust would be the initial step toward making this vision a reality. More than other Western political leaders, Eisenhower opposed war as a problem-solving mechanism. Having witnessed the near dissolution of the army during the interwar years, when Americans had been isolationist toward the outside world, he pondered how long his fellow countrymen—especially his fellow Kansans and other heartland Americans—would accept the price necessary to sustain the peacetime military machine. A conservative in monetary matters, Ike worried that rendering America insolvent to erect such a martial colossus would have the consequence of destroying the very society it was supposed to protect. During a White House meeting in 1946, called to assess the likelihood that the Soviets would initiate an armed assault against Western Europe, Eisenhower expressed his opinion that such an event was unlikely and would be disadvantageous to the Soviets. But, as the Cold War deepened and Eastern Europe fell under Moscow's domination, Eisenhower ultimately changed his views. A September 1947 entry in his diary contained the observation: "Russia is definitely out to communize the world. . . . We face a battle to extinction between the two systems."

By the time he ran for President in 1952, Eisenhower had recast himself as a Cold Warrior, though one who still hoped that East-West hostilities could be resolved. While declaring that if he were elected, the U.S. would never acknowledge Soviet control of Eastern Europe, Eisenhower also pledged that only peaceful measures would be used to roll back the Iron Curtain.

The death of Russia' longtime Communist despot Joseph Stalin early in Eisenhower's administration signaled a turning point. Advocating friendlier relations with the United States, the new Russian leader Georgi Malenkov declared: "There is not one disputed or undecided question that cannot be decided by peaceful means."[43]

Malenkov's declaration precipitated a "peace offensive" on the Soviets' part—one that required a response from Eisenhower. During an Oval Office meeting in late March 1953 with aide Emmet Hughes, Ike said, "Look, I am tired . . . of just plain indictments of the Soviet regime. . . . Just *one* thing matters: what have *we* got to offer the world? . . . If we cannot say these things—A, B, C, D, E, F, G, just like that—then we really have nothing to give, except just another speech. For what? Malenkov isn't going to be frightened with speeches. What are we *trying* to achieve?" Continuing, he told Hughes: "*Here* is what I would like to say. The jet plane that roars over your head costs three-quarters of a million dollars. That is more money than a man . . . is going to make in his lifetime. What world can afford this sort of thing for long? We are in an armaments race. Where will it lead us? At worst, to atomic warfare. At best, to robbing every people and nation on earth of the fruits of their own toil."

Eisenhower desired to see the world's resources utilized to furnish "all the good and necessary things for a decent living," not additional guns. To help realize this, Ike wanted to deliver an address that would *not* include the customary indictment of the Soviet Union. He directed Hughes and another White House aide, C. D. Jackson, to begin working on a speech on peace.[44]

The result of their labor was delivered in Washington to the American Society of Newspaper Editors on April 16, 1953.[45] As Eisenhower began his remarks, he experienced a sudden attack of ileitis. Despite his discomfort, he forced himself to continue. Following some ritual Soviet bashing, Eisenhower began his plea that the nations of the world set out on a new path. The Cold War had divided humanity and filled it with fear.

---

[43] *Ibid.*, 67-71.

[44] Stephen E. Ambrose, *Eisenhower. Volume II: The President* (New York: Simon and Schuster, 1984), 91-93.

[45] Herbert S. Parmet, *Eisenhower and the American Crusades* (New York: The Macmillan Company, 1972), 277.

"The worst to be feared and the best to be expected can be simply stated. The *worst* is atomic war. The *best* would be the this: a life of perpetual fear and tension; a burden of armies draining the wealth and labor of all peoples; a wasting of strength that defies the American system or the Soviet system or any system to achieve abundance and happiness . . .

"Every gun that is made, every warship launched, every rocket fired signifies, in the final sense, a theft from those who hunger and are not fed, those are cold and are not clothed.

"... This is not a way of life at all, in any true sense. Under the cloud of threatening war, it is humanity hanging from a cross of iron."[46]

Eisenhower's greatest fear concerning the arms race—and his most compelling reason to seek disarmament—was a surprise nuclear attack. In an effort to retard the arms race, Eisenhower in late 1953 appeared before the United Nations with his Atoms for Peace proposal, whereby the United States, the Soviet Union, and Great Britain would jointly contribute from their nuclear stockpiles to a UN atomic agency which would utilize these donations for peaceful endeavors. Such contributions would slow the arms race at an early phase—minus the on-site inspections the Soviets had always vetoed. "Eisenhower," wrote historian Michael Beschloss, "knew that the United States could afford to reduce its stockpile by several times the Soviet rate and still remain ahead." Privately Eisenhower believed that a superpower required only a small number of bombs to possess sufficient deterrent power; "the Russians wanted nothing badly to risk losing the Kremlin." The Soviets, however, wouldn't tolerate a continual American lead in nuclear stockpiles.[47]

Directly related to the protection of the United States against such a catastrophe was the need to know precisely what the enemy was up to. After assuming the Presidency in 1953, Eisenhower had frequently expressed dissatisfaction about the absence of hard intelligence information regarding the USSR—be it Kremlin politics or Russian military strength. Eisenhower's displeasure in this area stemmed from his experience during World War II. The Battle of the Bulge played an especially instructive role. Recalled one White House staffer, "where the Germans secretly amassed a major force unbeknownst to Allied intelligence, deeply impressed upon him the value as well as the limitations of intelligence, together with the dangers of be-

---

[46] Geoffrey Perret, *Eisenhower* (New York: Random House, 1999), 453-454.
[47] Beschloss, *Mayday*, 72-73.

ing caught off guard."[48] Eisenhower's sense of frustration was heightened by the absence of any advanced notice of the Soviets' test of an H-bomb in August 1953—a mere nine months after America's first test of such a weapon. "Our relative position in intelligence, compared to the Soviets," he privately lamented, "could scarcely have been worse. The Soviets enjoyed practically unimpeded access to information of a kind in which we were almost wholly lacking." The open nature of American society explained how easy it was for the Soviets to obtain such data. Information regarding some U.S. nuclear facilities was available in print, while accurate, small-scale maps of the United States were easily obtainable in local bookstores and service stations. The key to America obtaining equivalent data regarding the USSR, Eisenhower concluded, was aerial reconnaissance. The Soviet military arsenal appeared to be even more formidable when the Soviet Bison heavy bomber made its debut at the 1954 May Day parade in Moscow. The number of such aircraft on view that day appeared to be far more than what was believed available. The evidence suggested that the Soviets possessed both the H-bomb and the air force necessary to deliver such weapons to the United States. In reality, the Soviets had misled American intelligence into thinking that a gigantic bomber force existed, when the same squadron repeatedly flew over Red Square every few minutes.[49]

To prevent a nuclear Pearl Harbor, Eisenhower in March 1954 directed the Office of Defense Mobilization's Science Advisory Committee to find a solution to the threat. Out of the committee's labor emerged the Technological Capabilities Panel (TCP) Report—also known as the "Killian Report" (after Committee Chairman and MIT president James F. Killian) and the "Surprise Attack Study." The panel recommended the highest importance be accorded to the United States Air Force's intercontinental ballistic missile (ICBM) program. It called for development of an intermediate range ballistic missile (IRBM) capable of being launched from land or ship, the swift construction of a distant early warning (DEW) line in the arctic, a strong and balanced program on the interception and annihilation of ballistic missiles, the greater utilization of science and technology in techniques of waging peripheral conflicts, and increased intelligence capabilities. "We *must* find ways," declared committee member Edwin H. Land, the inventor of the Polaroid camera, "to increase the number of hard facts upon which our intelligence estimates are based, to provide better strategic warning, to minimize

---

[48] Philip Taubman, *Secret Empire: Eisenhower, the CIA, and the Hidden Story of America's Space Espionage* (New York: Simon & Schuster, 2003), 25.

[49] Christopher Andrew, *For the President's Eyes Only: Secret Intelligence and the American Presidency from Washington to Bush* (New York: HarperCollins Publishers, 1995), 221.

surprise in the kind of attack, and to reduce the danger of gross overestima-tion of the threat."[50]

Aerial reconnaissance was not a new idea. The earliest known instance was that of French Army Captain J.M.J. Coutrelle who, in 1794, utilized teth-ered manned balloons during the battle of Fleuries.[51] In the early months of the Civil War, Abraham Lincoln witnessed a demonstration by Thaddeus S.C. Lowe, a twenty-eight-year-old balloonist and self-styled professor, who, while occupying a balloon five hundred feet above Washington, telegraphed a message to the President via a cable linking the balloon to the ground. Lin-coln threw his support to the creation of a balloon corps comprising seven balloons and nine balloonists—all under Lowe's direction. Lowe's balloon corps scored a major success during the Peninsula campaign when it located an enormous aggregation of Confederate soldiers preparing to attack before the battle of Fair Oaks, Virginia. Despite such successes and the fact that the balloon corps won over some supporters in the military, its life-span was short, mainly because both the balloon trains and their gas generators were too cumbersome for rapid movement and was dissolved in June 1863.[52]

The first use of an airplane for reconnaissance in wartime occurred in 1911 when an Italian captain flew his monoplane over Ottoman positions near Tripoli. All the major combatants of World War I employed reconnaissance planes. By war's end, at least one fourth of all aircraft seeing service in that conflict were employed for photography purposes. The first known case of clandestine aerial reconnaissance occurred during the period immediately preceding World War II when British and French commercial airline pilots secretly photographed Germany's military preparations. After Pearl Harbor, aerial reconnaissance fully matured and played a crucial role, furnishing the Allies the major share of their intelligence information.[53]

In the immediate aftermath of the Soviet acquisition of the atomic bomb in 1949, the CIA's Office of Special Operations (OSO) began infiltrating agents into the Soviet Union for the purpose of reporting data on military movements that indicated that a Soviet nuclear attack on the West was in the works. Agents were placed within Soviet territory by air drops (the favored method) but also by land and sea. Recruits for these assignments were drawn from emigre groups and displaced-persons camps in Europe as well as from those who had recently defected from the Red Army. During the ensuing five years, these agents gathered information regarding military

---

[50] Walter A. McDougall, …The Heavens and the Earth: A Political History of the Space Age (New York: Basic Books, Inc., 1985), 115-116.

[51] Beschloss, Mayday, 76.

[52] Andrew, For the President's Eyes Only, 20.

[53] Beschloss, Mayday, 76.

intelligence targets from the Baltic Coast to Sakhalin in the Sea of Japan. The majority were eventually captured; when this happened their transmissions included a pre-arranged signal indicating they were now in Soviet hands. The OSO agents in Germany played along to keep the agent alive and breathing as long as possible. Others simply quit reporting, possibly because they had discarded both their radios and espionage assignments. Though the OSO operation established that the Soviets weren't preparing for immediate hostilities against the West, the reports on Soviet strategic military potential the operation generated were hardly satisfactory, with a trained scientist or engineer the sole people capable of deciphering the information within. Aerial reconnaissance was the best option.[54]

Reconnaissance flights commenced during the Truman administration. Originating in Alaska, they flew across the Bering Strait, then along the coast of northern Siberia. Flying along or near Soviet territory, reconnaissance aircraft could acquire considerable data regarding Soviet air defenses, including radar and communications systems. Other warplanes equipped with electronic sensors identified Soviet radar installations, studying their signals as Soviet defenders surveyed the skies, providing war planners in Washington an inkling of what American aircraft could expect should they attack Soviet territory. These limited intelligence-gathering missions were followed, in the early 1950s, by deliberate violations of Soviet airspace.

The true magnitude of these missions would not be known until many years later, when the veil of secrecy surrounding them was removed. They were the only aspect of the Cold War where Soviet and American forces actually came to blows militarily. The families of those crew members who disappeared on such flights never knew if their loved ones were killed when their planes were attacked or if they endured protracted imprisonment by the Soviets.[55]

Both American and British intelligence were vitally interested in the Soviet missile test site at Kapustin Yar, a town situated some sixty-five miles east of Volgograd, on the Western border of the Kazakh Soviet Socialist Republic. Anglo-American intelligence first became aware of the facility's presence in the spring of 1947; the following year the installation became the target of a British intelligence operation: British agents, impersonating archaeologists, went to northern Iran, where they conducted electronic surveillance of the facility. By 1953 the same installation had acquired heightened significance: reports of Soviet missile advances were such that an overflight of Ka-

---

[54] G.J.A. O'Toole, *Honorable Treachery: A History of U.S. Intelligence, Espionage, and Covert Action from the American Revolution to the CIA* (New York: The Atlantic Monthly Press, 1991), 463-464.

[55] Taubman, *Secret Empire*, 46-47.

pustin Yar became a matter of critical importance. A Royal Air Force RB-57, the reconnaissance version of the British Canberra twin-jet tactical bomber, was chosen for the mission which took place in July 1953. After flying out of West Germany and then crossing the Ukraine and the Russian republic, the plane flew down the course of the Volga, took photographs of the Kapustin Yar facility, then flew south before reaching the terminus of its flight: Iran. While the photos taken proved advantageous, the RB-47 had almost been intercepted—the plane reportedly bore numerous bullet holes when it landed. Additional missions over the Soviet Union would require a plane able to fly at far greater altitudes.[56]

It was this matter that prompted retired Marine General Philip Strong to consult Kelly Johnson of Lockheed. Johnson's solution was to outfit the Lockheed F-104 with wings like a tent. Johnson then collaborated with four Lockheed engineers to devise a spy plane that would fly over seventy thousand feet for as much as four thousand miles, then presented both the plan and a construction schedule for turning out thirty such planes at a briefing for Pentagon representatives in Washington. The Air Force had already authorized study contracts to Bell, Martin and Fairchild for work on a high-altitude plane. Though the Johnson's proposed plane received scrutiny, some Air Force men didn't believe it would work. Bell received tentative authorization to proceed.

Johnson was undeterred. Among others he approached in Washington was CIA Director Allen Dulles, who found the idea of Lockheed building a high-altitude reconnaissance plane for his agency while the rival Air Force project deflected attention from it a very attractive notion. Trevor Gardner, assistant to the Secretary of the Air Force for research and development, showed Johnson's proposal to the Killian panel's Edwin Land, then invited Johnson to return to Washington "to see whether I could make any sense," as Johnson would subsequently remember. The Johnson plan won Land and his fellow panel members over. Not waiting for the Killian panel to formally submit its proposals to President Eisenhower, Land and Killian took it upon themselves to see Ike immediately. Meeting with Eisenhower in November 1954, the two men argued that even if the amount of intelligence information deep flights over Russia produced was slim, the flights might motivate Russian leaders to divert funding from offensive to defensive weapons and prove just how ineffective Moscow's preoccupation with secrecy was. Perhaps the latter point would convince Russia to ratify disarmament accords with sufficient inspections. To Killian and Land's surprise, Eisenhower immediately tentatively authorized the project—providing that the Air Force not fly the

---

[56] O'Toole, *Honorable Treachery*, 465.

missions. The Air Force should provide assistance, but it would be the CIA's responsibility to actually fly the missions.

Meeting with his top defense and intelligence people early in the morning of November 24, 1954, Eisenhower was formally asked to authorize the development of thirty planes for roughly $35 million. The CIA, Allen Dulles explained, would be unable to handle the total sum without attracting attention to it. Secretary of Defense Charles Wilson agreed that the Pentagon would pick up the tab for a "substantial part" of the bill.

"Go ahead and get the equipment," Eisenhower said, "but before initiating operations, come in to let me have one last look at the plans." The meeting had taken only fifteen minutes.

Later that same day, Trevor Gardner, the man who had advocated the project over strong opposition from the Air Force and others, made a long-distance call to California: "Kelly, begin cleaning out that hangar this afternoon!"[57]

The actual construction of the CIA's new reconnaissance plane took place in the Skunk Works facility at the Lockheed Aircraft Corporation in Burbank, California. The challenge was formidable. In the thin air over seventy thousand feet, jet engines would hardly function. As the plane would be flying over hostile territory, which precluded refueling along the way, it had to remain aloft for a period of up to ten hours. In all likelihood, the engine, at such extreme altitude and distance, would consume fuel in such quantity that a conventional fuel tank would be of insufficient size, while a sufficiently large tank would so weigh down the aircraft it couldn't remain aloft at such a high altitude.

The craft devised essentially was a glider equipped with a Pratt & Whitney turbojet engine. The latter would save fuel by turning on and off—meaning that during its protracted time aloft over such long distances, the plane would function periodical as a glider and a jet, all the while using hardly more than a thousand gallons of fuel. The Angel, as the plane was initially dubbed, was fashioned with titanium and other lightweight materials. Its final wing design weighed a mere three pounds per square foot, one third that of a conventional aircraft. Still the lengthy wingspan presented problems when it came to installing the landing gear and aircraft stability on landing and takeoff. The engineers recommended placing the primary landing gear within the fuselage and pogos, the latter tiny landing gear, near the wingtips. When the plane took off, the pogos would fall away, to be reattached by ground crews running next to the plane when it lost its forward momentum after landing. One author felt that watching the plane takeoff and land was

---

[57] Beschloss, *Mayday*, 79-84.

similar to viewing cop drills in a Keystone comedy. Seeing the plane for the first time, one man called it a black vulture on crutches.[58]

Perfecting a new telescopic lens was the responsibility of James Baker, a member of the Land intelligence committee. Eastman Kodak developed a new Mylar film sufficiently thin to be carried aloft in huge quantities. Under Land's supervision, Hycon manufactured the gargantuan camera that oscillated from horizon to horizon, "covering a swath of land literally 750 miles wide—" approximately "one tenth of this in three dimensions." Eighty-eight days after the program began the test version of the plane was ready. The final cost was $19 million. Placed in the "U" classification—"U" meaning utility planes—the craft was christened with the name it would become famous under: the U-2. In reality, it wasn't the first plane to be so named. That distinction belonged to a pre-World War II single-engine Soviet biplane![59]

"Open Skies"

Knowing that the U-2 would soon be operational, Eisenhower decided to present his proposal for joint Soviet-American aerial inspection at Geneva.[60] The last time Soviet and American leaders had sat down together at a conference table had been in 1945. Not even Stalin's passing diminished Eisenhower's own hesitancy to meet with the Soviets. He did not wish to inflame the ire of the Republican Old Guard who likened summitry with Yalta—the latter, in their minds, the ultimate example of FDR's sellout to Stalin. Moreover, Eisenhower doubted whether the Soviets sincerely wanted to negotiate or merely desired a summit encounter as nothing more than an opportunity for them to wage a propaganda campaign.[61]

When it came to sitting down with Communist chieftains, Eisenhower remained reluctant "unless there was some likelihood that the confrontation could produce results acceptable to the peoples of the West." After becoming President, Eisenhower continued to declare his readiness to meet with anyone, anywhere, so long as there existed, "any logical reason to hope" such a gathering would improve the international situation.[62]

Late in 1954, Eisenhower made Soviet ratification of a long delayed Austrian peace treaty a precondition for a summit. The Soviets consented to the Austrian accord six months later. A big power meeting of the United States,

---

[58] Beschloss, *Mayday*, 90-92; Brugioni, *Eyeball to Eyeball*, 20.

[59] Beschloss, *Mayday*, 92-93.

[60] Stephen E. Ambrose, with Richard H. Immerman, *Ike's Spies: Eisenhower and the Espionage Establishment* (Garden City, New York: Doubleday & Company, Inc., 1981), 270.

[61] Chester J. Pach, Jr., and Elmo Richardson, *The Presidency of Dwight D. Eisenhower* (Lawrence, Kansas: The University Press of Kansas, 1991), Revised Edition, 108-109.

[62] Eisenhower, *Mandate for Change*, 504-505.

the Soviet Union, Great Britain, and France was then announced. One who was "terribly worried" about the impeding summit, Secretary of State John Foster Dulles, felt there were no quick answers to Cold War problems and feared the British and French might too easily accede to Soviet demands. These concerns, however, paled in comparison to what Foster Dulles feared his own boss, President Eisenhower, might do. Prior to Geneva, Dulles divulged his worries to former presidential assistant C.D. Jackson: he worried that Ike might misconstrue Soviet cordiality as sincerity and give his consent to something that would "upset the apple cart. I would hate to see the whole edifice undermined in response to a smile."

Dulles sought to educate the President in how the latter should conduct himself at Geneva. Instead of making new proposals, Eisenhower should merely seek to foment a mood favorable for additional talks. When discussing such weighty matters as German reunification or Soviet influence in Eastern Europe, Eisenhower shouldn't compromise and instead suggest that these issues and others be discussed by the Big Four foreign ministers.

Dissenting with such counsel, Special Assistant Nelson A. Rockefeller felt that Eisenhower "was going to have to take the initiative [at Geneva]. It had to be something that immediately electrified everybody."[63] In June 1955, acting with Eisenhower's blessing, he assembled eleven experts at Quantico Marine Base in Virginia to prepare a set of recommendations.

Verification had been the major impediment to realizing an arms control agreement. Just before the Rockefeller team got down to business at Quantico, the Russians acknowledged for the first time that on-site inspections was a necessity for any such accord to work. The West greeted the Soviet acknowledgment with skepticism; after all, in Korea, the Chinese had thwarted such inspection by diverting their forces where the surveillance teams couldn't see them.

Aerial inspection presented another option. Though the idea wasn't new, during the tense early years of the Cold War, few held hope that it would win Soviet approval. Possibly things would be different at Geneva. "Open Skies," as the plan became known, was among the recommendations the Rockefeller group presented to Eisenhower at the close of its deliberations, but no immediate action on the proposal was forthcoming.

The CIA took an interest in the matter. Many in the Agency would have opted for legal flights over the Soviet Union, as this course would avoid an international incident with the Russians and spare the American government and the CIA any embarrassment. The openness of America meant that any intelligence benefits the Russians would reap from Open Skies would be

---

[63] Pach and Richardson, *The Presidency of Dwight D. Eisenhower*, Revised Edition, 109-110.

comparatively scant while the United States would reap a harvest. The U-2, Allen Dulles observed, was "ideally suited" for this purpose.

In the period immediately preceding the Geneva meeting, Rockefeller urged Eisenhower to make the Open Skies proposal a major one at the conference. Foster Dulles opposed it. Recalling a White House meeting between himself, Ike, and the Secretary of State, Rockefeller explained that the latter counseled Eisenhower to utilize the forthcoming summit only to "identify the problem areas" for referral to the foreign ministers. "You can't do that," Rockefeller objected. "Nobody is going to take seriously that General Eisenhower, President Eisenhower comes all the way to Geneva to a summit meeting and says, 'I am going to identify the problems.'"

Just the same, Eisenhower found Open Skies attractive on several counts: It would burnish America's peaceful reputation without risking vital concessions to the Soviets and it might speed the way to arms control. If the Russians accepted, the plan would spare him from ordering U-2 planes to violate Soviet air frontiers. If they refused, illegal overflights would be more justifiable.

Eisenhower temporarily placed Open Skies on the back-burner—an action possibly meant to pacify Foster Dulles. Before departing for the summit, however, the President directed Rockefeller to stand by in Paris in case he was needed at Geneva.[64]

Meeting with Congressional leaders, Eisenhower stressed that he wouldn't enter into accords that needed no clearance from Congress. Eisenhower then laid his case before the American people in a televised address three days later, delivered just minutes before he boarded his flight for Geneva. While conceding that the conferees couldn't resolve the dilemmas posed by the arms race during one meeting, the President nevertheless pledged that the Geneva deliberations would be conducted in an atmosphere of conciliation, toleration, and understanding. "I say to you, if we can change the spirit in which these conferences are conducted we will have taken the greatest steps toward peace, toward future prosperity and tranquility that has ever been taken in the history of mankind." Eisenhower concluded his remarks by requesting that all Americans pray for peace that Sunday.[65]

The opening sessions of the conference didn't augur well for its success. Eisenhower challenged the Russians on the most serious issues dividing East and West: free elections in a unified Germany, Eastern Europe, Communist expansionism. The German people, Khrushchev rejoined, "have not yet had time to be educated to the great advantage of Communism," while Bulganin

---

[64] Beschloss, *Mayday*, 98-100.
[65] Pach and Richardson, *The Presidency of Dwight D. Eisenhower*, Revised Edition, 110.

stated that Soviet "internal affairs" like Eastern Europe were beyond consideration at the conference. As a beginning toward arms control, Eisenhower proposed that possibly they should seek "dependable ways to supervise and inspect military establishments so that there can be no frightful surprises." When the President's proposal failed to elicit a Russian response, Eisenhower summoned Rockefeller to the conference.

The night before Eisenhower submitted the Open Skies proposal to the Russians, the President's villa was the scene of a gathering of top-level American officials: Secretary of State Dulles, Admiral Radford, General Alfred Gruenther of NATO, and Rockefeller. When Eisenhower mentioned Open Skies, the latter received Radford and Gruenther's backing. The military chief's sanction apparently caused Foster Dulles to change his opinion of the plan. Speaking to the President's son John the following morning, Rockefeller said, "You have *got* to be in the conference this afternoon. Your dad is going to throw a bombshell." When the time came for the bombshell, Rockefeller whispered to the younger Eisenhower, "Now listen, here it comes."[66] As soon as the President completed his statement, an unexpected clap of thunder shook the conference which "was plunged into Stygian darkness. Our astonishment," Ike wrote, "was all the greater because in our air-conditioned and well-lighted room there had been no inkling of an approaching storm. For a moment there was stunned silence," followed by Ike's observation that he hadn't dreamed he was so eloquent as to turn off the lights. "This was rewarded with laughter, only because it was an obvious break in the tension, and in a few moments the lights came back on."[67]

Bulganin said it had "real merit" and warranted "further study." Whatever hopes Eisenhower may have derived from Bulganin's words were soon dashed by Khrushchev: "I disagree with our chairman. The trouble is, this is just espionage. We do not question your motives in making this proposal but who are you trying to fool! . . . This kind of plan would be fine for you because it would give your strategic forces the chance to gather target information and zero in on us." When Eisenhower's old wartime comrade-in-arms Zhukov joined the discussion, Ike said he was certain that Zhukov would have given "a great many rubles to have had good photography of the enemy's positions," to which Khrushchev and Zhukov rejoined that such a thing may have been true, but that was during the war.

Eisenhower urged the Russians not to dismiss the idea. What he sought was to "outline one first concrete step" which would "dispel fear and suspicion and thus lighten international tension by reassuring people against

---

[66] Beschloss, *Mayday*, 102-103.
[67] Eisenhower, *Mandate for Change*, 521.

the dangers of surprise attack." This would provide evidence to the world of their "joint intention not to fight against each other." Khrushchev adhered to his position that the plan constituted nothing but a "bald espionage plot." Eisenhower now clearly knew who Russia's true leader was.[68]

What became known as "the spirit of Geneva," gave rise to the impression that foreign relations were taking a turn in a new direction and lessened the fear of nuclear war. While a subsequent foreign minsters' conference would handle the details of genuine negotiations concerning the proposals that came out of the Geneva summit, it was Open Skies, not Soviet initiatives that produced the major headlines emanating from the Big Four meeting transforming Eisenhower into an anti-war soldier. Even the Russians, according to journal accounts, believed that Ike, unlike Foster Dulles, was a man of peace. In a post-summit address to the American people, Eisenhower revealed that agreement seemed close at hand, "increased visits by the citizens of one country into the territory of another, doing this in such a way as to give each the fullest opportunity to learn about the people of the other nation."[69]

In truth the conference did nothing to end or impede the Cold War. This isn't to say that the summit was totally devoid of real progress: it allowed subsequent U.S. Presidents to confer with their Soviet counterparts without being demonized with the appeasement tag. Eisenhower, the man whose standing as the leader of the victorious anti-Hitler coalition military forces allowed him to conclude the Korean armistice on the same terms Truman had sought without being vilified- could have sat down with the Red demons of the Kremlin at the conference table. At a post-summit White House meeting with Congressional leaders, Eisenhower said both sides sincerely sought a new beginning. He also revealed a secret not to be "let out of this room": Khrushchev and Bulganin had asked to visit the United States. "They would come fast. They want to be more in the public eye." The President's initial instinct had been to invite them but Foster Dulles "thought I had been impulsive enough," so Ike informed Bulganin that he would give thought to the proposed visit.[70]

Meanwhile the U-2 was being prepared for its initial test flight.

Taking Flight

On July 15, 1955, just before the opening of the Geneva conference, the first U-2 was completed. There followed a series of tests. Eight days later the

---

[68] Beschloss, *Mayday*, 103.
[69] *Ibid.*, 406-407.
[70] Beschloss, *Mayday*, 104-105.

U-2 was dismantled and packed into special shipping containers; the latter were then loaded aboard a C-124 cargo plane situated in an out-of-the-way area of the Burbank airport which, followed by Johnson in another aircraft, flew to the U-2's secret desert test facility. Once there, the plane was reassembled and readied for flight.[71]

Known variously as Groom Lake, Watertown Strip, or Paradise Ranch, the test facility was a dry lake bed in Nevada, within the atomic test area and adjoining the Nellis Air Force base gunnery range.[72] On July 29, 1955, Tony LeVier strapped himself into the U-2's cockpit to initiate a series of dry runs along the runway. Chosen by Johnson, LeVier was Lockheed's foremost test pilot and had flown more than a dozen of the company's new aircraft, including the F-94 Starfire interceptor and the F-104 Starfighter into the sky for the first time. At the slow ground speed specified for the tests, the U-2 wasn't expected to become airborne. The plane, however, failed to perform as expected: during the second run, as LeVier accelerated toward the maximum speed Johnson specified, 70 knots, the U-2 did indeed take-off because of the remarkable lift produced by the sailplane design. It continued flying with the engine essentially operating at idle.

Accompanying Johnson in a ground vehicle that followed the U-2 down the runway was the plane's main flight test engineer, Ernie L. Joiner. "The airplane disappeared in a cloud of dust and sand," he recalled. "We could see those long flexible wings flapping about. As we frantically chased after it, I thought Kelly was going to have a heart attack."

As the U-2 finally stopped, the overhead brakes, which appeared too small for the plane, caught fire and was extinguished by Johnson and Joiner. The former's log-entry for the day merely noted: "No harm done. Airplane was subjected to terrific test. Pogo sticks worked real well."[73]

The U-2's first real test flight, again with LeVier at the controls, took off at approximately four P.M., August 4, against a backdrop of rapidly forming enormous black thunderclouds. In LeVier's account of the flight:

> I took her up to eight thousand feet, with Kelly following behind me in a T-33 piloted by my colleague Bob Mayte. I got on the horn: "Kelly, it flies like a baby buggy." Rain was starting to splatter the windshield, so we decided to cut the first flight short because of the weather. Kelly was getting edgy as I circled around to make my approach for a landing. "Remember, I want you to land it on the nose wheel." I said I would. I came down as gently as I knew how and just

---

[71] Ben R. Rich and Leo Janos, *Skunk Works: A Personal Memoir of My Years at Lockheed* (Boston: Little, Brown and Company, 1994), 133-134.

[72] Brugioni, *Eyeball to Eyeball*, 24.

[73] Taubman, *Secret Empire*, 142-144.

touched the nose wheel to the ground and the . . . airplane began to porpoise. I immediately pulled up. "What's the matter?" Kelly radioed. The porpoising effect could break up that airplane—that was the matter. I told him I just touched the . . . thing down and it began to porpoise on me. He told me, "Take it around and come in lower than last time." I did that exactly and the . . . thing started to porpoise again. I gunned it again. By now it's really starting to get black and the rain and wind are kicking up. Kelly is in full panic now. I can hear it in his voice. He's afraid the fragile airplane will come apart in the storm. He yells at me, "Bring it in on the belly!" I say to him, "Kelly, I'm not gonna do that." I came around the third time and I held the nose nigh, just like I had wanted to, and put her down in a perfect two pointer. Bounced a little, but nice enough.[74]

The testing phase uncovered problems not only with the U-2 itself but with the suits and additional gear the pilots would have to wear while in flight. Pilot nutrition also presented challenges. The ultimate solution was to have the pilot administer food and water to himself via a plastic tube that was inserted through the opening of the helmet's face plate. "Liquids were stored in a plastic bottle and food (much like baby food) was stored in toothpaste-like tubes and squeezed through the tube as desired. Commonly used foods were applesauce, peaches, beef and gravy. Liquids used were water and fruit juices. The food and liquid were normally carried in a pocket of the leg of the pilot's coverall which was worn over the partial pressure suit."[75]

Curtis LeMay and other Air Force generals had initially opposed the U-2; now, as the plane came to fruition, they suddenly wanted to run the U-2 program themselves. Nothing doing, said CIA director Allen Dulles and Richard Bissell. "I wanted this project very much," Bissell would later write. "It was a glamorous and high-priority endeavor endorsed not only by the president but by a lot of very important scientific people on the outside. It would confer a great deal of prestige on the organization that could carry it off successfully." President Eisenhower, who had previously made it plain that he didn't want the Air Force running the U-2 program, again sided with the CIA. "I want this whole thing to be a civilian operation. If uniformed personnel of the armed forces of the United States fly over Russia, it is an act of war, legally, and I don't want any part of that."

Eisenhower had stipulated that although prospective U-2 pilots would be drawn from the Strategic Air Command (SAC), they had to obtain civilian status and fly under contract with the CIA.[76] The recruitment routine

---

[74] Rich and Janos, *Skunk Works*, 135-136.
[75] Brugioni, *Eyeball to Eyeball*, 24-25.
[76] Ambrose, *Ike's Spies*, 270.

had a clock-and-dagger quality about it. U-2 pilot candidates went to motels where they were asked to fly for the Agency.

After receiving aliases and bogus addresses from the Agency (the candidates worked to memorize this information), the recruits were directed to register at Washington's Du Pont Plaza, where they took rooms and waited for a summons. When the latter came, they were instructed to report to another room, which a CIA operative examined for listening devices. To prevent others from hearing their conversations, a radio was turned up high. After complaining about the deficiencies of the border flights, Bill Collins produced a picture of the plane they would be flying. When someone turned off the screaming radio to hear better, an annoyed Collins fell silent until the radio was turned up again.

Apparently every pilot candidate received authorization for top secret, yet as they viewed themselves as pilots instead of secret agents, they found the cloak-and-dagger atmosphere amusing. To the displeasure of some, all were required to submit to a lie detector test. Every time a meeting with Collins in Washington was held, a different hotel was used. When the men traveled, they did so in groups of one to four, occasionally with Collins; occasionally without.

The next stop was Albuquerque—and the Lovelace Clinic, where the staff subjected the recruits to a strenuous physical examination. Once the recruits passed the Lovelace ordeal and an FBI security investigation, they officially became part of the U-2 program. Under the terms of their contracts, they were bound to the CIA for a period of eighteen months—$1,500 a month while they were in the United States; $2,500 a month overseas. The pilots were promised reinstatement with the Air Force with no time lost toward elevation in rank or retirement.[77]

Money alone failed to provide sufficient explanation for why someone would want to fly the U-2 with all the attendant dangers. Neither did simple patriotism—though the latter was a welcome quality. What Bissell sought were those who enjoyed living on the edge and disdained the prospect of death. They were also to be people who shunned recognition in favor of anonymity—the more of the latter quality the better.[78]

Watertown Strip received its first batch of U-2 pilots in November 1955. At night they played pool and poker; by day they broke the world's known altitude record (65,889 feet) flying to Canada, Texas, Wyoming, Tennessee, Baja California. The only thing wrong with flying to such altitudes, one pilot

---

[77] Beschloss, *Mayday*, 108-109.
[78] Matthew Brzezinski, *Red Moon Rising: Sputnik and the Hidden Rivalries that Ignited the Space Age* (New York: Time Books, 2007), 122; Halberstam, *The Fifties*, 619-620.

remembered, was, "You couldn't brag about it." The CIA took the pilots to a safe house in the East where they were trained in escape and evasion.

By the spring of 1956, the initial group of U-2 pilots had almost completed their training and nine planes, a sufficient number to comprise a U-2 squadron abroad, had been fabricated. Other components of the program, including an improved Pratt & Whitney J57 engine less likely to flame out, as well as photographic equipment, were falling in place. By this time knowledge of the U-2's existence had been disclosed to a select few members of Congress—the latter having footed the bill for the program through the CIA's budget for more than a year without knowing what purpose the money was spent for. Allen Dulles had briefed the ranking members of the Senate Armed Services Committee about the new plane. Dulles also informed ranking members of the House Appropriations Committee. These four men were the only members of Congress who would officially know of the U-2 and the reason for its existence until the Powers incident in 1960.

A small number of key members of Congress who were apprised of CIA operations made certain the Agency received sufficient funds through secret accounts concealed in Defense Department appropriations.

By the end of March 1956, the U-2 had reached an altitude of 73,000 feet. To make certain Eisenhower understood how valuable the plane truly was, Bissell had it photograph Ike's Gettysburg, Pennsylvania, farm; the resulting pictures revealed some of Eisenhower's cattle and their feeding troughs. The detail they produced astonished the President.

A suitable cover story for the U-2's operation would have to be devised before the first planes were stationed abroad. It was decided that the U-2 would pose as a high-altitude weather research craft under the management of the National Advisory Committee of Aeronautics (NACA), later to become NASA. In the event a U-2 went down over unfriendly territory, it would be announced that the plane had been conducting weather research at the time of the incident. Upon learning of the cover story just before the U-2's initial penetration of Soviet airspace, both Killian and Land advised that should a plane be downed, Washington should assume complete responsibility for the affair, justifying the flights as a means to prevent surprise attack. On May 1, a C-124 transport carrying four disassembled U-2s arrived at Lakenheath air base in East Anglia; once there, the U-2s were assembled. This was followed, on May 7, by an announcement in Washington from NACA chief Hugh Dryden that a new aircraft developed by Lockheed and flown by the Air Force Air Weather Service would analyze the natural forces occurring at high altitude. For the public's benefit, Detachment A, as the U-2 squadron was known, was christened the 1st Weather Reconnaissance Squadron,

Provisional. Provisional Air Force units weren't obligated to report to higher headquarters.[79]

Permission to place the U-2s at Lakenheath, a SAC base, had been granted by British Prime Minister Anthony Eden. An event soon after caused him to reconsider. In the spring of 1956 Khrushchev and Bulganin paid a goodwill visit to Great Britain. The trip marked Khrushchev's first visit to the West and was viewed by many as a dress rehearsal for a later trip to the United States. The Soviet cruiser *Ordzhonikidze* had conveyed the Russian leaders to Britain and had docked at Portsmouth harbor. Anxious to continue the cordial relations begun at the Geneva summit conference, Eden forbade British intelligence to initiate any operations against the Russian vessel during Khrushchev and Bulganin's visit. The Admiralty was interested in the pitch of the cruiser's screws. A "free-lance" frogman, Commander Lionel Crabbe, "offered" his services for the assignment.

During an evening dinner, a Russian asked the First Lord of the Admiralty, "What was the frogman doing off our bows this morning?" No one ever saw Crabbe alive again. Subsequently his body, minus its head, washed ashore. The evidence indicated he had been murdered by Soviet counterintelligence agents waiting for him in a secret compartment beneath the ship. The furor resulting from the episode caused Eden to change his mind about basing the U-2s in Britain: "This isn't the moment to be making overflights from here," he informed Washington.

Seeking a new staging area, Bissell approached West German Chancellor Konrad Adenauer, who green-lighted the relocation of the U-2 operation to Wiesbaden.[80]

Eden wasn't the only Western leader to have second thoughts about the U-2. So was Eisenhower—the man who had initiated the program. By 1956, with the plane ready to commence operations, making a decision to begin reconnaissance missions mandatory, Eisenhower had good reason to hold back on deployment. With a slight improvement in Soviet-American relations evident, Ike was in no hurry to spoil a further detente by sending the new spy plane over Soviet frontiers, especially if the possibility existed that such flights would be observed and downed. Such fears had to be weighed against compelling reasons for obtaining solid information concerning the Soviets' military might: there was the need both to ascertain that strength and to quiet the mounting domestic political tempest generated by the issue of how satisfactory America's own defenses were. The accusation that the

[79] Taubman, *Secret Empire*, 166-168.
[80] Beschloss, *Mayday*, 112, 116-117.

Russians were acquiring military supremacy could well be an effective Democratic campaign issue in the 1956 elections.[81]

Political pressure notwithstanding, Eisenhower withheld deciding to initiate U-2 operations when Allen Dulles conferred with him on the subject on May 28, 1956. The President's concern centered on the ramifications of dispatching an American reconnaissance plane, even an unarmed, non-military craft, into Soviet airspace. "Such a decision," he said, "is one of the most soul-searching questions to come before a President. We've got to think about what our reaction would be if they were to do this to us." In such an event, the United States would endeavor to shoot the intruder out of the sky. What Eisenhower desired were guarantees that the Soviets would be unable to easily monitor the U-2 or shoot it down. Test flights over the United States revealed that American radar was incapable of regularly monitoring the plane and numerous centers unable to even spot it. The CIA had frequently promised Eisenhower that Moscow's radar network, which had been constructed with equipment furnished by the Allies during the war, wouldn't detect the U-2. Nevertheless, according to a study prepared that spring by the CIA's Office of Scientific Intelligence, detection was likely. Yet the evidence indicates that Eisenhower was never told about this new finding.

Had the CIA informed him of its revamped appraisal, Eisenhower may well have further delayed authorizing the U-2's initial reconnaissance mission, or even terminated the program altogether. He wrote in his memoirs that based on what he had been told concerning Soviet air defenses, he was certain that "in the then-existing state of radar efficiency and the inability of fighter planes to operate at altitudes above some fifty thousand feet, U-2 reconnaissance could be undertaken with reasonable safety."

Eisenhower had also received CIA assurance that should the Soviets succeed in downing a U-2, it was unlikely that the pilot would survive, providing the Russians indisputable proof that the overflights were run by the United States. Leaving nothing to chance, the Agency gave the pilots suicide pills, with the option of bringing them along during flights over Soviet territory; they weren't under orders to use them. The pills were discarded when one pilot mistakenly reached for one, thinking it a Lemon Drop he used to moisten his throat during the lengthy missions and were replaced with a tiny needle containing a shellfish toxin.

Using existing presidential authority for Air Force flights over Eastern Europe, Bissell decreed that the first U-2 mission to be flown over the Soviet bloc—covering East Germany, Czechoslovakia, and Poland—was to occur June 20, 1956. Before dawn that day, a U-2 piloted by Carl Overstreet took

---

[81] Taubman, *Secret Empire*, 169.

flight from the Wiesbaden facility; the mission went off without a hitch and the resulting photographs arrived in Washington two days later.

Even though he now possessed authorization to conduct deep overflights of the Soviet Union, Bissell still had to notify West German Chancellor Adenauer that they were in the offing and had to wait until General Twining wrapped up a visit to Moscow, where Khrushchev invited him to attend the Moscow Air Show that began June 23. Khrushchev's guest asked that the overflights be delayed until after his visit was over.

On July 2, Bissell approved two additional overflights of Eastern Europe, covering Czechoslovakia, Hungary, Romania, East Germany, Poland, and Bulgaria, then, along with Dulles' aide General Cabell, briefed the President, during which time they reported on the June 20 mission. Eisenhower wanted to know if that overflight had registered on Eastern European radar. In reply, Bissell said that while some observation had occurred, radar operators had made the erroneous assumption that Overstreet had flown at 42,000 feet, nearly four miles lower than its genuine altitude. With the detection issue still weighing on his mind, Ike requested further info concerning the other flights over Eastern Europe.

Eisenhower authorized a ten-day interval for operations, to begin July 4. Designated Mission 2013, the first overflight would enter Soviet airspace above Belorussia and, from there, fly north to Leningrad to photograph numerous military airfields and the naval shipyards that turned out Soviet submarines. Mission 2014 was slated for Moscow, site of the factory that built the Bison bomber, and the bomber test-flight center at Ramenskoye, scene of the Bison's initial sighting three years earlier. Photographing a missile plant and a rocket-engine facility were also part of Mission 2014's agenda.[82]

At 6 P.M., July 3, Bissell entered the U-2 Operations Center in Washington. The U-2 base in West Germany had received word that "we may be flying a mission, and this will be the flight plan and you'd better get pilots, navigational aids and everything else set up." Bissell found that "the boys had laid out a flight directly to Moscow, ninety-degree turn, then directly over Leningrad, then down the Baltic coast—all coastal, air radar installations."

The six o'clock meeting was "the major briefing and a full review of weather," Bissell explained. "If everything looked good, a single code word went to the field saying, 'The mission is on, the flight plan as transmitted is approved.'" Bissell instructed them to flash the code word to West Germany. When Bissell returned to the Ops Center a half-hour before midnight, "The weather was still good, so I sent the 'go' message."

---

[82] *Ibid.*, 176-183.

Simultaneous with the U-2's initial deep penetration of Soviet territory, Nikita Khrushchev, in keeping with the spirit of Geneva, was attending the American Embassy's annual Independence Day reception, hosted by the American ambassador to Russia, Charles Bohlen. The latter, though aware of the U-2 project, didn't know that the plane's initial flight over Moscow was being made that very day. This allowed him plausible deniability: he could candidly state that he was completely in the dark about the overflight should it become public knowledge.[83]

The third U-2 overflight of the Soviet Union occurred on July 8. In the cockpit that day was Marty Knutson, who had been the first pilot chosen for the U-2 program:

> I flew over Leningrad and it blew my mind because Leningrad was my target as a SAC pilot and I spent two years training with maps and films, and here I was, coming in from the same direction as in the SAC battle plan, looking down on it through my sights. Only this time I was lining up for photos, not a bomb drop. It was a crystal-clear day and about twenty minutes out of Leningrad I hit pay dirt. This was exactly what the president of the United States was waiting to see. I flew right over a bomber base called Engels Airfield and there, lined up and waiting for my cameras, were thirty Bison bombers. This would prove the worst, I thought. Because the powers that be back in Washington feared that we were facing a huge bomber gap. I proved the gap—or so I thought. As it turned out, my pictures were rushed by Allen Dulles to the Oval Office. For several weeks there was real consternation, but then the results by other flights began coming in and my thirty Bisons were the only ones spotted in that whole massive . . . country, so our own people began to relax a little and we turned out attention to their missile production. I flew hundreds of missions for the agency after that, but that moment over Engels Airfield I considered the most important of any ride I took[84]

On July 10, Moscow's ambassador to Washington lodged an official protest with the State Department concerning pirate flights by "a U.S. Air Force twin-engine plane" originating from West Germany. The protest, which mentioned exact times, dates and routes, declared that the encroachments were apparently "intentional and for purposes of reconnaissance." Moreover, they were conducted at a moment "when relations between governments are improving and when mutual confidence is growing." The protest assigned the blame for the violations to "Reactionary circles hostile to the cause of

---

[83] Beschloss, *Mayday*, 121, 122.
[84] Rich and Janos, *Skunk Works*, 146, 148-149.

peace" who were "worried by the relaxation of mutual tensions." State Department spokesmen denied any knowledge of such overflights.

Drafting a reply to the Soviet protest on July 11, Secretary of State Dulles telephoned his brother with it; the latter replied, "Fine—perfect—good luck!" Reviewing the draft, Eisenhower requested that Foster Dulles "button it up" with the additional explanation that U.S. flight plans "carefully exclude such overflights as the Soviet note alleges."

While attending the Bastille Day reception at the French Embassy in Moscow, Bulganin asked Ambassador Bohlen if he was aware of the overflights, to which Bohlen replied that he possessed "no information whatsoever" about the matter. The Kremlin, Bulganin continued, possessed "indisputable evidence" from radar proving the U.S. encroachment of Soviet airspace: "This is a very serious matter." Soviet Marshal R.A. Rudenko said the Kremlin hadn't downed the intruders out of its desire not to heighten international tensions, but should the flights continue, it would take "all necessary measures." Eisenhower summoned CIA director Dulles to the White House.[85]

Accompanying Dulles to that meeting were the initial batch of photographs taken by the U-2—all of which originated from the first overflight mission. Bissell recalled:

> It took us four days to get our hands on the photographs from that first mission. I remember vividly standing around a long table with Dulles next to me, both of us chuckling with amazement at the clarity of those incredible black-and-white photos. From seventy thousand feet you could not only count the airplanes lined up at ramps, but tell what they were without a magnifying glass. We were astounded. We had finally pried open the oyster shell of Russian secrecy and discovered a giant pearl. Allen rushed with the first samples over to the Oval Office. He told me that Eisenhower was so excited he spread out the entire batch on the floor and he and Allen viewed the photos like two kids running a model train.[86]

Yet, at the same meeting, Eisenhower complained to Dulles that the CIA had promised him that "not over a minor percentage of these [flights] would be picked up," and told the CIA director that he had "lost enthusiasm" for the U-2 project. Eisenhower continued that if Moscow overflew the United States, "the reaction would be drastic." Another source of presidential concern was how the Americans would react if they were to learn their government was blatantly violating international law. "Soviet protests were one thing; any loss of confidence by our own people would be quite another.

[85] Beschloss, *Mayday*, 124-125.
[86] Rich and Janos, *Skunk Works*, 165.

We'd better stand down more or less indefinitely," Eisenhower told Dulles. "Don't start again until you get permission." Going forward, the President would personally review every proposal for a U-2 mission before clearing it.[87]

"So we had very, very tight ground rules," Bissell explained, "very tight control by the President. Then, once the mission was approved, it was my responsibility to watch the weather forecasts three times a day, and select the actual time, and then notify all concerned that the mission was about to take off."[88]

Covert operations such as the U-2 afforded Eisenhower the means to accomplish his objectives in the foreign policy realm without disaffecting domestic or international public opinion—that is unless or until such operations became public knowledge. Eisenhower felt the U-2 performed a significant role early on. In 1955 Air Force intelligence estimates asserted that the Soviet Long Range Air Force would by decade's end occupy a more powerful position than SAC. Production of Bear bombers during late 1956 was estimated at twenty-five per month. The estimates also held that the number of Bison bombers in the Soviet air force by 1959 or 1960 would be six hundred to eight hundred. Largely owing to the data produced by the U-2 missions, these ominous estimates were regularly diminished during 1957 and 1958. By 1959 the Soviet air force possessed a combined total of fewer than two hundred Bisons and Bears.[89]

In August 1956 the Second Weather Observational Squadron, Provisional, completed U-2 training at Watertown Strip. From there it would be assigned to Incirlik AFB, Adana, Turkey. While the U-2s assigned to the unit were dismantled and transported to Adana, the unit's members, one of whom was Francis Gary Powers, were given two weeks' leave. During that interlude, Powers visited his family in Pound, Virginia. While there, his father asked him numerous questions, "more, in fact, than I had anticipated. But I got around them fairly well, or so I thought." Before flying out for his new assignment, Powers made a final telephone call home.

"I've figured out what you are doing," his father said.

"What do you mean? I told you what I'm doing."

"No," replied the elder Powers. "I've figured it out. You're working for the FBI."[90]

The facilities at Incirlik closely resembled Watertown Strip. Owing to the absence of women, "our appearances went to hell," explained one U-2

[87] Taubman, *Secret Empire*, 188-189.

[88] Ambrose, *Ike's Spies*, 272-273.

[89] Andrew, *For the President's Eyes Only*, 224.

[90] Francis Gary Powers, with Curt Gentry, *Operation Overflight* (New York: Holt, Rinehart and Winston, 1970), 38, 39.

technician. The poor quality of the food rendered pilots scrawny. Occasionally they ventured forth into town to dine at a restaurant, but the CIA cautioned them about throat-slashers lurking in the shadows.

As time passed, the Incirlik detachment waited for their chance to overfly Russia, unaware of the presidential prohibition on such missions. To occupy their empty time, the pilots played poker and toured local tourist sites. The only missions they did fly concerned weather and flying east along the southern Soviet border for the purpose of detecting radio and radar signals. Adding to their discontent was the almost complete absence of news concerning the world beyond Incirlik. Presently the outside world would come crashing in on them. The flashpoint would be the Middle East. The crisis would center on British, French, and Israeli grievances toward Egypt.[91]

When the United States extended diplomatic recognition to Israel in 1948 few politicians or journalists contemplated any future problems would arise with the Arab world. Such forecasts proved erroneous. Reacting to an Israeli raid on the Gaza Strip in 1955—an act precipitated by border clashes on the part of Egypt—that country's leader, Gamal Abdel Nasser arranged an arms agreement with Russia and Czechoslovakia. Seeking to keep Egypt out of the Soviet orbit, President Eisenhower committed the United States to help underwrite the building of the Aswan Dam on the Nile River that was intended to be the highlight of Nasser's modernization program. The deal fell through in 1956 when Nasser recognized Communist China. Nasser's provocations didn't stop there. When the Israelis, who were enraged by Arab guerrilla attacks, undertook preparations for a full-fledged war against the Egyptians in the summer of 1956, Nasser excoriated France for its munitions sale to Israel and provoked the wrath of Great Britain by nationalizing the Suez Canal. Moreover Nasser announced that Egypt herself would erect the Aswan Dam, financing the project with revenue from the canal. For France, which held sizable stock in the canal, the latter's nationalization wasn't the only source of irritation with Nasser: the Egyptian leader also backed the Algerian rebels. Israeli hostility was further inflamed when Nasser denied it the right to use the Canal—the only nation to be so treated.[92]

Because they very likely believed that Eisenhower would not go along with their scheme, Britain's Eden and France's Guy Mollet kept the Americans in the dark as to their intentions. John Foster Dulles confided his anxieties about British and French aims in the Middle East to his brother. Equally concerned, Eisenhower asked Allen Dulles to put U-2s in the air over the region to ascertain the situation. On September 27, 1956, Francis Gary

---

[91] Beschloss, *Mayday*, 136.

[92] John Patrick Diggins, *The Proud Decades: America in War and in Peace 1941-1960* (New York: W.W. Norton & Company, 1988), 299-300.

Powers received his initial directive to overfly the Mediterranean with the assignment to be on the alert for gatherings of two or more ships. In the days to follow, he and other U-2 pilots photographed most of the Middle East region as they sought to detect the presence of an invasion flotilla. What the U-2s revealed by mid-October was that Israel was making preparations for war, with Eisenhower noting, "Our high-flying reconnaissance planes have shown that Israel has obtained some sixty of the French Mystere pursuit planes, where there had been reported the transfer of only twenty-four." The planes appeared to be endowed with "a rabbit-like capacity for multiplication." In the coming weeks, the U-2 would play a vital role in keeping Ike informed on developments in the unfolding Middle East crisis.

On October 29, under the protection of French fighter planes, Israeli paratroopers descended on the Sinai. Israeli tank forces made ready to advance west and south into Egypt. The President sought an immediate cease-fire. The number of U-2 flights increased. Flying over Egypt the day before Halloween, Francis Gary Powers beheld what most likely were the initial shots fired in the first daytime conflict in the Sinai. The next day, during a flight over the primary Egyptian military field near Cairo, a U-2 pilot noticed burning planes and hangars. Supposedly the CIA provided this evidence to the Royal Air Force in London, which merely expressed its gratitude for the "QUICKEST BOMB DAMAGE ASSESSMENT WE'VE EVER HAD." The U-2 evidence disclosed that a two-hundred-ship British-French task force was converging on Egypt.

The Suez crisis wasn't the only item on Eisenhower's agenda that fall. He was also campaigning for reelection to a second term and had to contend with a second international crisis—the Hungarian revolt against Soviet rule. The latter, along with the East German and Polish revolts, seemed to indicate that the Iron Curtain was breaking up. Eisenhower feared that the Russians might resort to "extreme measures"—"even global war"—to maintain their hold on Eastern Europe. Hungarian separatists pleaded for Western assistance for their cause. This would be the best opportunity for the CIA to activate its network in Eastern Europe.

Instead Eisenhower decided not to challenge the Soviets in a crisis closely adjacent to Soviet borders. He refused to authorize the aerial delivery of weapons and supplies. Nor would he deploy troops in the region. Hungary, Ike explained, was "as inaccessible to us as Tibet."

On November 5, British and French paratroopers landed on the Suez Canal, a move that was followed up with amphibious landings. Bulganin both invited the United States to partner with the Soviets to halt the Middle East crisis and threatened London and Paris with nuclear devastation.

Shortly before the Eisenhowers left at nine A.M., Election Day, November 6, to cast their ballots in Gettysburg, the President received word from CIA chief Dulles that the Russians had made a pledge to Nasser to "do something" in the Middle East—possibly sending their air force into Syria. In response, Eisenhower ordered that the U-2 overfly Syria and Israel, but not to fly into Russia. Should the latter attack the British and French, "we would be in war." Eisenhower asked if U.S. forces in the Mediterranean possessed atomic anti-submarine weapons.

After voting in Gettysburg, the Eisenhowers returned to Washington. Goodpaster reported that the U-2 missions had failed to disclose the presence of Soviet planes in Syria or moving into Egypt. The prospects for the Suez crisis escalating into World War III had diminished considerably. Eisenhower spent Election Night waiting for Adlai Stevenson's concession speech. The Suez crisis ended in a cease-fire.[93]

The ultimate outcome of Suez was the fall of Britain and France as major world powers and the beginning of America's role as the dominant western power in the Middle East. U.S.-Soviet relations in the post-Suez period were tense, making future U-2 overflights over Russia an extremely important issue. Asked to reassume such missions, Eisenhower replied, "Why do we need to go in? What good will it do? Everyone in the world says that in the last six weeks, the U.S. has gained a place it hasn't held since World War Two. To make trips now would cost more than we would gain in solid information."

Seconding this view, a State Department official said losing a plane at this point would be nearly catastrophic.

Bissell provided a solution: the new U-2 facility in Turkey, where Francis Gary Powers was stationed, was "a better way to get at most of the targets in Russia." Bissell wanted the U-2 to inspect Soviet bomber fields, Kapustin Yar, the Ukraine and Caucasus, the cities on the Volga. Reflecting his concerns about what the Russians might do in the wake of the Hungarian and Suez crises, Eisenhower authorized a pair of shallow U-2 missions, stipulating that they remain as close as possible to the border and still cover the fields.

"*You're it, Powers.*" Thus did Francis Gary Powers learn from his U-2 base commander in Turkey that he had been chosen to fly the first U-2 mission originating from Adana to enter Soviet airspace. Apparently there were additional flights covering Eastern Europe as well. When these missions drew private complaints from the Russians, Eisenhower informed John Foster Dulles he was "going to order complete stoppage of the entire business." The

---

[93] Beschloss, *Mayday*, 138-139.

Secretary of State concurred. Given the present restive state of American-Soviet relations, any provocative actions were indeed unwise.[94]

By the time the U-2 flights resumed in 1957, the program was a securely established operation. This included overflights of the USSR on those occasions when presidential sanction was granted. U-2 operations abroad now centered on bases in Turkey and Japan, each of which housed 150 men. "We quite literally had the ability to cover almost any part of the surface of the earth for photograph reconnaissance, within twenty-four hours of notice," said Bissell.[95]

The U-2 bases in Turkey and Japan also served as staging grounds for missions that either took off or landed in Pakistan, Iran, Norway and other locations. The U-2 program entered a new phase in 1957 when it became a joint venture between the United States and Britain.

Royal Air Force pilots were trained at Watertown strip. RAF officers were also sent to Washington and Adana. Using information supplied by the British, the CIA plotted numerous flights into Russia that were flown by British pilots in American U-2s. As these missions were undertaken at Macmillan's sanction, theoretically they were British, not American, operations. U-2 missions were also flown from Taiwan to cover China.[96]

Eisenhower appreciated the risks inherent in sending out the U-2. "Well, boys," he recalled saying, "I believe the country needs this information, and I'm going to approve it. But I'll tell you one thing. Some day one of these machines is going to be caught, and we're going to have a storm."[97]

Eisenhower suggested that the Air Force take over the program in part for monetary concerns but Dulles was in no mood to relinquish CIA control over the U-2. The Agency calculated that the Russians as yet could not down a U-2. In light of this, why surrender the plane?

Still pressing his case, Eisenhower, meeting with his Board of Consultants on Foreign Intelligence Activities in December 1958, recommended a "re-evaluation of the U-2 program." Both the President and the Board had been "highly enthusiastic" about the reconnaissance plane, but by now, "we have located adequate targets." Ike now wondered "whether the intelligence which we receive from this source is worth the exacerbation of international tension that results." Instead of taking Eisenhower's "hint," the Board members praised the U-2 as "highly worthwhile." The President said nothing

---

[94] Beschloss, *Mayday*, 139.
[95] Ambrose, *Ike's Spies*, 274.
[96] Beschloss, *Mayday*, 144-148.
[97] Parmet, *Eisenhower and the American Crusades*, 538.

more. In this instance, he would have done well to follow his instincts instead of his advisers.[98]

And so the U-2 continued to fly while, back on earth, the quiz show craze continued to flourish.

---

[98] Beschloss, *Mayday*, 160-161.

3. TWENTY-ONE, HERBERT STEMPEL AND CHARLES VAN DOREN (1956–1957)

By the fall of 1956, over a year after *The $64,000 Question* had ignited television's big-money quiz show craze, the network schedules were inundated with them. *Question* retained its position as king of the hill in the quiz pantheon while its spin-off, *The $64,000 Challenge*, continued to do well, as did NBC's venerable *You Bet Your Life*. The latter, though its cash prizes were in no way comparable to the $64,000 contests, owed its continuing success to host Groucho Marx.

Of all the new quizzes that debuted during the 1956-1957 season, none equaled the sensation created by NBC's *Twenty-One*, which owed its success to the public acclaim showered on its most famous contestant—the one who indeed became the most famous quiz show champ of the 1950s.[99] Unknown to the general public at the time was the behind-the-scenes drama involving *Twenty-One*'s producer and a disgruntled former contestant whose resentment at being dethroned in favor of *Twenty-One*'s brightest star contributed to the eventual revelation of the quiz shows' fraudulence.

"How Would You Like to Win $25,000? ... Play Ball With Me ... and You Will ..."

Twenty-One was created by Barry and Enright Productions, named after its bosses Jack Barry and Daniel Enright. Of the two, Barry was the one the public saw on television. He so enjoyed being on camera that he was described by a friend and a co-worker "as a kindergarten egomaniac. He suffers the same as most people do who like to appear on television and be recognized

---

[99] Castleman and Podrazik, *Watching TV*, 114.

on the streets." In 1947 Barry teamed up with Enright, who had gotten his start in radio in 1939, and was currently program supervisor at New York's WOR.[100] The duo enjoyed a successful collaboration creating and producing numerous quiz shows: *Juvenile Jury*, which featured a panel of young people who answered questions forwarded by audience members, both at home and in the studio, and by celebrity guests; *Life Begins at 80*, only this time the panelists were far older; and *Wisdom of the Ages*, which featured both juvenile and senior citizen panelists.[101]

Their next production, *Tic Tac Dough*, airing in daytime, featured two contestants who played the game on an enormous board with nine squares, each bearing a labeled category and each *X* or *O* needing a correct answer to win that particular category. Unlike the big-money quizzes, *Tic Tac Dough*, like the majority of other daytime contest shows, offered small monetary prizes—in *Tic Tac Dough's* case a mere $100 a game. Yet, in *Tic Tac Dough's* case, should a tie occur, the next game raised the ante. Because *Tic Tac Dough* was an open-ended contest, the contestant could remain on the show for an unlimited period of time, winning greater sums of money.

With Jack Barry as host, *Tic Tac Dough* first aired in July 1956, and soon became a popular daytime show.

Combining the contestant format of *The $64,000 Question* with the open-ended format of *Tic Tac Dough*, Enright created *Twenty-One*, a more intricate variation on the card game of the same name. Borrowing a technique from *The $64,000 Challenge, Twenty-One* featured rival players competing against each other in dual isolation booths. Contestants sought to score twenty-one points by correctly answering questions valued in difficulty from one to eleven points. Unlike other quiz shows where the contestant answered questions in categories of their own selection, *Twenty-One's* players had to answer questions in numerous categories chosen at random. When the emcee announced the chosen category, the contestant could select the number of points he wanted to play for. Should he correctly answer a ten-point question, then an eleven-point question, he scored the winning twenty-one points.

Barry and Enright filmed a preliminary rehearsal of their proposed quiz show which they then ran for their long-time sponsor, Pharmaceuticals, Incorporated, and the latter's advertising agency, Edward Kletter Associates. Pharmaceuticals, most famous for manufacturing Geritol, an iron restorative for "tired blood," signed onto Barry and Enright's latest creation, agreeing to pay the producing team $15,000 a show, along with an extra $10,000 week-

---

[100] Anderson, *Television Fraud*, 43.
[101] www.pbs.org/wgbh/amex/quizshow/peopleevents/pande04.html.

ly for prize money. The contract was slated to run twenty-six weeks, after which it could be renewed every thirteen weeks. NBC agreed to carry *Twenty-One* during the fall 1956 season.

The very first *Twenty-One* broadcast wasn't rigged. Indeed, Enright felt it was so good a show that rigging wouldn't be necessary. In truth, that initial broadcast "was a dismal failure," he recalled. "It was just plain dull."[102] Because be viewed quiz shows as vehicles for drama and entertainment—and nothing more—Enright had no particular qualms about rigging *Twenty-One*. "You cannot ask random questions of people and have a show," explained one game-show producer. "You simply have failure, failure, failure, and that does not make entertainment." Given such a philosophy, quiz-show rigging prevailed and Enright was a master of the art. Recalling that era long afterward, Enright admitted he wasn't very nice. He was ambition-driven: "I was determined to be successful no matter what it cost, and I was greedy, greedy, not for money, but for authority, power, prestige and respect." Thus, whatever he did to attain his goals was permissible to his way of thinking. People, as he saw it, were tools to be exploited; otherwise they would exploit you. The rigging of *Twenty-One* not only benefited the show, it enabled Enright to attain the stature he sought, convincing him that nothing he did was wrong.

Thus, *Twenty-One* became the model of a totally fraudulent quiz show. To Enright, contestants weren't simply winners and losers but heroes and villains. His first try at casting a hero, Richard Jackman, a writer from Oneonta, New York, had only recently been a contestant on *Tic Tac Dough*, where he hadn't been coached and was quickly eliminated. He then successfully tried out for *Twenty-One*.[103] Just before Jackman initially appeared on Barry and Enright's latest quiz October 3, 1956, Enright met with him to go over numerous questions, then told Jackman, "You are in a position to destroy my career." Jackman quickly found out what Enright meant by his ominous statement: on his first appearance on *Twenty-One*, he discovered that the questions he answered on-air were the same ones Enright had asked him during the pre-quiz run through. Jackman won $24,500, but informed Enright that he had no desire to be involved with a rigged show and withdrew. Enright eventually persuaded him to take $15,000 for his initial *Twenty-One* appearance and appear on one more show to make a graceful exit instead of abruptly dropping out without explanation.[104]

It didn't take long for Enright to find his next *Twenty-One* champion. The very night the quiz first aired, Herbert M. Stempel, an ex-G.I. working his way through City College of New York, viewed the show at his residence,

---

[102] www.pbs.org/wgbh/amex/quizshow/filmmore/transcript/index.html
[103] Halberstam, *The Fifties*, 649; Anderson, *Television Fraud*, 46.
[104] Halberstam, *The Fifties*, 649.

and felt that the questions on it weren't that outstanding. He told his wife he believed he could answer nearly every one from whatever category they originated. In his letter of introduction to Barry and Enright Productions, he explained:

> "Doctors have told me and many of my friends say that I have a retentive, if not photographic memory, and I have thousands of odd and obscure facts and facets of general information at my fingertips. I have stayed home continuously watching many television shows and I answer so great a bulk of the questions that my wife has continually urged me to try out for your fine show."[105]

There was more to Stempel's mental endowments than simply a retentive memory; he was, in reality, a super genius with an IQ of 170. Following his graduation from the renowned Bronx High School of Science, Stempel for a time worked for the Post Office, then entered the army during World War II. He left the service in 1952 to attend college on the G.I. Bill. Stempel's intellectual genius made it unnecessary for him to devote considerable amounts of time to his college studies. He harbored ill-defined dreams of becoming a thespian or playwright, but, for the moment, he readily acknowledged his primary issue was to free himself from his wife's family's financial domination.[106]

Shortly after submitting his application to appear on *Twenty-One*, Stempel was summoned to Manhattan where he took the test for the quiz. He then received another summons, this time from *Twenty-One* producer Howard Merrill, directing him to report to a meeting where he met Enright, Barry, Robert Noah, co-creator and briefly executive producer of *Twenty-One*, At this session, Stempel learned he had scored 251 correct answers on the exam, the highest of all would-be candidates for *Twenty-One* to date. He was then asked questions on a wide-range of obscure facts as well as his background.[107] What happened next Stempel subsequently described in his testimony before a congressional committee investigating quiz show rigging:

> ". . . . I received a call from a gentleman who identified himself as Mr. Daniel Enright and said that he had to see me in his office upon a very urgent matter. I thereupon told him that my wife had gone to the theater and I was babysitting that evening. He said he had to see me desperately and he would come out. He came out about a half hour later. I recognized him from having met him before. At that time when

---

[105] Anderson, *Television Fraud*, 47-48; www.pbs.org/wgbh/amex/quizshow/peoplecvents/pande01.html 5 November 2007.
[106] Stone and Yohn, *Prime Time and Misdemeanors*, 28.
[107] Anderson, *Television Fraud*, 48.

he entered my house he was carrying an attaché case. Without further ado, he opened up the attaché case while sitting on my couch, pulled out a bunch of square cards, such as were eventually used as category cards on "Twenty-one," and proceeded to say the category is blank-blank, whatever it happened to be, and then would ask me questions sequentially from 1 to 11. . . .

"I managed to answer the bulk of the questions and those which I did not know, he helped me on, and supplied the answers. After having done this, he very, very bluntly sat back and said with a smile, "How would you like to win $25,000?" I said to him, I was sort of taken aback, and I said, "Who wouldn't". . . . He said something to the equivalent, "Play ball with me, kid, and you will do it," or words to that effect. Then he explained to me that I had been selected to go on the air as a contestant that very next evening. He was rehearsing me. Then he asked me, incidentally, where my wardrobe was, and I told him. He went and checked all my suits and selected a blue double breasted ill-fitting suit which had belonged to my deceased father-in-law, which I was intending to give to charity. Then he asked to look at my shirts. I went to the chest which I have and showed him my shirts. He said essentially that a blue shirt would be worn for television, whereupon he picked out a frayed collar blue shirt. He also instructed me to wear a wristwatch which ticked away like an alarm clock. It was a very cheap $6 wristwatch. He also instructed me that I had to get what is known, as I understand it, a marine-type white-wall haircut. This was the way I had to dress up."[108]

Commenting further on how he was to appear before the television cameras, Enright, in a television interview years after his congressional testimony, said, "The whole idea was to make me appear like an ex-G.I. working his way through college—to make me appear as what you would call today, a nerd, a square."[109]

Enright's coaching of Stempel continued the following afternoon when he came to the studio for a pre-show rehearsal session. As Stempel again told the congressmen:

"He . . . told me at this time exactly how the questions were to be answered. In other words, I was to write down something like "Take 5 seconds, pause, stutter, say nine points." In other words, everything was explicit. He showed me how to bite my lip to show extreme tension. How to mop my brow. He taught me how to stutter and say in

---

[108] "A Sop to the Public at Large': Contestant Herbert Stempel Exposes Contrivances in a 1950s Television Quiz Show," historymatters.gmu.edu/d/6565 30 October 2007.
[109] www.pbs.org/wgbh/amex/quizshow/filmmore/transcript/index.html

a very plaintive voice, 'I will take nine, nine points.' Remembering the questions was quite easy, but the actual stage directions were the most difficult thing because everything had to be done exactly."[110]

During the first minutes of the *Twenty-One* broadcast he made his initial appearance on, Stempel stayed in a private dressing room while two contestants played to a scoreless tie, whereupon a new rule took effect, eliminating scoreless players with consolation prizes valued at $100. His first opponent was an accountant, Maurice Peloubet. Following Enright's script, Stempel trounced Peloubet in an eighteen to nothing game, quickly winning $9,000. From there, Stempel went on to boost his winnings to over $50,000. Two times a week before each appearance, Stempel and Enright rehearsed how many points Stempel would play during each round, the questions he would be asked, and the answers he would give, including giving intentionally incorrect answers to enliven the pace of the show when warranted. Everything about Stempel's performance was precisely rehearsed—in part to keep the rounds from exceeding their allocated time, thereby intruding into commercial breaks. Stempel was also drilled on how to answer questions in such a manner as to enhance the tension. When he was actually on the air, his performance was made to look more authentic by switching off the air conditioning in his isolation booth so he would perspire.

Stempel complied with Enright's instructions even on those occasions when he knew the latter was wrong. Prior to the November 7, 1956, broadcast of *Twenty-One*, Stempel was informed that he would be identifying the Pacific island from which the "Enola Gay" departed on its historic flight to Hiroshima during World War II. Stempel knew the correct answer: Tinian. No, said Enright, the island was Okinawa; after all, his research people couldn't have made an error. When the time came to answer the question on-air, Stempel said "Okinawa," which emcee Jack Barry said was accurate. This produced a strong public reaction, including a phone call from the Enola Gay's copilot's widow. Stempel's rival on that week's *Twenty-One*, Dr. Carlos Carballo, was brought back for a rematch the following week, during which time Barry asserted the error had resulted when he read the answer from the wrong card; Okinawa was the correct answer to another, unused question about islands. Stempel emerged victorious in the rematch.[111]

Stempel may have objected to having to unquestioningly obey Enright's dictates, yet the attention he received from fellow CCNY students was gratifying. He overheard one student tell another, "Herb Stempel's in one of my classes," while another student, a complete stranger, told him he and his

---

[110] "A Sop to the Public at Large," historymatters.gmu.edu/d/6565.
[111] Stone and Yohn, *Prime Time and Misdemeanors*, 30-31.

friends were proud that he attended CCNY. Girls gave him secret, admiring looks. "It was heady stuff."[112]

About five weeks into Stempel's reign on *Twenty-One*, he learned that, owing to budgetary considerations, he couldn't take home all the winnings he had amassed. Still he would be assured a high amount even though he could theoretically forfeit all of it according to the regulations governing the quiz. (A lengthy sequence of tie games with an eventual defeat could obliterate a considerable sum of prize money). Enright went so far as to tell Stempel that if he declined to sign such an agreement, he would quickly become a loser on the quiz. Given the circumstances, Stempel had no other option but to sign; the document he did sign was neither notarized nor witnessed.

During one pre-game warm-up with Enright, Jack Barry happened to drop by. This unexpected appearance on Barry's part caused Enright to conceal the question-and-answer cards he was using with Stempel. When the latter asked whether Barry knew about the drill, Enright told Stempel, "Mind your own business and pay attention to your lessons." There was no indication that Barry knew anything about the production aspects of *Twenty-One*. For that matter, both *Twenty-One*'s sponsor and advertising agency were also ignorant of such matters. When it came to the budgetary issue Enright raised with Stempel, this was a matter that was the sole responsibility of the producers. The contract between *Twenty-One* and Pharmaceuticals, Incorporated stipulated that the sponsor provide $10,000 a week for prize money. Should the typical weekly winnings come to less than that figure, the difference was to be refunded to Pharmaceuticals at the conclusion of the initial twenty-six broadcasts of *Twenty-One* and every thirteen weeks thereafter. If the situation were reversed, with the prize money going over the $10,000 weekly limit, the responsibility for paying the additional outlay of money fell to the producers themselves. Thus, adhering to his budget as clearly as possible was one factor motivating Enright's desire to shape the fortunes of contestants during their time on *Twenty-One*. With both Enright and Freedman deciding who on the quiz remained and who left, the weekly sums of prize money paid out occupied a mere range between $500 and $750 over $10,000 per broadcast during the entire time the show aired: two years. If Pharmaceuticals, Incorporated had known it was due a refund, it would have paid more attention to how things were managed on *Twenty-One*, but with the production company contributing small amounts over the $10,000 limit, the sponsor had no reason to examine how the quiz operated.

Enright had a bigger matter on his mind in the fall of 1956: Herb Stempel. Despite the latter's winning streak on *Twenty-One*, the ratings for the show,

---

[112] Halberstam, *The Fifties*, 651.

despite the unlimited opportunity it afforded contestants to win prize money, were dismal, compared to the top-ten positions the more limited $64,000 contests occupied. The solution to this unacceptable state of affairs, Freedman and Enright believed, was to replace Stempel with someone the viewers would find more appealing.[113]

The beginning of the end of Stempel's time on *Twenty-One* can be traced to November 28, 1956. On that date, when the total amount of his winnings stood at $69,500, Stempel played a series of predetermined ties against a competitor he instantly perceived was his adversary. As the outcome of that evening's contests were three ties, Stempel could only presume that his rival was being coached as well. A rematch between the two was scheduled, with the stakes increased to $2,000 a point.[114] Stempel finally learned the certainty of his fate when he reported for his pre-game coaching session on December 4:

> "I arrived at Mr. Enright's office, and suddenly on the couch in his office found an enormous pile of records which he very, very bluntly told me were mementos from the program of all the programs I had been on. In other words, all recordings of all the programs. After his assistants had left, I was told very bluntly, as he walked over to the blackboard, that I had done very well for the show, reached a certain plateau, and he drew a chalk mark, sort of going up the blackboard and then leveled it off, but said, "Now we find we are sort of at a plateau. We have to find a new champion. That is why you are going to have to go." Then he outlined the program for the evening, telling me I would miss on a question pertaining to what picture won the Academy Award in 1955, . . . and I was also in the last question told to miss the last part of a three-part question dealing with the topic I had discussed in American history course 2 days before."[115]

"The Wizard of Quiz"[116]

The man who brought Herb Stempel's reign as quiz champ to an end first came to Dan Enright's attention though Albert Freedman, who made the prospective new champion's acquaintance at a cocktail soiree. The man Enright and Freedman were discussing, the one *Time* would christen "The Wizard of Quiz," was a young English instructor at Columbia University— Charles Van Doren.[117] Born in 1927, his background was far removed from

[113] Anderson, *Television Fraud*, 51-53.

[114] Stone and Yohn, *Prime Time and Misdemeanors*, 31.

[115] "A Sop to the Public at Large," historymatters.gmu.edu/d/6565.

[116] Title drawn from *Time*, "The Wizard of Quiz," February 11, 1957, www.time.com/time/printout/0,8816,809055,00.html 18 February 2008.

[117] www.time.com/time/printout/0,8816,809055,00.html; Halberstam, *The Fifties*, 651.

that of Herbert Stempel. Van Doren's mother, Dorothy, in addition to being a novelist, had been an editor of the *Nation;* Uncle Carl had authored a Pulitzer Prize winning biography of Benjamin Franklin; Charles' father, Mark, who also nabbed a Pulitzer (for poetry), had written a nearly consummate work on Nathaniel Hawthorne, and was regarded as one of America's best literary critics and was one of the great instructors in the realm of higher education. The Van Dorens divided their time between their expansive Cornwall, Connecticut, farmhouse, and their residence on Greenwich Village's Bleecker Street. At the latter, in addition to Uncle Carl, one could find such high-caliber conversational company as Mortimer Adler, Clifton Fadiman, critic Joseph Wood Krutch, columnist Franklin P. Adams, lawyer Morris L. Ernst, and novelist Sinclair Lewis.

According to his records at Greenwich Village's City and County School, at four he was "one of the best block builders in the group; his dramatic play is very vivid"; at six, "outstanding for clear thinking and intelligent planning"; at eight, "a ready fund of first-hand knowledge." When he was five-years-old, his mother taught him to read. By the time he was eight, his parents discovered him staying up late, reading whatever he could lay his hands on. Presently, his passion for books came to include the subject of baseball. His father instilled within him another mania—that of making validating facts by consulting reference books. He also came to read the dictionary as a form of living literature. One weekend during his adolescence, he read the Bible cover to cover. As a candidate for a Ph. D in English literature, he "systematically read his way through the Columbia library stacks on the subject, averaging 20 books a week for two years."[118] Continually shifting goals characterized Van Doren's early years as a student of higher education. Initially he studied music, then shifted to philosophical studies. He impressed cartoonist-satirist James Thurber (a Connecticut neighbor) with his performance in a 1947 amateur production of Thurber's *The Male Animal*—so much so that Thurber sought to convince Van Doren to take up a professional acting career. As a graduate student at Columbia, he studied science with the aim of becoming an astronomer. As a doctoral candidate majoring in English, Van Doren obtained a fellowship to Cambridge University; there he studied the life and writings of poet William Cowper, about whom he ultimately wrote his dissertation. During his time abroad, he briefly attended the Sorbonne and spent an interval taking stock of himself; during the latter he was especially disturbed that he was following his father Mark Van Doren's career track. He went so far as to begin working on a novel about patricide. Returning to the United States in the mid-1950s, he embarked upon a teaching career.

---

[118] Www.time.com/time/printout/0,8816,809055,00.html

He initially became involved in television when he worked two-and-a-half years as a researcher for Clifton Fadiman's projects, including *Down You Go* and *Conversation*. He also served as assistant editor for another Fadiman enterprise, the anthology *The American Treasury*. He co-wrote a biography, *Lincoln's Commando*, about Civil War naval commander William B. Cushing. He finally obtained a pre-doctoral instructorship in English at Columbia, where his father taught. In the words of Columbia's president, Grayson Kirk, Charles was "an able and exciting teacher."[119]

Despite his impressive background, Charles Van Doren confronted a quandary common to people in his situation: as the product of so distinguished a family, the big question was—what truly was *his* own, a conundrum made even more difficult by the fact he was entering a vocation already inhabited by one or more renowned and successful parents. Quite possibly the true motivation for Van Doren to become a quiz show contestant was the opportunity it gave him to achieve a renown independent of and fair greater than that of his family. At the height of his *Twenty-One* fame, he appeared on the cover of *Time*—a prominence his father and uncle never attained.[120]

Van Doren also sought another kind of independence from his family—financial. His Columbia salary was barely more than sufficient. A casual acquaintance suggested he apply to *Tic Tac Dough*. While not a television set owner and dimly aware that there was such a show being broadcast, Van Doren, just the same, went to Barry and Enright's office, where he took, not only the *Tic Tac Dough* exam, but the one for *Twenty-One* as well. Contacted the following week, Van Doren learned he had been chosen to appear on *Twenty-One* instead of *Tic Tac Dough*—the reason being, he was told, was that he was far too smart for the latter show. Van Doren consented to appear on the more profitable *Twenty-One*. The fact that the latter quiz offered more prize money undoubtedly persuaded the financially hard-pressed Van Doren to go with *Twenty-One*. After waiting as a standby contestant for two consecutive *Twenty-One* broadcasts, Van Doren finally played Stempel for the first time on November 28, 1956.[121]

Like Stempel before him, Van Doren met privately with a member of the *Twenty-One* production staff—in his case Albert Freedman. Testifying before the same Congressional committee after Stempel's appearance, Van Doren explained:

---

[119] Anderson, *Television Fraud*, 53-54.

[120] Halberstam, *The Fifties*, 656; www.pbs.org/wgbh/amex/quizshow/filmmore/transcript/index.html

[121] Anderson, *Television Fraud*, 54-55.

"Before my first actual appearance on "Twenty-one," I was asked by Freedman to come to his apartment. He took me into his bedroom where we could talk alone. He told me that Herbert Stempel, the current champion, was an unbeatable contestant because he knew too much. He said that Stempel was unpopular, and was defeating opponents right and left to the detriment of the program. He asked me if, as a favor to him, I would agree to make an arrangement whereby I would tie Stempel and thus increase the entertainment value of the program.

"I asked him to let me go on the program honestly, without receiving help. He said that was impossible. He told me that I would not have a chance to defeat Stempel because he was too knowledgeable. He also told me that the show was merely entertainment and that giving help to quiz contests was a common practice and merely a part of show business. This of course was not true, but perhaps I wanted to believe him. Whenever I hesitated or expressed uneasiness at the course events were taking during my time on the program the same sort of discussion ensued, and, foolishly and wrongly, I persuaded myself that it was all true. Freedman guaranteed me $1,000 if I would appear for one night . . . I was sick at heart. Yet the fact is that I unfortunately agreed, after some time, to his proposal.

"He instructed me how to answer the questions: to pause before certain parts and return to them, to hesitate and build up suspense, and so forth. On this first occasion and on several subsequent ones he gave me a script to memorize, and before the program he took back the script and rehearsed me in my part. This [was] the general method which he used throughout my 14 weeks on "Twenty-one." When I could answer the questions right off he would tell me that my answers were not given in an entertaining and interesting way, and he would then rehearse me in the manner in which I was to act and speak."[122]

The first time they played against each other on-air, challenger Van Doren and reigning champ Stempel scored a trio of tie matches. If one were looking for two dissimilar men to pit against each other on a quiz show, one needn't have looked any further than Stempel and Van Doren. That he appreciated the fact that he must leave *Twenty-One* at some point failed to appease Stempel when he finally did learn that his quiz show contestant days were over. The source of his misery, he subsequently explained, stemmed from his loathing of Van Doren and envy of the benefits he had had.[123] "I felt here

---

[122] "The Truth Is the Only Thing with Which a Man Can Live': Quiz Show Contestant Charles Van Doren Publicly Confesses to Deceiving His Television Audience," history-matters.gmu.edu/d/6566 30 October 2007.
[123] Anderson, *Television Fraud*, 56.

was a guy, Van Doren, that had a fancy name, Ivy League education, parents all his life, and I had just the opposite, the hard way up," he would tell Enright.[124] Stempel's sense of inferiority toward Van Doren wasn't the only matter at stake: school pride had entered the picture. Because of the press, the contest between the two men had been transformed into a rivalry between their respective institutions—CCNY and Columbia. Though he was never specifically told so, Stempel believed that Van Doren, like him, was being coached—a suspicion that was reinforced by Enright's announcement to him that he would tie Van Doren in the initial confrontation on December 5 and lose the second match eighteen to ten. Seeking to mollify Stempel, Enright tendered a pair of olive branches: a possible, salaried job as research consultant with Barry and Enright Productions and a possible appearance on *The Steve Allen Show*.[125]

On the day of his scheduled dethronement from *Twenty-One*, Stempel passed the time at home viewing television. Throughout that morning, WNBC announced: "Is Herb Stempel going to win over $100,000 tonight?" In addition to losing to the likes of Van Doren, Stempel was agitated by the fact that Enright had directed him to miss the question on which film won the Oscar for Best Picture of 1955. The correct answer—*Marty*—was one of Stempel's all time-favorite movies, one he undoubtedly identified with as its title character closely resembled him. "A few seconds before that as I was trying to came up with the answer, I could have changed my mind. I could have said, 'The answer is *Marty*, instead of *On the Waterfront*.' I would have won. There would have been no Charles Van Doren, famous celebrity. Charles Van Doren would have gone back to teaching college and my whole life would have been changed." Stempel adhered to Enright's script, took his dive, and ended his time on *Twenty-One*. Compounding his injury was an incident that occurred as he was walking backstage: a pair of technicians were engaged in conversation; one of them said, "At least, we finally have a clean-cut intellectual on this program, not a freak with a sponge memory."

For Stempel, these words were as painful, "as if somebody had taken a knife and shoved it right into me."[126]

For Van Doren, on the other hand, his win on *Twenty-One* marked the beginning of a whirlwind that in time became nightmarish—a sensation compounded no doubt by his awareness of the deceit he was party to. He made a record fifteen appearances on *Twenty-One*. He was inundated with letters telling how he signified the nation's hope for a more sober, intellectual future, especially after the recent McCarthy era had cast learning in a

[124] Halberstam, *The Fifties*, 656.
[125] Anderson, *Television Fraud*, 56-57.
[126] Www.pbs.org/wgbh/amex/quizshow/filmmore/transcript/index.html

nefarious, un-American light. He received both offers from other universities for tenured professorships and movie roles. NBC signed him to a three-year contract to appear on *The Today Show* as the latter's resident intellectual. His yearly NBC salary—$50,000—far surpassed his Columbia earnings. "I felt like a bullfighter in a bull ring with thousands and thousands of people cheering me on and all I wanted to do was get out of there," he later said. After paying the taxes on his ultimate quiz show winnings, $129,000, Van Doren was left with approximately $28,000.[127]

Undoubtedly most of his fans were parents of the baby-boomer generation and others aghast at the emerging "rock'n'roll" music and its primary champion—Elvis Presley.[128] "The Wizard of Quiz" and "Elvis the Pelvis" were as much polar opposites as Van Doren and Stempel had been—with a difference. Where Van Doren came across as self-possessed, conservative, and cerebral, sexual innuendo characterized Presley's persona: he moaned and gasped as he sang and whacked his guitar with his hips, all the while attired in skin-tight, flashy apparel—an image clearly at variance with the era's predominant, dispassionate "organization man" archetype.[129] When Elvis appeared on television, some producers only allowed him to be seen from the waist up. Their elders' disapproval of him only made Elvis a more attractive figure.[130]

In the *Sputnik* era, Van Doren was touted as the ideal American youth needed to follow if the United States was to surmount the latest Russian challenge. Ironically one cultural historian detected a similarity between the quiz shows and Presley's performances: a sense of spontaneity, the feeling that both, unlike scripted motion picture or television dramatic performances, were authentic. Van Doren was a godsend for *Twenty-One* as well. During his time on the quiz, NBC made the bold move to switch the show from its initial Wednesday night time-slot to Monday, where it took on the CBS powerhouse, *I Love Lucy*—with surprising results. While the Barry and Enright production never trounced *Lucy* in the ratings competition, the fact was that by March 1957 *Twenty-One* became NBC's first show to hold out the potential of beating *Lucy*. The primary explanation for *Twenty-One*'s success in its new time period opposite *I Love Lucy* was the continued presence of Van Doren on the quiz—which prompted viewers to continue tuning-in to see how he fared.

[127] Halberstam, *The Fifties*, 658.

[128] Anderson, *Television Fraud*, 70.

[129] Karal Ann Marling, *As Seen on TV: The Visual Culture of Everyday Life in the 1950s* (Cambridge, Massachusetts: Harvard University Press, 1994), 183; Bernard A. Weisberger, *Cold War, Cold Peace: The United States and Russia since 1945* (New York: American Heritage Publishing Co., Inc., 1984), 185.

[130] Diggins, *The Proud Decades*, 195-196.

Success did nothing to calm Van Doren's anxiety:

> "As time went on the show ballooned beyond my wildest expectations. I had supposed I would win a few thousand dollars and be known to a small television audience. But from an unknown college instructor I became a celebrity. I received thousands of letters and dozens of requests to make speeches, appear in movies, and so forth—in short, all the trappings of modern publicity. To a certain extent this went to my head. I was almost able to convince myself that it did not matter what I was doing because it was having such a good effect on the national attitude to teachers, education, and the intellectual life. At the same time, I was winning more money than I had ever had or even dreamed of having. I hoped people would not think I could do nothing besides stand in an isolation booth and answer questions. I realized that I was really giving a wrong impression of education. True education does not mean the knowledge of facts exclusively. I wrote trying to express this feeling, but few were interested. Instead I was referred to as a "quiz-whiz," a "human book of knowledge," a "walking encyclopedia." I wanted to be a writer and a teacher of literature. I seemed to be moving farther and farther away from that aim.

> "I told Freedman of my fears and misgivings, and I asked him several times to release me from the program. At the end of January 1957, when I had appeared 8 or 10 times, I asked him once more to release me, and this time more strongly. He agreed to allow me to stop, but it was some time before it could be arranged. He told me that I had to be defeated in a dramatic manner. A series of ties had to be planned which would give the program the required excitement and suspense. On February 18 I played a tie with Mrs. Vivian (*sic*—her real first name was Vivienne[131]) Nearing, and the following week played two more ties with her. Freedman then told me that she was to be my last opponent, and that I would be defeated by her. I thanked him. He told me that I would have to play twice more after February 25. The next program was on March 11. When I arrived at the studio Freedman told me that since there were now only three programs a month, this was not time enough to "build up" another contestant and so I was to lose that very night. I said: "Thank God." Mrs. Nearing defeated me in the first game played that night."[132]

Just before Van Doren's final departure from *Twenty-One*, *New York Post* correspondent Dave Gelman, to whom Herb Stempel had earlier notified in

---

[131] *Ibid.*, 72.
[132] "The Truth Is the Only Thing with Which a Man Can Live," historymatters.gmu. edu/d/6566.

the face of his own impending exit to make way for Van Doren, got back in touch with Stempel, who told him the entire story of his *Twenty-One* experience. Heeding the counsel of its libel lawyer, the *Post* decided against publishing Stempel's story. For Stempel, who was now seeing a psychiatrist, the paper's decision was another bad break for him. Moreover, he was facing financial difficulties. Most of his pretax winnings from *Twenty-One* had been spent in numerous ways.

Stempel now turned to Enright for financial assistance, hinting that he would reveal the truth about *Twenty-One* if he didn't receive additional funds or employment. Enright promised to give a Stempel a job with his production company when he graduated from CCNY in a few months. In order to forestall a perceived blackmail effort, Enright convinced Stempel to put his signature to a document declaring he hadn't been assisted in any way on the quiz and offered a panelist's seat on a "possible" future show. As an additional safeguard, Enright surreptitiously tape-recorded his conversation with Stempel. Finally, he volunteered to pick up the tab for Stempel's psychiatric care. After all these pledges, Enright related Stempel's blackmail threat to Davis and Franklin, instructing them to disavow the "fix" story in the event it came to the attention of the press.

Stempel neglected two important avenues who would have given him serious attention: he neglected to talk to any officials from NBC, and neither did he contact Matthew Rosenhouse. As head of *Twenty-One*'s sponsor, Rosenhouse surely would have wrung down the curtain on the rigged quiz had he been aware of such shenanigans.[133]

Enright certainly has his fears that his dirty secret would one day come to light but calmed his anxieties with the belief that no one who participated in the rigging would acknowledge having done so. What he and his colleagues failed to consider was that "a contestant might reveal his role in rigging because he might be subjected to such trauma and such hurt that it would overcome whatever reluctance he had to tell the truth." This is exactly what happened to Stempel. His objective now was revenge, no matter what the cost.[134]

The Ticking Time Bomb

For the moment the Stempel issue had receded into the background, allowing Enright once more to devote his full energies to *Twenty-One*. Vivienne Nearing, the woman who dethroned Charles Van Doren, was presently top-

---

[133] Anderson, *Television Fraud*, 73-74.
[134] Www.pbs.org/wgbh/amex/quizshow/filmmore/transcript/index.html; Halberstam, *The Fifties*, 658.

pled by *Twenty-One*'s latest superstar, Hank Bloomgarden. A medical research consultant, Bloomgarden, like Van Doren before him, had been enticed into going along with *Twenty-One*'s deceptive practices by being persuaded that his appearances would promote a worthwhile cause—in Bloomgarden's case the National Association for Mental Health. Bloomgarden hoped to increase contributions to the association. For Bloomgarden, Enright and Freedman devised what would be *Twenty-One*'s longest running series of tie matches, boosting the tension such games would produce and, hopefully, the show's ratings. Bloomgarden's opponent in these matches, James Snodgrass, was an artist in his late thirties and a graduate of Cleveland's Western Reserve University, who had initially pursued a screenwriting career before switching his vocation to painting and studying art in New York. A friend, captivated by the vast store of overall knowledge housed in Snodgrass' brain, told him about *Tic Tac Dough*, recommending he apply to be a contestant.[135]

Snodgrass' excellent performance on both the *Tic Tac Dough* and *Twenty-One* exams led to him becoming a standby player and ultimately facing-off against Bloomgarden on April 22, 1957. After the initial Snodgrass-Bloomgarden encounter, Freedman notified the former he would be playing the prearranged tie games and that Snodgrass would lose the May 20 contest after the tie matches had elevated the stakes to $3,000 per point. What truly annoyed Snodgrass about all this was the fact that, like Stempel before him, he was being instructed to deliberately miss a question concerning a favorite subject—in Snodgrass' case, the poet Emily Dickinson. Resolved to correctly answer the question, Snodgrass prepared a letter containing the questions he was to be asked on the forthcoming *Twenty-One* broadcast, along with the answers to them and the directions he had been given to miss, then sent it by registered mail on May 17, 1957. At the time, Snodgrass had no way of knowing that his action in this instance would be of great future significance.

True to himself, Snodgrass correctly named "Emily Dickinson" during the May 20 telecast. During the ensuing commercial break, Freedman and Enright both came out on stage to inquire if Snodgrass was all right. During the second round, Bloomgarden and Snodgrass chose the eleven-point and hardest question: identifying the five groups of vertebrae in the human spinal column. Instead of naming the bones by listing them in their grouping—as the question required and which Bloomgarden did—Snodgrass instead began by naming the bone itself. He lost by twenty-one points, allowing Bloomgarden to win $73,500 for the evening. The outcome of the match produced an outcry from physicians nationwide that if Snodgrass had incorrectly identified the bone group, Bloomgarden had also been wrong for saying "coccyx"—a

---

[135] Anderson, *Television Fraud*, 74-75; Stone and Yohn, *Prime Time and Misdemeanors*, 88.

noun—instead of "coccygeal." The controversy grew so intense that the two contestants were brought together for a rematch, with the contest beginning once more at $3,500 per point, and Bloomgarden promised the $52,500 he possessed as he embarked upon what appeared to be his final confrontation with Snodgrass.

In the immediate aftermath of the tumultuous May 20 *Twenty-One* broadcast, Freedman, completely ignorant of the rising medical controversy the quiz had ignited, confronted the uncooperative Snodgrass, and, in the latter's account of events, went ballistic, claiming that Snodgrass' audacity in refusing to play ball as instructed, had led to Freedman's ruination. Because he had lost by twenty-one points at $3,500 per point rather than the predetermined lesser sum, *Twenty-One* had gone over budget, presenting the possibility of financial ruin.

Because he no longer trusted Snodgrass, Freedman merely partially prepped the former for the match scheduled for June 3. Snodgrass, who still hoped to emerge victorious over Bloomgarden, saw his dreams crushed when he couldn't identify the prime minister of Ghana. His ultimate winnings for his entire time on *Twenty-One*, $4,000, paled in comparison to Bloomgarden's $92,500.

Shortly before the Snodgrass-Bloomgarden rematch necessitated by the medical question episode, NBC purchased all the assets of Barry and Enright Productions, Incorporated, for a reported sum of $4 million—though the actual purchase price of $2 million was never revealed. As the Barry and Enright—NBC deal was in the final stages of completion, Enright pondered whether the network should be told that it was purchasing a rigged show and decided to seek the counsel of his agent, Sonny Werblin—later the owner of the New York Jets football team.

"Dan," asked Werblin, "have I ever asked you whether the show was rigged?"

No, said Enright.

"And has NBC ever asked you whether the show was rigged?"

Again, Enright said no.

"Well, the reason that none of us has asked is because we don't want to know."[136]

Over at *The $64,000 Challenge*, the big name of the 1956-1957 season was Teddy Nadler, a forty-seven-year-old St. Louis supply clerk, whose formal education ended at the age of thirteen when he quit school, and, who at the time of his quiz show celebrity, was earning seventy-five dollars a week at

---

[136] Halberstam, *The Fifties*, 660.

his clerk's job.[137] Nadler wasn't reticent about touting his qualifications for appearing on the quiz, as his letter of application made clear: "I have a remarkable memory. My knowledge is fabulous; analyzing monumental. I am a human almanac of information." It took several more letters before he finally got the chance to meet with the producers, who were incredulous about Nadler's bona fides. Nadler had been forced to drop out of school in order to support his family. He then became a ravenous reader, listened to radio music in his free time, and discovered that he retained nearly everything of interest to him. Nadler claimed that he could recite data pertaining to any world leader in history as well as 500 historic battles and could hum entire symphonies.[138]

Beginning as a challenger in late 1956, Nadler quickly established himself as a major quiz show player, using his prodigious reservoir of knowledge to face numerous contenders. He would surpass Charles Van Doren, both in the length of quiz show appearances—thirty-eight different, though not consecutive, times—and in total winnings for one quiz show—$152,000. He would appear for a few weeks on *Challenge*, then disappear, then be brought back to play again. He defeated opponents in the area of the Civil War, baseball, and geography—the latter category, along with history, Nadler's strong points. That he appended answers with extraneous information or completed his rival's answers made him unpopular with viewers proved no deterrent to his continued return appearances on *The $64,000 Challenge*. Producers may well have viewed him as the epitome of the "common man" for the big-money quiz shows. Characterizing himself in his typically blunt fashion, Nadler said, "I'm not like Van Doren who is educated and appeals to the ladies because of his looks. I'm ugly and I'm a nitwit, except for my memory."

The $64,000 Question was responsible for producing the biggest record holder for winning the biggest sum of prize money for one broadcast or continued program: ten-year-old Robert Strom who won $192,000! The expanded sum of prize money available to *Question's* contestants resulted from a suggestion on the part of Revlon chief Charles Revson that the quiz add $32,000 plateaus beyond the initial $64,000, stopping at a potential amount of $256,000. Young Strom won his money by answering questions in the field of science, halting his winning streak at $192,000 in accordance with his parents' requests. When the truth about quiz show rigging became public knowledge, Strom, who received no coaching, was demoralized: "I hope

---

[137] Anderson, *Television Fraud*, 81.
[138] "Human Almanac," www.time.com/time/printout/0,8816,809214,00.html 18 February 2008.

the public doesn't lose faith in the contestants who really knew their stuff," he said.[139]

After a poor season, *The Big Surprise* vanished from the air for good in May 1957 but not before becoming embroiled in a dispute that raised the first public hint that the quiz shows were fraudulent. Contestant Dale Logue missed a question at the $10,000 level. She contested that the question she missed was the same one she was asked in a pre-game rehearsal. Employing an attorney, she filed suit against the quiz show's producers for $103,000 on the grounds that she was intentionally "sacked" from the program. The Federal Trade Commission (FTC), which learned about Logue's complaint from her attorney, initiated a probe of the matter at the lower staff tier—though the commission felt it lacked any jurisdictional authority in the affair. The main substance of the FTC's inquiry, which never went beyond the staff level and was concluded in May 1958, consisted of little more than the commission obtaining statements from the producers and the latter's promises that quiz was above-board. Outside the FTC, the only other official interest in the matter came from Martin Revson, who asked EPI's Harry Fleischmann and Steve Carlin if the accusations against *The Big Surprise* were true and was told they weren't. The Logue affair went virtually unnoticed by the press.[140]

In the midst of the continuing quiz show mania, the initial speculation that the quizzes might be fixed appeared in print. *Time* magazine was the first to raise the issue in its April 22, 1957, edition. The article began with a question that bluntly asked: "Are the quiz shows rigged? The answer: the producers of many shows control the outcome as closely as they dare—without collusion with contestants, yet far more effectively than most viewers suspect." From there, *Time* went on to describe how writers scripted the repartee between contestants and quiz show hosts. Regarding the big-money quizzes, while stating that the latter couldn't risk collusion with the contestants appearing on them, the magazine, nonetheless, cited the words of one big-money quiz old-timer who declared that "you have 70% or 80% control of what happens. To keep a contestant winning, all you have to do is figure out how not to hit a question he doesn't know. That's the basis of all quiz shows." "The producers," *Time* said, picking up the story there, "hand-pick their contestants for personality, occupation and geographical spread as well as specialized knowledge, then arm themselves with a shrewd, thorough insight into the contestant's strength and weakness, and have full control of the questions he will be asked."

---

[139] Anderson, *Television Fraud*, 82-84; Paul Sann, *Fads, Follies and Delusions of the American People* (New York: Bonanza Books, 1967), 328.
[140] Anderson, *Television Fraud*, 84, 88-89.

There was also the matter of the locked vault that safeguarded the questions used on *The $64,000 Question.* "There is all this rigmarole about locked vaults," said someone close to the show, "but who has the key to the locked vault? The producer, of course

Time concluded its analysis with the observation that, despite all the controls they exercised over their quizzes, the producers confronted a pair of dilemmas over which they were seemingly powerless:

> The sum of $64,000 no longer inspires audience awe. Viewers have become so blasé that the producers arbitrarily changed their rules to enable . . . Strom to win as much as $256,000, and devised new rules to let . . . Nadler keep winning too. More important, a kind of inflation has also hit the contestants: instead of the kind of ordinary people who struck a responsive chord in viewers, they now run to narrow specialists and photographic minds—"freaks," as the trade calls them. Given a margin of error for the contestants' human foibles, the producers seem to be able to control virtually everything—except their own fears of losing their audience.[141]

Time's inquiry was followed, four months later, by a similar probe in *Look* magazine. While saying that most quiz show producers rejected the notion that their programs were "fixed," *Look* noted that such denials had failed to pacify TV critics, one of whom, Harriet Van Horne of the *New York World-Telegram*, cited the words of Ralph Waldo Emerson: "The louder he talked of his honor, the faster we counted our spoons!" Citing *Twenty-One, Look* explained that once the producers know what a contestant's expertise is, the next step was to pair the contestant with a competitor knowledgeable in the same fields. "One of the appeals of the show rests on the great number of categories in which contestants are expert, and not on the difficulty of each question." After examining Van Doren," Dan Enright explained, "we knew that he knew almost nothing about babies, one of our categories. We went through the categories he knew first. He was lucky. We never got around to babies."

Quoting Bill Ladd, TV editor of the Louisville, Ky., *Courier-Journal* then explained that a contestant himself could manipulate the outcome of a quiz show. Based on a telephone conversation he had with Van Doren, Ladd believed the latter intentionally missed the question that knocked him off *Twenty-One:* "He had told me on the phone that 'a long series of ties, with the stake increasing every week, could ruin my bankroll, and I'll never let it happen.' Two weeks later, after several ties and at $2,000 a point, he missed." While the question appeared easy for someone of Van Doren's intelligence,

---

[141] "The $60 Million Question," www.time.com/time/magazine/article/0,9171,824828,00.html 18 February 2008.

"the pressure of competing," *Look* observed, "can make the best of memories fail."

"If a sponsor wants to give away loot, it's his own business how he does it!" was the forthright opinion of *Treasure Hunt* producer Bud Granoff, who acknowledged that the question segment of his show was frequently fixed. "We often ask a contestant the same question he has already answered correctly in his pre-show interview."

Concluding that none of the quiz shows were fixed "in the sense of being dishonest," *Look* opined that "It may be more accurate to say that they are controlled or partially controlled. The one certainty is that, of all today's big-money quiz shows, only two come anywhere near being completely spontaneous." The two *Look* had in mind, both airing on CBS, were *Two for the Money*, where "Contestants take no tests and don't have to meet any special requirements," and *Name That Tune*, where contestants were randomly chosen, "either from letters, from the studio audience or off the streets of New York." Questions used on the show were supplied, not by the producer, but by viewers who submitted them.[142]

In probing the workings of the quiz shows, both *Time* and *Look* made one serious oversight: they failed to touch upon the practice of collusion between a producer and a contestant, with the latter fully cognizant of what was going on, in engineering the outcomes of matches. The reason for this lapse, theorized Kent Anderson, was that either the two news-weeklies were so caught up by Van Doren's appeal or they believed that it would have been almost impossible to control non-specialized knowledge within a framework of questions.

In the interim between the publication of the *Time* and *Look* pieces, Harriet Van Horne, whom *Look* had cited as one of the doubting Thomases when it came to quiz show producers protestations of innocence of fixing, dove into the quiz show issue with her own series of articles in the *New York World-Telegram and Sun:* "Some of the cynics and the contestants who didn't make it say a lot of rehearsal goes on behind closed doors, that, contestants are given hundreds of 'practice questions' and that some of them, with slight variations in wording, later turn up on the show."

Van Horne's series, unlike the *Time* and *Look* reports, did elicit some outside reaction—in this instance, that of Martin Revson, who asked Carlin and Fleischmann if Cates' statement had any validity; the two EPI men said no. Revson's concerns were also calmed by the results of another probe, this one

---

[142] David Aldrich, "Are TV Quiz Shows Fixed?" *Look*, August 20, 1957, 45-47.

by William Ewald of United Press, which failed to unearth any questionable practices.[143]

Martin Revson's distress was the sole tangible reaction Van Horne's and the other published articles aroused concerning the true nature of the quiz shows at that juncture. Stempel's accusations regarding *Twenty-One* had yet to receive serious consideration. Yet a time bomb was ticking—and it would be only a matter of time before it went off.

Charles Van Doren as a member of the Today Show staff. Back row: Van Doren (left) and Dave Garroway (right). Front row: Jack Lescoulie (left) and Frank Blair (right). Credit: NBC/Photofest.

---

[143] Anderson, *Television Fraud*, 91-92.

4. SPUTNIK (1957–1958)

In early 1957 a U-2 mission flying over Turkestan made a startling discovery: the existence of the Tyura-Tam missile test center. Within a week of the facility's detection CIA photo interpreters would assemble a cardboard model of it, complete with railway sidings and feeder roads, and take it to the White House for viewing. A National Intelligence Estimate (NIE) of March 12, 1957, forecast that the initial Soviet ICBM might become operational in 1960 or 1961. On August 1, CIA director Dulles advised the National Security Council (NSC) that there was "no evidence of anything new or dramatic in the Soviet missile program."[144]

A subsequent announcement from *Tass*, the official Soviet news agency, made a mockery of Dulles' confident assertion. Issued August 26 under Khrushchev's orders, it read:

> A few days ago a super-long-range, intercontinental multi-stage ballistic missile was launched. The tests of the missile were successful; they fully confirmed the correctness of the calculations and the selected design. The flight of the missile took place at a very great, hereto unattained, altitude. Covering an enormous distance in a short time, the missile hit the assigned region. The results obtained show that there is a possibility of launching missiles into any region of the terrestrial globe.[145]

The news of the successful Soviet ICBM test forced not only a revision of American estimates; it also made Tyura-Tam a significant place of interest for U.S. intelligence, mandating further U-2 surveillance of the facility. On August 28 ground crews at an airstrip outside Lahore, Pakistan, prepared for

---

[144] Andrew, *For the President's Eyes Only*, 240.
[145] Brzezinski, *Red Moon Rising*, 128.

a U-2 flyover. Once presidential authorization for the mission was secured, the pilot pointed his plane north and entered Soviet airspace. When CIA analysts studied the resulting photographs they saw that the Tyura-Tam facility was quite large. The vast dimensions meant only one thing: the R-7, as the Soviet ICBM was designated, was a colossal vehicle.

The date of the first successful Soviet test of an ICBM, August 3, had been two days after Allen Dulles assured the NSC that nothing new or dramatic on the Soviet missile front was evident. Following another successful test, Moscow revealed the existence of its ICBM in the *Tass* announcement. The ICBM test now set the stage for an even greater Soviet achievement. On September 17, Russia disclosed that a satellite launch was impending. This was followed on October 1 by news concerning which radio frequency the satellite would be broadcasting on.[146]

"Business as Usual"

The evening of October 4, 1957, the Soviet Embassy in Washington was the scene of a reception of space scientists from nations participating in the International Geophysical Year (IGY). American scientists sought to learn from their Russian colleagues when they would attempt to launch a satellite into space during the International Geophysical Year (IGY). Events at Tyura-Tam that same evening were about to confirm that prediction. After a series of delays in the countdown came the moment when the satellite was launched:

> The clear tones of a bugle were heard above the noise of the machines on the pad. Blinding flames swirled about, and a deep rolling thunder was heard. The silvery rocket was instantly enveloped in clouds of vapor. Its glittering, shapely body seemed to quiver and slowly rise up from the launch pad. A raging flame burst forth and its candle dispelled the darkness of night on the steppe. So fierce was the glare that silhouettes of the work towers, machines, and people were clearly outlined. . . .[147]

> After the rocket bearing the satellite had vanished, everyone hurried to radio receivers to hear the satellite's initial signal: beep, beep, beep. . . .

Back in Washington a Soviet Embassy official summoned Walter Sullivan to take a phone call from *The New York Times'* Washington bureau. Taking down a message from the call, Sullivan gave it to Lloyd V. Berkner, who

---

[146] McDougall, *. . . The Heavens and the Earth,* 61.
[147] Ibid., 61.

clapped his hands for silence: "Radio Moscow has just reported that the Rus-sians have placed a satellite in orbit 200 kilometers above the earth."

Khrushchev had just returned to Moscow from his dacha in the Crimea. "When the satellite was launched, they phoned me that the rocket had tak-en the right course and that the satellite was already revolving around the earth. I congratulated the entire group of engineers and technicians on this outstanding achievement and calmly went to bed."[148]

Once again *Tass* broke the official word: "The first artificial earth satel-lite in the world has now been created. This first satellite was successfully launched in the U.S.S.R. Artificial earth satellites will pave the way for space travel and it seems that the present generation will witness how the freed and conscious labor of the people of the new socialist society turns even the most daring of man's dreams into reality." Two radio transmitters within the craft constantly fed scientific data back to Earth.[149] Originally christened *Prosteshyy Sputnik* ("simplest fellow traveler"), the satellite would soon be-come famous by the far simpler designation—*Sputnik*.[150]

As nuclear weapons became more powerful, work intensified to devise a missile capable of carrying a bomb to the enemy in the fastest possible time. The Soviet effort focused on a top-secret rocket project dubbed "the mech-anism," the production of a missile that would convey H-bomb warheads. The project bore fruit in the successful Soviet ICBM tests of August 1957.[151]

When it came to *Sputnik*, the existence of the Soviet satellite program was known to President Eisenhower. U-2 overflights of the Soviet Union yielded photographs of the ICBM installation that had hurled *Sputnik* into the cos-mos. That the Russians were about to launch their satellite was known to U.S. scientists and intelligence by the late summer of 1957. The American in-tention to launch its satellite during the IGY and the selection of the Navy's Vanguard missile, which was developed for scientific purposes, was meant to stress the peaceful nature of the U.S. space program.

Vanguard had been chosen over the Army's Project Orbiter to guarantee a strong civilian cast to the American satellite project. Orbiter, by contrast, seemed to assure faster results but speed wasn't the top priority. It proved to be a major mistake for the Americans.[152]

When news of *Sputnik's* launching was revealed, the initial response on the part of official America was to downplay the Soviet space success. With

---

[148] *Ibid.*, 61-62.
[149] Goldman, *The Crucial Decade–And After*, 307.
[150] D'Antonio, *A Ball, a Dog, and a Monkey*, 10-11.
[151] Jeremy Isaacs and Taylor Downing, *Cold War: An Illustrated History, 1945-1991* (Boston: Little, Brown and Company, 1998), 154-155.
[152] Pach and Richardson, *The Presidency of Dwight D. Eisenhower*, Revised Edition, 171.

Eisenhower away from Washington at the time, the task of preparing the official presidential response fell to Secretary of State John Foster Dulles. While acknowledging that the launch was "an event of considerable technical and scientific importance," Foster Dulles continued that "that importance should not be exaggerated. What has happened involves no basic discovery and the value of a satellite to mankind will for a long time be highly problematical." *Sputnik* was "without military significance," declared White House aide Maxwell Rabb. The United States wasn't about to become involved "in an outer space basketball game," declared Eisenhower's White House Chief of Staff Sherman Adams. *Sputnik* was a worthless "hunk of iron," grumbled the chief of the Vanguard program, Admiral Rawson Bennett.

White House voices were joined by those belonging to Congressional Republicans. *Sputnik* was merely "a propaganda stunt," intoned Senator Alexander Wiley of Wisconsin. It was like a "canary that jumps on the eagle's back," said Representative James Fulton of Pennsylvania, apparently hinting that the Soviets, as one historian described it, "were hitchhiking off American technology."

The media's approach to *Sputnik* was to inflate it into a significant news story. "Listen now for the sound that will forever more separate the old from the new," declared NBC when it aired *Sputnik's* characteristic beep on October 5. *The New York Times'* headline fairly screamed: "Soviet Fires Earth Satellite into Space," ran the headline in the style ordinarily brought out to announce declarations of war. Adding to the *Sputnik*-inspired journalistic feeding frenzy was the prospect it offered to scapegoat those responsible for this catastrophic American defeat in the Cold War—which would also allow newspapers to sell more of their product and reap additional profits.[153]

Sputnik struck a blow to America in another sense: the idea that American technology reigned unchallenged. When the Russians acquired their own atomic bomb in 1949, it had simply been a case of them catching up with the United States. *Sputnik* was an all-together different matter: while the U.S. had its own rocket and space effort, there was no denying the reality that the Russians had a head-start in the cosmos.[154]

Sputnik also signaled that the days when America felt itself impregnable to enemy attack were over. A missile that could carry a satellite into orbit could likewise carry a nuclear warhead directly to the continental United States. Eisenhower administration assurances notwithstanding, there existed an innate bond between satellites and ballistic missiles. *Sputnik*, in the final analysis, was about the security of the American people. "If the inter-

[153] Brzezinski, *Red Moon Rising*, 171-172.
[154] Weisberger, *Cold War, Cold Peace*, 177-178.

continental missile is, indeed, the ultimate, the final weapon of warfare," said CBS's Eric Sevareid, "then at the present rate, Russia will soon come to a period during which she can stand astride the world, its military master."

Where the senior officials of Eisenhower's administration treated *Sputnik* with nonchalance, others—Richard Nixon, Henry Cabot Lodge, and Nelson Rockefeller—instantly appreciated *Sputnik's* propaganda value. They realized that in the nuclear age, any Soviet scientific achievement was viewed as threatening. At a dinner party, budget director Percival Brundage predicted that *Sputnik* would be forgotten in six months. "Yes, dear," replied his dinner companion, hostess Perle Mesta. "And in six months we may all be dead."[155]

Wrapping up his weekend getaway in Gettysburg, Ike returned to Washington the first Sunday night after *Sputnik* had been launched. "To his amazement," wrote his biographer Geoffrey Perret, "on Monday the Oval Office was virtually besieged. Generals were descending on him from the Pentagon to talk missiles, congressmen were rushing over from Capitol Hill insisting that he talk to them, diplomats from State were coming into the executive offices wanting to know what they were supposed to say to a dumbfounded world and reporters were clamoring for a press conference so that he could reassure a jittery nation. He remained calm, smiling, unconcerned, the man in charge, waiting for the fever to pass. Eisenhower had his pre-lunch rest and in late afternoon he went outside and spent nearly an hour hitting golf balls."[156] Business as usual" was the office stance at the White House.[157]

None of this appeased the White House press corps, who smelled blood and were in no mood to give the President any slack. Their hostile tone was evident from the very first question asked by UPI's Merriman Smith: "Mr. President, Russia has launched an earth satellite. They also claim to have had a successful firing of an intercontinental ballistic missile, none of which this country has. I ask you sir, what are you going to do about it?"

Smith's question elicited a protracted presidential reply, again stressing the intention of the United States to launch a satellite as part of its contribution to the IGY, yet provided little in the way of solid evidence of a new course of action or any arresting memorable phrase.

The journalists' pounding continued. "Mr. President," asked CBS correspondent Charles von Freed, "Khrushchev claims we are now entering a period when conventional planes, bombers and fighters will be confined to museums because they are outmoded by the missiles which Russia claims she has perfected. Khrushchev's remarks would seem to indicate he wants

---

[155] Halberstam, *The Fifties*, 625.
[156] Perret, *Eisenhower*, 559.
[157] Brzezinski, *Red Moon Rising*, 176-177.

us to believe our Strategic Air Command is now outmoded. Do you believe that SAC is outmoded?"

"No," answered the President, who then proceeded to explain the process would be an evolutionary, not revolutionary, one, and would take twenty years.

May Craig of the *Portland Press Herald:* "Mr. President, you have spoken of the scientific aspects of the satellite. Do you think it has immense significance in surveillance of other countries?"

"Not at this time," said Eisenhower, who did not mention the fact that only the day before he had questioned Deputy Secretary of Defense Donald Quarles about what headway was being made in the air force's slackening space reconnaissance program. "I think that period is a long ways off when you consider that even now, and apparently they have, the Russians, under a dictatorial society, where they have some of the finest scientists in the world, who have for many years been working on it, apparently from what they say they have put one small ball in the air."

"Is it a correct interpretation of what you said about your satisfaction with the [U.S.] missile program as separate from the satellite program," asked the *Washington Post* correspondent, "that you have no plans to take any steps to combine the various government units which are involved in this program and which give certainly the public appearance of a great deal of service rivalry, with some reason to feel that this is why we seem to be lagging behind the Soviets?"

On and on it went until Hazel Markel of NBC finally cut to the heart of the matter: "Mr. President, in light of the great faith which the American people have in your military knowledge and leadership, are you saying at this time that with the Russian satellite whirling about the world, you are not more concerned nor overly concerned about military security?"[158]

"As far as the satellite itself is concerned," replied Eisenhower, "that does not raise my apprehensions, not one iota. I see nothing at the moment, at this stage of development, that is significant ... as far as security is concerned."[159]

Meeting with Sergei Korolyov the day after Eisenhower's tense encounter with the press, Khrushchev reminded him that the October Revolution jubilee—the fortieth anniversary of the Bolshevik revolution—was imminent. Having issued invitations to the leaders of world communism to come to Moscow for the celebration, Khrushchev was eager to impress them—particularly China's Mao Zedong—with another extraordinary demonstration of Russian power. Anastas Mikoyan of the Soviet Presidium suggested

---

[158] *Ibid.,* 179-181.
[159] Ambrose, *Eisenhower: Volume II,* 450.

"a Sputnik that will broadcast the 'Internationale'—the pan-Communist anthem—from space." Khrushchev immediately vetoed the proposal.

"What if we launch a Sputnik with a living being?" asked Korolyov, entering the breach. The idea wasn't new: the military had been sending canines on high-altitude suborbital rocket flights and parachuting them back to earth in special hermetically sealed chambers. All Korolyov need do was barrow such a chamber, install a life-support system in it, and ready it for flight.

Khrushchev immediately jumped at the idea of Russia sending the first life form into space.

"That's what we need," he said. "A dog. Give us a dog." He had only one stipulation: "make sure you are ready for the holidays."[160]

At midday on October 31, 1957, the dog chosen to become the first canine to orbit the Earth was placed inside *Sputnik II*. Her original name, Kudryavka (Russian for "Little Curly"), had been shortened to the name she would become known to history as: Laika (a Russian name for husky-type dogs). Once the capsule carrying Laika was fitted to the R-7 missile that would carry her into space, and the additional pre-launch activities had been completed, *Sputnik II* was launched at 7:30 A.M., November 3. Because neither Korolyov or, for that matter, anyone else within the Soviet Union, had any idea how to protect the satellite from the heat produced by atmospheric friction when an object reentered the Earth's atmosphere, Laika had no chance of returning to Earth alive. So as to spare the dog the agony of suffocating in space when her oxygen supply was spent, *Sputnik II's* designers had equipped the capsule with an automatic lethal injection system.

As far as could be determined from Earth, Laika did well on her initial two or three orbits. Her image was transmitted to earth via a television camera inside her space home. When it became clear that Laika's trip would be one-way, her impending demise drew protests from national humane societies in the United States, Great Britain, and elsewhere. Not until many decades had passed would the true facts concerning Lakia's demise be revealed: most likely the dog expired due to heat exhaustion, and possibly stress within a short span of time after she was launched into space. [161]

The impact of *Sputnik II* was even greater than that of the initial Russian satellite success because this time it caused Americans to cast doubts on their country and their President. Secretary of State Dulles was anxious. "The President alone can give the leadership which will restore a feeling of reasonable security—and faith in the Administration," a Dulles aide wrote

---

[160] Brzezinski, *Red Moon Rising*, 206-210.
[161] D'Antonio, *A Ball, A Dog, and A Monkey*, 85-88, 90-91.

in a memo that received dissemination in the White House. "This leads on every side to the desirability of finding a suitable date, in the not too distant future, to make a strong fighting speech."

Eisenhower, who believed that the only malady troubling the nation was a simple case of anxiety that could be easily remedied, decided to deliver a series of uplifting speeches to the nation. The presidential remarks were christened Operation Confidence, or "Chin Up" speeches. The first one, delivered on November 7, came the same day newspapers nationwide featured the jingoistic words of Nikita Khrushchev. "The fact that we were able to launch the first Sputnik, and then, a month later, launch a second shows that we can launch ten, even twenty satellites tomorrow," he declared, while failing to point out that Korolyov had now used the last R-7 available to him. "The satellite is the intercontinental ballistic missile with a different warhead. We can change that warhead from a bomb to a scientific instrument," he continued.

Eisenhower delivered his rebuttal to Khrushchev's boast in his speech. "The United States can practically annihilate the war-making capabilities of any other nation," he declared, itemizing America's defenses. "We are well ahead of the Soviets in the nuclear field both in quantity and in quality," he continued. "We intend to stay ahead."

As Eisenhower spoke, the camera revealed the presence in the Oval Office of a white triangular object: the nose cone from a Jupiter C test rocket; the cone, Eisenhower said, had been sent into space during successful missile reentry tests—proof that the American space and rocket programs were advancing forward, and that everything was fine. "It misses the whole point to say that we must now increase our expenditures on all kinds of military hardware and defense," cautioned the President. "Certainly, we should feel a high sense of urgency. But this does not mean that we should mount our charger and try to ride off in all directions at once.[162]

By the time the *Sputniks* soared across the skies and into the headlines, the sixty-seven-year old President had experienced an exceptionally strenuous two-year period. There had been a pair of health crises: a heart attack in 1955, followed, several months later, by ileitis surgery. And immediately before the *Sputnik* hysteria, the fall of 1957 had brought the school desegregation crisis in Little Rock, Arkansas, which had forced Eisenhower to dispatch federal troops to ensure compliance with the integration of Central High School. The combination of Little Rock and *Sputnik* exacted a great toil on Eisenhower, physically. Under doctor's orders, he left Washington in the middle of November to rest up at his golfing retreat at Georgia's Augusta National

---

[162] Brzezinski, *Red Moon Rising,* 217-218.

Golf Club, where he both labored at his presidential duties and relaxed. Returning to Washington, he began preparing his next "Chin Up" address, to be delivered the following week in Cleveland.

The truth of Eisenhower's worsening condition became known soon after: Eisenhower had suffered a minor stroke. Sherman Adams and Nixon took over some of Ike's duties—all the while maintaining that the President had suffered only minor impairment. He experienced difficulty finding the appropriate words to express himself; otherwise he was strong, alert, and able to communicate. None of this, however, quieted rumors that Eisenhower's condition was graver than that and that he might even have to resign from office.[163]

Eisenhower himself scotched such rumors by staging a rapid recovery from his ailment—attending the NATO summit meeting in Paris in December, delivering the conference's opening address, followed, on January 9, 1958, by his State of the Union message to a joint session of Congress.[164]

Immediately after *Sputnik* had gone up, Jim Hagerty had announced that the Navy—much to the latter's surprise—intended to launch their satellite.[165] The satellite in question was "a small satellite sphere," to be followed, a few months later, by a fully instrumental scientific payload. Both launches were to adhere to the dates set for them as part of the IGY. However, the initial launch of the sphere, scheduled for December 1957, was meant to be nothing more than a mere dress rehearsal that would check Vanguard's booster and upper stages, which had yet to be fired in tandem and were still classified as experimental. Vanguard's maiden flight would be televised live as it happened—whatever the outcome.[166]

In the wake of Hagerty's announcement, the Vanguard crew put their backs into readying their craft to stake America's claim in space. In mid-November the object of their toil, TV-3 (Test Vehicle-3) was rolled out to the launch pad. While the rocket was prepped, media outlets (television and newspapers) organized their coverage of the impending event.[167]

December 4, 1957, was the date set for Vanguard's launch from Florida's Cape Canaveral. However, a series of mechanical failures delayed lift-off until December 6. The failure to launch the satellite as originally planned touched off howls of derision in the foreign press. British newspapers labeled the grounded American satellite "Flopnick," "Stayputnik," "Kaputnick," while the Communist East German newspapers, using *spat*—German

---

[163] D'Antonio, *A Ball, A Dog, and A Monkey*, 98-103.
[164] Parmet, *Eisenhower and the American Crusades*, 517.
[165] Halberstam, *The Fifties*, 627.
[166] Brzezinski, *Red Moon Rising*, 186-187.
[167] D'Antonio, *A Ball, A Dog, and A Monkey*, 114, 110.

for late—called it *Spatnick*. Closer to home, *The New York Times* reported that Washington had come up with its own designation for the troubled space vehicle: "The American satellite ought to be called Civil Servant. It won't work, and you can't fire it."[168]

Finally, conditions cleared to permit the launch. What happened when the countdown climaxed stood out in stark contrast to *Sputnik I*'s triumphant lift-off. Engineer Kurt Stehling remembered:

> It seemed as if the gates of hell had opened up. Brilliant stiletto flames shot out from the side of the rocket near the engine. The vehicle agonizingly hesitated for a moment, quivered again, and in front of our unbelieving, shocked eyes, began to topple. It sank like a great flaming sword into scabbard down into the blast tube. It toppled slowly, breaking apart, hitting part of the test guard and ground with a tremendous roar that could be felt and heard even behind the two-foot concrete wall of the blockhouse and the six-inch bulletproof glass. For a moment or two there was complete disbelief. I could see it in the faces. I could feel it myself. This just couldn't be. . . . The fire died down and we saw America's supposed response to the 200-pound Soviet satellite—our four-pound grapefruit—lying amid the scattered glowing debris, still beeping away, unharmed.[169]

The Los Angeles Herald and Examiner headlined its coverage of the Vanguard disaster "9-8-7-6-5-4-3-2-1-Pfft." "Oh dear," read *The New York Daily Mirror's* caption accompanying a photograph of the explosion. By contrast, *The Des Moines Register* noted that "Soviet newspapers have not told us whether any failures preceded the first success of the Sputniks. That's the difference between the free government of the people and the suppressive power of the police state." Khrushchev jeered that the *Sputniks* were "lonely, waiting for American satellites to join them in space." He added, "Who wants to overtake whom in science? The United States would like to overtake the Soviet Union."[170]

It now fell to Werner von Braun and his team to redeem America's fortunes in space. After being ordered to launch a satellite after the second *Sputnik*, von Braun's team promised to carry out their directive within 90 days. Lift-off for von Braun's rocket was scheduled for January 29, 1958. This time there was no publicity blitz of the sort surrounding the disastrous first attempt. The initial phase of the countdown was smooth but unfavorable weather conditions prompted a postponement. A member of the launch team feared

---

[168] Carl Solberg, *Riding High: America in the Cold War* (New York: Mason & Lipscomb Publishers, 1973), 341.

[169] Halberstam, *The Fifties*, 627.

[170] Solberg, *Riding High*, 342.

the rocket's fuel might begin corroding the tanks. Finally, at 10:47:56 P.M., January 31, the rocket was launched. Six minutes, fifty seconds after lift-off, the final rocket, or kick stage, ignited and burned for six seconds, sending the first American satellite into the heavens. Presidential Press Secretary Hagerty finally received permission to notify his boss. "That's wonderful," said Eisenhower. "I surely feel a lot better now." But he was cautious. "Let's not make too great a hullabaloo about this," he continued.[171]

In contrast to *Sputnik II's* 1,100-lb. payload, *Explorer I*, America's first satellite, weighed in at merely 18.2 lbs. Nevertheless, the *Explorer* scored a significant scientific discovery: the existence of belts of intense radiation encircling Earth. Their presence worried experts who thought they would prevent manned space flight to the rest of the solar system. The radiation zone was christened the Van Allen Belt.[172]

Once the United States finally entered space, she exceeded Russia in the number of satellites. In contrast to Russia, which only launched *Sputnik III* in 1958, America launched five satellites and three lunar probes. America scored two additional space milestones in 1958. On December 13, she sent the first primate into space. Gordo, a nine-month old squirrel monkey, was rocketed aloft aboard Bioflight I to study his reaction to lift-off, weightlessness, and return to Earth. Every aspect of the flight was successful—except the splashdown: the capsule overshot its expected landing site by approximately five miles, and Gordo apparently drowned when the nose cone of his craft broke and flooded. *Life* magazine honored him by publishing his picture in its pages. Just days later the launch of an Atlas 10-B containing instruments that broadcast the first ever voice heard from space to Earth: that of President Eisenhower presenting a Christmas message to all mankind:

> This is the President of the United States speaking. Through the marvels of scientific advances my voice is coming to you from a satellite traveling in outer space. My message is a simple one. Through these unique means I convey to you and all mankind America's wish for peace on earth and goodwill toward men everywhere.[173]

Still Russia claimed the significant firsts in the early years of the space race. They sent a space probe past the moon and into solar orbit (January 1959); landed a probe on the moon and sent pictures of the moon's dark side back to Earth (October 1959); and orbited a man around the Earth (April 1961). The first American to orbit the Earth did so in February 1962.

---

[171] Halberstam, *The Fifties*, 627-628.
[172] John M. Mansfield, *Man on the Moon* (New York: Stein and Day, 1969), 74.
[173] D'Antonio, *A Ball, A Dog, and A Monkey*, 233-235, 241-243.

Yet the United States wasn't that far behind. It remained for additional spending on the Eisenhower administration's part and the Kennedy administration's total commitment to finally push the United States ahead in the space race, culminating in American astronauts becoming the first men to land and walk on the moon in 1969.[174]

The "Missile Gap" and the "National Purpose"

All of that lay in the future. For now, *Sputnik* was the catalyst for a searching reexamination of America's defense and education systems and its national purpose. Some Americans believed that *Sputnik* demonstrated that their country had gone soft, compared to the more disciplined and serious Russians—a feeling that proved a major challenge for Eisenhower to dispel.[175]

Since World War II, Americans had believed that theirs was the world's greatest nation in all aspects. In reality, America's geographical isolation during the war was primarily responsible for her postwar industrial and economic might. Safe from enemy attack, American industry prospered during the war. Moreover, the wartime Manhattan Project which armed the United States with the atomic bomb wasn't an exclusively American undertaking as it also involved the contributions of anti-Nazi scientists from Europe.

President Eisenhower was also credited with America's economic vigor and other good fortune during the 1950s. But says biographer Stephen E. Ambrose,

> It was plain good luck. The economic boom would have taken place even if Taft or Stevenson had won in 1952. America's preponderant position in military and financial power was a legacy Eisenhower inherited. Eisenhower had been a participant in the process of changing the isolationist America of 1939 into the world colossus of 1952, but not the maker of that policy. His task as President was one of managing America's rise to globalism, not bring it about. As Eisenhower himself was always first to point out, it was plain silly to give all the credit, or blame, to one man.[176]

For the Democrats, who had been on the receiving end of McCarthy-era Republican attacks about being "soft on communism" a short time earlier, *Sputnik* now provided the same kind of opening to similarly pound Republicans with—this time being "soft" on national defense. Senator Henry Jackson of Washington spoke of "shame and danger." Of all the Democrats to

---

[174] J. Ronald Oakley, *God's Country: America in the Fifties* (New York: Dembner Books, 1986), 347.

[175] O'Neill, *American High*, 270.

[176] Ambrose, *Eisenhower: Volume II*, 424, 425.

benefit the most, politically, from *Sputnik*, it was Senator Lyndon B. Johnson of Texas. October 4, 1957, found LBJ relaxing with guests at his Texas ranch when word of the Russian satellite came. During an after dinner stroll with them, Johnson decided to helm a Senate inquiry into missile and space matters and promptly set about laying the groundwork for the probe. The perfect forum to conduct what Johnson had in mind was had been created in 1950 by Johnson's political mentor, Richard Russell of Georgia—the Preparedness Subcommittee of the Senate Armed Services Committee. Russell's original intention was to furnish LBJ a political stage on which the Texan could make a name for himself. During its early years of existence, the subcommittee had occupied its time studying the defense effort during the Korean War, much as the renowned "Truman Committee" had done during World War II. The subcommittee fell by the wayside as a result of the GOP's capture of the Senate in 1952—yet the latter proved only temporary: the outcome of the 1954 elections provided both the subcommittee and now Senate Majority Leader Lyndon Johnson a new lease on political life.

Despite his eagerness to jump into the maelstrom *Sputnik* had ignited, Johnson stayed his hand—with good reason. Eisenhower was a revered national figure and, as had been shown earlier, attacking him on defense issues entailed great risk. Not until subsequent events—the public's frenzied reaction to *Sputnik I*, the obvious befuddlement on the administration's part, and the added shock of *Sputnik II*—did the Democrats known with certainty that they had plausible grounds for conducting such an inquiry.[177]

On November 25, 1957, Johnson's Inquiry into Satellite and Missile Programs began its hearings. Edward Teller wanted America to aim for the moon:

> Shall I tell you why I want to go to the moon? . . . I don't really know. I don't know, but once we make it we will find some use. And I think going to the moon is in the same category. It will have both amusing and amazing and practical and military consequences.[178]

Vannevar Bush advocated more backing for science and education and respect for the scientist "as a fellow worker for the good of the country"—not a "highbrow or egghead."[179] General Jimmy Doolittle cautioned that Russia would presently surpass America in every field unless military research and development received greater backing. When it came their turn to testify, administration spokesmen were unable to rebut the critics. LBJ ended day one of the hearings by saying that America had suffered a scientific Pearl

---

[177] McDougall, ...*The Heavens and the Earth*, 141-142.
[178] O'Neill, *American High*, 276; McDougall, ...*The Heavens and the Earth*, 152-153.
[179] O'Neill, *American High*, 276; McDougall, ...*The Heavens and the Earth*, 153.

Harbor. When the hearings concluded the following January, they had given the Democrats tremendous mileage.[180] For Johnson, they had provided him the knowledge that the Soviets held the lead in missile development and numbers of submarines, and were catching up in aircraft, were more skilled in research and development, led the way in space, and were faster in producing scientists and engineers. He presented the Senate, the White House, and journalists a list of seventeen recommendations. Not only had America lost the competition to fashion a weapon, it had lost the battle of organized intellectual power:

> There can be no adequate defense for the U.S. except in a reservoir of trained and educated minds. The immediate objective is to defend ourselves. But the equally important objective is to reach the hearts and minds of men everywhere so that the day will come when the ballistic missile will be merely a rusty relic in the museums of mankind. . . .[181]

While the *Sputniks* proved that the Soviets did possess an advantage in the ability to carry satellites into orbit, they trailed badly behind in the production of workable warheads and failed to deploy an ICBM during the Eisenhower presidency. The enormous American lead in military missile development and nuclear weapons grew even greater during the second Eisenhower administration, and a Russian attack would have precipitated a catastrophic American response.

The photographic evidence provided by the U-2 overflights of the Soviet Union conclusively proved in 1956-1957 that the Soviets were far behind in ICBM development. "The President," self-assured about his military expertise," wrote historian James T. Patterson, "carefully examined the U-2 evidence, for he took pride in his attention to American security," which he rated a higher priority than space exploration.*[182] In his view, it was far

---

[180] O'Neill, *American High,* 276.

[181] McDougall, *...The Heavens and the Earth,* 155.

[182] Numerous historians have asserted that Eisenhower never worried much about the supposed missile gap because the U-2 photographs revealed a small and unimpressive Soviet missile program. "This oft-repeated assertion," William I. Hitchcock has written, "is misleading." He continues that the 13 U-2 missions flown over the Soviet Union between June and October 1957 "provided no comfort at all." The U-2 photographs taken in the month before *Sputnik* disclosed an enormous and burgeoning Soviet nuclear weapons and missile testing program. Precisely how far the Soviet Union's new rockets could travel, how many it intended to construct, how accurate they were remained unknown. .

The U-2 missions furnished invaluable data, "yet because of the extreme risk of the illegal overflights" writes Hitchcock, Eisenhower believed the downing of one might incite a war—he didn't continue them. In the interval between mid-October 1957 and December 1959, he authorized only two flights into Soviet airspace. With the U-2 all but grounded, CIA analysts had to depend on a second option to monitor Soviet rocketry. In early 1955

better to have "one good Redstone nuclear-armed missile than a rocket that could hit the moon. We have no enemies on the moon." Refusing to let *Sputnik* stampede him, Eisenhower clung to the doctrine of "sufficiency," where the United States' principle necessity was to sustain enough armed might to survive an enemy attack, with nuclear weapons available to retaliate with, yet not incessantly add to its stockpiles. How many times, he asked in 1958, "could [you] kill the same man?" As he told the Cabinet, "Look, I'd like to know what's on the other side of the moon, but I won't pay to find out this year."[183]

Because he was loathe to reveal the existence of the U-2, Eisenhower asked that the American people simply believe his assurances that the United States maintained its military lead over Russia, *Sputnik* notwithstanding, only to discover—to his astonishment—that they didn't. Eisenhower found *Sputnik* as bedeviling an issue as Senator Joseph McCarthy and his Communists-in-government hearings had been a short while earlier for Truman. Then, Eisenhower had derived political benefit from McCarthy's assaults on the Democratic administration, which had been one reason why he took no action against McCarthy. Now Eisenhower found himself ensnared in the same predicament.[184]

Eisenhower made some concessions to alleviate popular anxieties. He backed the creation of the National Aeronautics and Space Administration (NASA), a civilian agency assigned to coordinate future missile development and space exploration. He further promoted federal assistance to education to further science and foreign languages.[185] The ensuing legislation, the National Defense Education Act of 1958, provided, among other things, $295 million in low-interest loans to college students (particularly those studying to become teachers); $280 million in matching funds for laboratories and other facilities and materials for teaching science, math, and foreign languages in public schools; $82 million for over 5,000 fellowships annually for graduate students who were pursuing careers as college teachers and additional funding to improve the teaching of foreign languages and for encouraging

---

the U.S. had installed a sophisticated radar system to monitor Soviet missile tests. The ensuing information revealed the astonishing frequency of Soviet missile tests—almost 300 between 1953 and 1957—and the approximate range and altitude of the missiles the Soviets were developing. "Although most of the missiles they tested were short- or intermediate-range, it was clear they were trying to achieve long-range ICBM capability. CIA analysts combined the radar data, the U-2 photographs, and their analysis of the rocket that carried *Sputnik* into orbit, and concluded that they had *underestimated* Soviet missile capabilities." Hitchcock, *The Age of Eisenhower*, 384-385.

183 Patterson, *Grand Expectations*, 419-420.

184 William L. O'Neill, American High: The Years of Confidence, 1945-160 (New York: The Free Press, 1986), 274.

185 Patterson, *Grand Expectations*, 420-421.

---

the utilization of television and other tools for audiovisual instruction. Still the NDEA was intended to further the national defense—and nothing more. The bill stipulated that those receiving financial assistance under it must sign a proviso confirming their allegiance to the United States and to swear that they had never taken part in subversive activities. That clause elicited subsequent objections and was ultimately eliminated.[186] Eisenhower's performance in the *Sputnik* crisis (and his conduct of defense policies overall in his second term) has for the most part been viewed favorably by many historians. By focusing on missile development, he oversaw major advances in the nation's air-based and nuclear capability in comparison to the Soviet Union. Eisenhower's level-headed response to *Sputnik* and the domestic criticism of his defense policy in the wake of the Russian space achievement also kept defense spending from skyrocketing.

Still Eisenhower failed to completely alleviate popular anxieties arising from *Sputnik*. Americans believed they were the world's leader in science and technology and, if they slipped from that position, someone was at fault. Indicating this sentiment, a number of luminaries publicly lamented what they felt to be the absence of "national purpose," yet couldn't quite clarify what that was. Other voices chimed in on the subject. Addressing the Women's National Democratic Club in Washington in 1959, George Kennan said:

> "If you ask me . . . whether a country in the state this country is in today: with no highly developed sense of national purpose, with the overwhelming accent of life on personal comfort and amusement, with a dearth of public services and a surfeit of privately sold gadgetry, with a chaotic transportation system, with its great urban areas being gradually disintegrated by the headlong switch to motor transportation, with an educational system where quality has been extensively sacrificed to quantity, and with insufficient social discipline even to keep its major industries functioning without grievous interruptions—if you ask me whether such a country has, over the long run, good chances of competing with a purposeful, serious, and disciplined society such as that of the Soviet Union, I must say that the answer is 'no.'"[187]

When Eisenhower stepped down from the presidency in 1961, the number of ICBMs in the American arsenal was approximately two hundred. At the end of the Kennedy presidency, that figure had risen to one thousand and was still multiplying. Subsequently JFK's Defense Secretary, Robert McNamara, admitted that the "missile gap" was a myth, or if it had existed, it

---

[186] Oakley, *God's Country*, 352; Patterson, *Grand Expectations*, 421; Solberg, *Riding High*, 351.
[187] Patterson, *Grand Expectations*, 421, 422; Goldman, *The Crucial Decade–And After*, 342-343.

favored the United States. McNamara's confession, however, came too late to halt the modern arms race.[188]

Thus the "truth" of the "missile gap" was finally exposed. Also fallacious was the impression that America's defenses and way of life were inferior to that of the Soviet Union. That notion had arisen from the media's exaggeration of the true significance of *Sputnik:* such overkill stampeded the public into believing the doomsayers' gloomy observations that *Sputnik* signified the descent of America's star. Aside from demonstrating that the Soviets held the lead in the space competition—for the moment anyway—*Sputnik* merely showed that forced industrialization and scientific development under an authoritarian system of government could achieve remarkable feats—nothing more. Unlike the democratic, capitalistic United States, which could simultaneously support its space effort and meet the basic needs of its people, Russia was incapable of doing the same. A French newspaper appreciated this, observing that *Sputnik I* was "a brilliant star" extending Soviet power into the heavens, but only "thanks to millions of pots and shoes lacking."[189]

Presently space mania in both the United States and Russia began to subside, to be replaced by more mundane issues—chiefly the health of both nations' economies. The Soviet Union returned to its quest to match the Western standard of living; the new battle cry was Catch UP! In America a recession that began at roughly the same time the first *Sputnik* had made its big splash produced high levels of both food prices and unemployment. By the end of 1958 all indications were that the recession was past. The stock market led the way with a 37% gain for the year. Income, employment, manufacturing, and savings rose. The space effort was credited with this recovery as it stimulated swift hikes in government spending which produced jobs and prompted spending. Others credited the economic turnaround more to the expansion of new, high-value American-borne technologies—chief of which was the semiconductor industry. Delivering a goodwill message of his own for the New Year over the Mutual Broadcasting Network, Khrushchev declared, "All of us Soviet people, from the bottom of our hearts, wish the American people well-being and happiness, a life of peace and tranquility for 1959 and the development and strengthening of friendly cooperation between our countries for the benefits of peace."[190]

---

[188] Ambrose, *Ike's Spies*, 278.
[189] Weisberger, *Cold War, Cold Peace*, 179.
[190] D'Antonio, *A Ball, A Dog, and A Monkey*, 191-192. 245-246.

5. BERLIN, THE "KITCHEN DEBATE," AND THE "SPIRIT OF CAMP DAVID" (1958–1959)

Nikita Khrushchev's expressed hopes for improved Soviet-American relations in the new year 1959 had been preceded, over two months earlier, by words that implied war over the divided city of Berlin. Speaking in Moscow's Sports Palace on November 10, 1958, the Soviet Premier declared that the time was obviously at hand "for the signatories of the Potsdam Agreement to renounce the remnants of the occupation regime in Berlin and thereby make it possible to create a normal situation in the capital of the German Democratic Republic." Because America and its NATO allies were ready to let West Germany develop a military more powerful than the British and French armies combined, apparently there was nothing in the Potsdam Agreement to the benefit of Moscow—save for one provision that the Allies continued adherence to: their occupation rights in West Berlin. "Who profits from such a situation?" Khrushchev asked, posing a rhetorical question, the implied answer being not the Soviet Union.

The Soviets intended to resolve the matter by relinquishing its responsibilities under the agreement to East Germany itself. East German soldiers would oversee the points of access running from West Germany to West Berlin and examine the visas of those visiting the city. Ultimately the East Germans would decide if they would allow the use of their territory—be it in the air or on the ground—to reach West Berlin.[191]

This wouldn't be the first time the Russians had sought to expel the Western allies from Berlin. Stalin had first sought this with the Berlin block-

---

[191] Aleksandr Fursenko and Timothy Naftali, *Khrushchev's Cold War: The Inside Story of an American Adversary* (New York: W.W. Norton and Company, 2006), 199-200.

ade in 1948 but had been thwarted by the Berlin Airlift, which forced Stalin to lift the blockade in 1949.[192]

Khrushchev followed his November 10 declaration with a formal note to Washington on November 27, accusing the West of transforming their half of Berlin "into a kind of state within a state and using it as a center" for subversive operations against the East German government. The continuance of the occupation rights was "tantamount to recognizing something like a privileged position of the NATO countries," necessitating measures to turn West Berlin into a free and demilitarized city. The Soviet Union was ready for negotiations for this transformation, during which time Allied access to West Berlin would remain unhindered. Should the negotiations prove unsuccessful, the Soviet Union and East Germany would then decide the matter between themselves in such a way that allowed the East Germans themselves to regulate access to West Berlin, with Moscow providing military assistance to back up the agreement.[193]

Until now there had been grounds for believing that relations between the superpowers could be improved: the preceding August 28, Eisenhower announced the American cessation of nuclear testing, followed, in November, by a similar announcement on the Russians' part.[194] Though both sides continued increasing the size of their nuclear arsenals in the wake of the testing halt, not since the beginning of the Cold War had the prospects of achieving some form of nuclear accord been so favorable.[195]

Why then did Khrushchev choose this particular moment to inflame Cold War tensions anew with his Berlin ultimatum? Born into a peasant family, Khrushchev had risen from his humble origins to the apex of Soviet power, chairman of the Council of Ministers, by 1958. Along the way he had survived Stalin's purges of the 1930s and the paranoia of his final years. After Stalin's death he shoved aside potential rivals to gain supreme power.[196] Khrushchev urged the de-Stalinization of Russia and Eastern Europe and the resumption of collective leadership, asserted that war between capitalism and communism wasn't predestined, and declared that socialism could be achieved in other ways.[197]

In addition to signaling a possible lessening of the Cold War, Khrushchev's de-Stalinization speech energized hopes for reforms in Eastern Eu-

---

[192] *Ibid.*, 197.

[193] Parmet, *Eisenhower and the American Crusades*, 529.

[194] Oakley, *God's Country*, 383.

[195] Patterson, *Grand Expectations*, 423, 424.

[196] Weisberger, *Cold War, Cold Peace*, 188.

[197] Oakley, *God's Country*, 221.

rope.[198] The latter most likely was the catalyst for the sequence of events that culminated in Khrushchev's Berlin ultimatum: if the reforming zeal went too far, it could seriously jeopardize Khrushchev's position; hence he had to demonstrate that he was at heart as dedicated a Communist as his peers were.

The hopes for reforms ignited subsequent nationalist uprisings in East Germany, Poland, and Hungary that nearly lead to Khrushchev's removal. His strong actions in quelling the revolts apparently redeemed—and chastened—him. This provided an opportunity for those, whom Khrushchev would condemn as the "Anti-Party Group," to seek his ouster. Convening the Presidium during Khrushchev's absence in Finland in June 1957, they demanded his resignation on the grounds that rapid liberalization had impaired the cause of international communism. Khrushchev would not stand aside until the verdict had received the approval of the vast membership of the Central Committee—a bastion of Khrushchev partisans, who, brought to Moscow aboard army planes, defeated the ouster of their patron. Khrushchev disposed of his adversaries, leaving him, by 1958, as Party and government head—putting him in the company of the only other men to hold both positions simultaneously, Lenin and Stalin.

Berlin was the sole Western enclave within the Soviet realm. It's open borders allowed a tidal wave of East Germans to escape the hardships of life under Communist domination. The result of this exodus was that the number of people living in East Germany dwindled; many of those fleeing were necessary to the maintenance of an advanced industrialized economy. The exodus was the source of Khrushchev's lament that Berlin was "a bone in my throat."[199]

Khrushchev's aim in seeking negotiations on a German peace treaty was to force the West to approach and accord implied acknowledgment of the existence of Soviet Russia's East German client state. That he had nearly been ousted as a result of the 1956 uprisings remained in his mind. In the opinion of American ambassador Llewellyn Thompson, Khrushchev was resolved to "nail down the eastern frontiers of Germany and of Poland," thus eliminating them as further trouble spots.

Khrushchev's greatest worry may have been that the Western Allies would transform West Germany into a nuclear-armed power—a possibility that added to Russia's longstanding fear of Germany. His public bombast aside, Khrushchev supposedly knew that, owing to the U-2 and other intelligence sources, Eisenhower needn't fear Soviet armed might. If Khrushchev

---

[198] Weisberger, *Cold War, Cold Peace*, 188; Patterson, *Grand Expectations*, 304.
[199] Pach and Richardson, *The Presidency of Dwight D. Eisenhower*, Revised Edition, 200.

lacked strategic strength to force the West to the bargaining table to achieve a German peace treaty and secure a pledge forswearing the nuclear arming of West Germany, his sole option was to rattle his nuclear saber at the West over one of its most vulnerable protectorates. "Berlin," Khrushchev said, "is the testicles of the West. Each time I yank, they holler."[200]

Following meetings of the Western foreign ministers and the NATO council, the U.S. vowed to hold firm in Berlin and expected the Soviets to honor the Allied agreements until the latter were ended by mutual concurrence. Secretary of State Dulles and Eisenhower further made it plain that they would not negotiate with the East German regime, which the United States refused to recognize. The only way Eisenhower would entertain the creation of a free city would be if such an arrangement extended to all of Berlin and if the UN was given responsibility for supervising the access routes from the West. Eisenhower reinforced these positions with military preparations that he directed be implemented in such a way as not to alarm the public, but sufficiently obvious as not to escape the notice of Soviet intelligence. He further made it clear that allowing East Germany to regulate Allied movement in and out of Berlin was unacceptable to the United States. Eisenhower defended his actions on the grounds that America would defend its position in Berlin in a way that would allow Khrushchev the option of changing his position without the Soviet chairman fearing that doing so would be a humiliating act on his part. Eisenhower made it plain that American strategy wouldn't be half-hearted: "Khrushchev should know that when we decide to act, our whole stack will be in the pot."[201] Should an attempt be made to halt a Western convoy from entering West Berlin after May 27, 1959—the date Khrushchev set for the conclusion of negotiations with the West—Eisenhower considered mounting a new Berlin airlift, severing diplomatic contact with Russia, and readying the American people for a possible world war.[202]

The Berlin crisis also produced calls at home for rash action that demanded Eisenhower's attention. The President regarded calls for stronger military actions as dangerous: one such course, a full mobilization of NATO forces, would merely inflame tensions. Regarding the use of nuclear weapons to free Berlin, "Well, I don't know how you could free anything with nuclear weapons." He vetoed a suggestion from the Joint Chiefs that, should Berlin be blockaded once the Soviets' deadline had passed, a division of troops be deployed to shatter the blockade.

---

[200] Beschloss, *Mayday*, 171-172.
[201] Pach and Richardson, *The Presidency of Dwight D. Eisenhower*, Revised Edition, 201-202.
[202] Beschloss, *Mayday*, 172.

Eisenhower also informed Congress that the Berlin matter didn't require emergency spending. Over congressional objections, he reduced army strength by 50,000. The troops, he argued, weren't needed as the administration placed great reliance on nuclear weapons to forestall aggression. He also explained that any attempt to equal the number of Soviet conventional forces could produce a garrison state that would jeopardize American democracy.

When it came to Western solidarity, Eisenhower more or less could depend on France's Charles de Gaulle—despite the fact that experience had taught Eisenhower during World War II that de Gaulle could be very difficult to deal with. Another wartime ally turned political leader who gave cause for concern was Britain's Harold Macmillan.[203] Concerned that the Berlin crisis was heading toward war, Macmillan flew to Moscow for talks with Khrushchev in February 1959. The meeting began on a friendly note but, when the British Prime Minister, acting in accord with a prior agreement with Eisenhower, merely proposed the convening of a meeting of the Big Four foreign ministers to discuss the Berlin matter, the Anglo-Soviet conference turned dark. Khrushchev wanted to know what a foreign ministers meeting could accomplish. Khrushchev then canceled his public invitation to escort his guest to Kiev and Leningrad on the grounds that he had a toothache! At this point Macmillan considered breaking off the summit and going home but chose to remain. Back in Moscow, he informed his host he wouldn't object if the foreign ministers conclave led the way to a big power summit meeting. [204]

During a subsequent meeting with Eisenhower in Washington, Macmillan declared that the British "were not prepared to face obliteration for the sake of two million Berlin Germans, their former enemies, especially over issues such as the color of passes for motor convoys and the nationality of those who stamped them." When Macmillan noted that eight atomic bombs were all that was necessary to kill 30 million of his countrymen and destroy the British economy, Eisenhower rejoined that far more Americans would perish in a nuclear conflict. In the wake of the Eisenhower-Macmillan parley, Khrushchev announced at the end of March his readiness to dispatch his foreign minister, Andrei Gromyko, to Geneva. This marked the end of the Berlin crisis—though the issue that sparked it remained unresolved.

May 27, 1959, the date set for the termination of Khrushchev's Berlin ultimatum, saw the arrival in Washington of the Big Four foreign ministers and other dignitaries for a somber event—the funeral of John Foster Dulles,

[203] Pach and Richardson, *The Presidency of Dwight D. Eisenhower*, Revised Edition, 202-203.
[204] Beschloss, Mayday, 173-175.

who had succumbed to cancer. The foreign ministers had already gathering in Geneva but failed to settle the Berlin matter.[205] Clearly neither Khrushchev or Eisenhower would budge from their respective positions: Khrushchev conducting serious negotiations only at the summit level; Eisenhower refusing to hold such a meeting in the absence of any headway at the foreign ministers' level.[206]

Nixon in Moscow

While the world awaited the ultimate outcome of the Berlin crisis, plans continued in both the United States and the Soviet Union for the opening of art and technological displays in New York and Moscow. Soviet Deputy Premier Frol Kozlov would have the honor of opening his nation's exhibition in New York, while Vice President Richard Nixon would do the same in Moscow. At this time, Khrushchev publicly intimated his desire to visit the United States; as he told visiting American governors in Moscow, he was "ready for travel."[207]

Khrushchev indeed got the invitation but the manner in which it was extended proved an embarrassment to Eisenhower. During Kozlov's appearance in New York to open the Russian Exhibition, Deputy Undersecretary of State Robert Murphy meet the Deputy Premier, at which time he extended the invitation for Khrushchev's visit to Kozlov. What Murphy failed to comprehend was that such a visit was contingent upon progress concerning Berlin, hence he failed to tell Kozlov of this stipulation. Eisenhower's shock—both when he learned that foreign ministers remained deadlocked over Berlin and that Murphy misunderstood the precondition attached to Khrushchev's invitation—was understandable. In the President's view, such an error on the part of the State Department would never have happened had the late Foster Dulles still been running Foggy Bottom.[208]

The faux pas over Khrushchev's invitation transformed Nixon's Russian visit from simply a goodwill courtesy call into a prelude for the main event: the Eisenhower-Khrushchev parley. Eisenhower made the Vice President's purpose in visiting Russia quite clear at the outset: Nixon would be acting merely as presidential envoy, with no authority to conduct any negotiations with Khrushchev.[209] Among those accompanying Nixon to Moscow were his wife Pat, President Eisenhower's brother Milton, Admiral Hyman Rick-

---

[205] Pach and Richardson, *The Presidency of Dwight D. Eisenhower*, Revised Edition, 203-205.
[206] Beschloss, *Mayday*, 177.
[207] *Ibid.*, 178.
[208] Pach and Richardson, *The Presidency of Dwight D. Eisenhower*, Revised Edition, 206-207.
[209] Beschloss, *Mayday*, 178.

over—the latter the Navy's foremost authority on nuclear energy—Professor William Elliott of Harvard, and staff people from the State Department and Nixon's office. One who failed to secure a place in the Vice President's entourage was a man currently engaged in promotion work for Nixon and the Republicans in Southern California— H.R. Haldeman, later of Watergate infamy in Nixon's own White House.

Just before the Vice President's departure, Eisenhower, in accordance with the provisions of the annual Captive Nations resolution, which Congress had passed since the GOP took over the Legislative branch in 1953, proclaimed Captive Nations Week, during which time Americans were urged to pray for those living under Communist rule. Unknown to the Americans was the fact that the proclamations deeply offended the Russian leadership. This may well explain the frosty reception accorded the vice presidential party upon its arrival in Moscow. When Nixon conferred with the American ambassador, Llewellyn Thompson, at Spaso House after the arrival ceremony, he learned of the Soviet leaders' displeasure with the Captive Nations resolution. Thompson explained "that they were particularly sensitive to such criticism because their relations with some of the satellite countries were strained," Nixon later recalled.[210]

Owing to the time change, Nixon hardly sleep that night. Around 5:30 that morning he awakened Jack Sherwood, the Secret Service agent assigned to him, informing him of his wish to visit the Danilovsky market, where farmers brought their produce and meat. "It would be," Nixon wrote, "a good way to get a sense of the city and its people before starting my official schedule." Once he arrived there, Nixon quickly attracted a crowd. Nixon spent nearly an hour with the throng, answering their questions, enjoying himself. He was about to leave when several people inquired if he had any tickets to the American Exhibition. Having none with him, Nixon said he would be delighted to buy some for his newly acquired friends in the market so they could be his guests. When he directed Sherwood to give the group spokesman a hundred-ruble note to buy a hundred tickets, the spokesman was unable to accept, saying that only selected individuals received tickets from the government. "We all laughed about the problem, and I shook hands and left." The episode provided the pretext for Soviet newspapers *Pravda*, *Izvestia*, and *Trud* to accuse Nixon of having attempted to "bribe" and "degrade" Soviet citizens by offering them money.

Later that morning, Nixon meet Khrushchev in the latter's Kremlin office. During this occasion the Chairman vehemently expressed his anger at

[210] Stephen E. Ambrose, *Nixon: The Education of a Politician 1913-1962* (New York: Simon and Schuster, 1987), 520-522; Richard Nixon, *RN: The Memoirs of Richard Nixon* (New York: Grosset & Dunlap, 1978), 206.

the Captive Nations resolution. Then the Soviet Premier and the American Vice President drove to the American Exhibition for a visit before its official opening that evening.[211]

Their first stop was the Glass Pavilion, which housed a display of consumer items. The Soviet press derided this part of the exhibit as unrepresentative of the average American's life. A "traditional Moscow fair" had suddenly appeared as well to sell similar items seldom seen in Russian stores. As Nixon and Khrushchev passed RCA's mock television studio, an engineer asked them if they wanted to view themselves on the new color monitors and try out a system that taped and replayed TV broadcasts.[212]

Khrushchev began the session by complaining about American trade practices, which elicited Nixon's comment, "There must be a free exchange of ideas." Indicating the television camera, Khrushchev then asked if the tape they were recording as part of this demonstration would be seen in America, in English translation? Nixon promised it would. Khrushchev then asked how long America had existed. "One hundred and fifty years," Nixon answered. (Nixon erred; later he provided the correct answer—180 years—in his memoirs).

"One hundred and fifty years?" Khrushchev asked. "Well, then, we will say America has been in existence for one hundred and fifty years and this is the level she has reached. We have existed not quite forty-two years and in another seven years we will be on the same level as America. When we catch you up, in passing you by, we will wave to you [here Khrushchev waved to an imaginary American]. Then if you wish, we can stop and say: Please follow up."

He then denounced the Captive Nations resolution, after which he embraced a Soviet worker on the set, rocking back and forth with him. "Does this man look like a slave laborer?" Khrushchev then waved at other Soviet workers: "With men with such spirit, how can we lose?"

Nixon conceded the Soviet lead in rockets, but indicated the American advantage in other areas—"color television, for instance." "No," said Khrushchev, "we are up with you on this, too. We have bested you in one technique and also in the other."

> NIXON: You see, you never concede anything.

> KHRUSHCHEV: I do not give up.[213]

---

[211] Nixon, *RN*, 2006-208.

[212] Marling, *As Seen on TV*, 272.

[213] Ambrose, *Nixon*, 523.

Future presidential speechwriter William Safire provided the opportunity for Nixon to score a comeback in round two of their argument. Seeing Nixon exit the studio in search of a way to recoup, Safire called out, "This way to the typical American house," setting the stage for the celebrated "kitchen debate."[214]

Nixon praised the merits of the model house, which, he said, cost $14,000 and was affordable for American workers. This was true in the Soviet Union, said Khrushchev, who continued that American homes would not last beyond 20 years. "We put that question to your capitalists and they said, 'In 20 years we will sell them another house. We [Russians] build firmly. We build for our children and grandchildren. We use bricks."

Nixon, in turn, lodged an accusation of his own against Khrushchev: that of filibustering. "You do all the talking and you do not let anyone talk. I want to make one point. We don't think this fair will astound the Russian people, but it will interest them. To us, diversity, the right to choose, the fact that we have a thousand different builders, that's the spice of life. We don't want to have a decision made at the top by one government official saying that we will have one type of house. That's the difference."

Khrushchev characterized the production of so many kinds of washing machines or houses as inefficient, then launched into another lecture on the superior quality of Soviet products. Nixon permitted Khrushchev to have his say, then asked, "Isn't it better to be talking about the relative merits of our washing machines than of the relative strength of our rockets? Isn't this the kind of competition you want?" "Yes," Khrushchev answered, "but your generals say, 'We want to compete in rockets. We can beat you.'"

By now the discussion had degenerated into a mutual finger-jabbing session. "Who wants to threaten?" Nixon asked. "I'm not threatening. We will never engage in threats."

Correspondent James Reston of *The New York Times* observed that while the discussion was a "disaster in terms of connectional diplomacy, Mr. Khrushchev was still smiling at the end. He had a good time. He had an argument with another politician today and an audience to go with it, and naturally this was a politician's idea of fun."

At the conclusion of the "kitchen debate," Khrushchev spotted an elderly Russian woman cheering him, and embraced her. Seeing Nixon, William Randolph Hearst yelled, "Hey Dick!" Khrushchev, whom Hearst had previously interviewed, shook Hearst's hands, exclaiming, "My capitalist, monopolist, journalist friend. Do you ever publish anything in your papers that you disagree with?"

---

[214] Brodie, *Richard Nixon*, 384.

Hearst's affirmative answer was greeted with incredulity on Khrushchev's part—a feeling that persisted when Nixon explained some of the things the newspapers printed about him. Nixon continued, "If there is one idea you must get out of your head, it is that the American press is a kept press."[215]

Time approvingly characterized the Nixon of the "kitchen debate" as "the personification of a kind of disciplined vigor that belied tales of the decadent and limp-wristed West." Adlai Stevenson conceded that Nixon had "scored heavily" and would undoubtedly prove "a formidable candidate" in the 1960 presidential election—"all of which fills me with a feeling that must be nausea and wonder about the new image of the American hero to inspire our little boys."[216]

Khrushchev gave his word that Nixon's remarks at the opening of the American Exhibition would be published in their entirety in *Pravda* and *Izvestia*. Nixon thus aimed them at the Russian people. "There are 44 million families in the United States," 25 million of which "live in houses or apartments that have as much or more floor space than the one you see in this Exhibit." Nixon asserted that 31 million families owned their own homes, that Americans possessed 56 million cars, 50 million television sets and 143 million radio sets. The typical American family purchased nine dresses and suits and 14 pairs of shoes yearly. What all this showed was that America "has from the standpoint of distribution of wealth come closest to the idea of prosperity for all in a classless society." Hence, "The caricature of capitalism as a predatory, monopolist-dominated society is as hopelessly out of date, as far as the United States is concerned, as a wooden plow." Wrapping up his remarks, Nixon emphasized peaceful competition:

> "Let us extend this competition to include the spiritual as well as the material aspects of our civilization. Let us compete not in how to take lives but in how to save them. Let us work for victory not in war but for the victory of plenty over poverty, of health over disease, of understanding over ignorance wherever they exist in the world."[217]

Nixon's remarks marked the first time a politician had presented a positive image of American life to the Russian people. "No matter what happens now," enthused a guest, "your trip to the Soviet Union will go down as a major diplomatic triumph."[218]

---

[215] Ambrose, *Nixon*, 524-525.
[216] Beschloss, *Mayday*, 181.
[217] Ambrose, Nixon, 525-526
[218] Ibid., 526.

At the conclusion of a subsequent lunch gathering, Nixon requested a private audience with Khrushchev:

> Walking over the grounds of the dacha with only Troyanovsky, his interpreter, with us, I brought up the invitation President Eisenhower had extended to him to come and visit the United States, which we had not discussed before. I explained that his visit would be met with mixed reactions in the United States. I urged him to do everything possible to create the proper atmosphere for constructive talks. Then I suggested that the eyes of the world were on the Geneva Foreign Ministers Conference and that some action on his part to break the impasse on the Berlin question could be a dramatic event which would make his visit to the United States not only successful but also historical in making progress toward a peaceful settlement of our differences.[219]

Hearing Nixon out, Khrushchev merely replied that he would remain in contact with Gromyko in Geneva. Nixon felt that his plea had failed as much as that of Eisenhower's brother Milton earlier during their lunch.[220] Nixon concluded his Russian visit by delivering an unprecedented radio and television address to the people of the Soviet Union. At Thompson's suggestion, Nixon's remarks included a reference to the incident at the Danilovsky market. "In my speech," Nixon later wrote, "I simply described what had happened, but this was the first time anyone could remember that *Pravda* had been criticized publicly." Nixon continued that "the incident stirred debate among the Russian people long after I was gone."[221]

"What we need today is not two worlds but one world where different peoples choose the economic and political systems which they want, but where there is free communication among all the peoples living on this earth."

Briefing Eisenhower and the White House staff after returning to Washington, Nixon characterized Khrushchev "as a man with a closed mind, who will not be impressed with what he sees in America. The only approach which will be useful will be to give him a subtle feeling of the power and will of America." The Soviet Chairman "will try to wear anyone down who talks to him. As to social matters," Nixon "recommended stag events in business suits since Khrushchev, by principle, eschews tuxedoes. The women are accustomed to being entertained separately." The Russians would bring a "great entourage," and Nixon counseled that "his trip should be managed

---

[219] Richard M. Nixon, Six Crises (Garden City, New York: Doubleday & Company, Inc., 1962), 271.

[220] Nixon, *Six Crises*, 270-271.

[221] Richard Nixon, RN: The Memoirs of Richard Nixon (New York: Grosset & Dunlap, 1978), 212.

by someone experienced in running political campaigns." Eliminating himself from the latter, Nixon did so on the grounds that it would be "improper since he had not done so with any other head of state." Twice Nixon suggested that Eisenhower "give Khrushchev the greatest exposure possible," as it would force the Soviet leader to extend the same courtesy to Eisenhower when the latter visited Moscow, and because "in the long run, exposure would hurt Khrushchev." Nixon's most important element of counsel was not to expect to change Khrushchev's opinions by debating the virtues of the American and Soviet systems—a lesson Nixon had learned first-hand from Khrushchev himself.[222]

Thus advised, Eisenhower prepared for the first visit to America of a Soviet head of state.

Khrushchev in America

On August 3, 1959, Eisenhower confirmed that he and Khrushchev would be visiting one another's countries—Khrushchev to set foot on American soil the following month, Eisenhower to visit Russia at a later date. During a subsequent press conference, Eisenhower refuted the impression that John Foster Dulles' departure signaled a new course in American foreign policy, with Ike taking a more active role in this area. He explained that both Foster Dulles and other State Department officers had been consulted about a personal encounter with Khrushchev. There was also the fact that Eisenhower himself had held reservations about such a meeting, though he himself was unable to publicly express his reluctance.

Naturally, the announcement of Khrushchev's impending arrival set off cries of outrage from conservative voices. As early as January, Senator Thomas Dodd, a Democrat from Connecticut, implored Eisenhower to resist meeting the Russians bilaterally as the Russians might seize upon this as an opportunity to divide America from the free world by exploiting "the fear and resentments of our allies." In April Eisenhower's fellow Republican, Senator Style Bridges of New Hampshire, expressed to Ike that "this Government is not going to be bluffed or blackmailed into a summit conference" and backed the President's opinion that "we need some prior assurance that a summit conference will produce real achievement." The news of the reciprocal visits on the part of the two heads of state prompted the archbishop of Philadelphia to offer a mass for the wellbeing of Eisenhower and the United States as well as cable the White House: "Today's announcement leaves a deep wound." Eisenhower himself felt it necessary to personally promise Fran-

---

[222] Ambrose, *Nixon*, 533-534.

cis Cardinal Spellman of New York that this venture in personal diplomacy meant no "surrender" and the maintenance of the firm stand on Berlin.[223]

Cardinal Spellman wasn't the only one who needed reassurance that Khrushchev's impending American visit didn't bode ominously. Flying to confer with America's Western European allies just before Khrushchev's arrival, Eisenhower assured them that he wouldn't be cutting a peace agreement with the Russian that left them out in the cold. The President's son John later said, "I don't think he said, 'I've been had by my own people,' but he said, 'I'm not going to represent my views without representing yours too.'"[224]

Accompanied by his family and entourage, Khrushchev departed for the United States in a new Soviet passenger plane on September 14, 1959. "It made me proud," he recalled, "to think that we were on our way to the United States" in the aircraft. "Not that we worshiped America. The reason we were proud was that we had finally forced the United States to recognize the necessity of establishing closer contacts with us. We'd come a long way from the time when the United States wouldn't even grant us diplomatic recognition." When Khrushchev learned that his plane was about to land in Washington, "In a few minutes, we'd be face to face with America. Now I'd be able to see it with my own eyes, to touch it with my own fingers. All this put me on my guard and my nerves were strained with excitement."[225]

Khrushchev's plane landed at Andrews Air Force Base, in Maryland, on September 15. In addition to Eisenhower and other American officials and journalists, thousands of onlookers—including a college student bearing a sign reading WELCOME KHRUSHCHEV—had turned out to greet the Russian visitor. The student told the reporters, "Better to greet him with an open hand than with a sneer."

The size of Khrushchev's plane, the world's largest passenger plane, had necessitated his arrival at Andrews instead of National Airport. Once the plane had landed and halted, another problem arose: it was too high for the motorized stairs to reach the door to allow its passengers to disembark. "Our pilot," Khrushchev recounted of the episode, "said we'd have to leave the plane not in the formal, dignified way" protocol dictated, "but practically climbing down, using our hands and legs!" The Russians turned the incident to their advantage: "It was an embarrassment for the Americans. They hadn't known our plane was such a giant."

Eisenhower delivered a formal statement of welcome to Khrushchev, who, when it came his turn, used his official opening statement to get in a

---

[223] Parmet, *Eisenhower and the American Crusades*, 545-546.
[224] Beschloss, *Mayday*, 184.
[225] Quoted in *ibid.*, 185-186.

jab at his host by reminding him that "Shortly before this meeting with you, Soviet scientists, technicians, engineers and workers filled our hearts with joy by launching a rocket to the moon. We have no doubt that the excellent scientists, engineers and workers of the U.S.A. will also carry the pennant to the moon. The Soviet pennant, as an old resident, will then welcome your pennant." (Later that same day Khrushchev presented Eisenhower a gift: a polished wooden box containing replicas of the spheres and pennants the Soviets had just launched into space). The official welcoming ceremony concluded, a limousine conveyed Eisenhower and the Khrushchevs to the latter's guest residence, Blair House, in downtown Washington.

After changing clothes and having his lunch, Khrushchev and his party met Eisenhower and his party in the West Wing of the White House for the purpose of finalizing the agenda for their discussions at Camp David, the presidential retreat, at the conclusion of Khrushchev's American tour. One issue, Berlin, came up at this time. While conceding that the Allied occupation there, fourteen years after the end of World War II, was "abnormal," Eisenhower explained, "Until the United States can discharge its obligation to the German people, there should be no unilateral action on the part of the Soviets embarrassing to us and making it impossible for us to discharge these responsibilities." Khrushchev's ultimatum had caused "a serious crisis."

"Believe me, we would like to come to terms on Germany and thereby on Berlin too," Khrushchev replied. "We do not contemplate taking unilateral action—though on your side, you took unilateral action in Japan in which we were deprived of rights we should have had. We had to accept that. We must find a way out which would not leave an unpleasant residue in our relationship." The problem, as Khrushchev saw it, was that fundamentally Americans feared Marxism.

After ninety minutes, photographers were brought in to snap pictures of Eisenhower and Khrushchev together in the Oval Office. This was followed by a private session between the two leaders, then Eisenhower took Khrushchev on a helicopter ride over Washington. That evening the Eisenhowers hosted the Khrushchevs at a state dinner at the White House. During this occasion, Khrushchev then met the CIA's Allen Dulles. The later commented, "You may have seen some of my intelligence reports from time to time."

"I believe we get the same reports," said Khrushchev, "and probably from the same people."

"Maybe we should pool our efforts," Dulles replied.

"Yes, we should buy our intelligence data together and save money. We'd have to pay the people only once!"

Another high American official Khrushchev met that evening was FBI Director J. Edgar Hoover, who subsequently told Congress that the Soviet Chairman's presence had produced an "atmosphere favorable to Communism among Americans."[226]

The following afternoon Khrushchev spoke to the National Press Club, then was exposed to the free atmosphere of an American press conference. Asked where he had been and what he was doing during Stalin's purges, Khrushchev declined to answer what he considered a provocative question. Concerning Hungary, the latter "has stuck in some people's throats [like] a dead rat." He paused then continued, "We could think of some dead cats we could throw at you."[227]

At five o'clock, Khrushchev met with the Senate Foreign Relations Committee for tea in the committee's ceremonial chamber in the Capitol: "I feel that I have known practically all of you a long time but until now, you have been sort of ethereal beings to me. Now you appear in the flesh." He counseled the senators to accept the existence of socialist states in the world. He emphasized the latter by indicating the wart on the bridge of his nose: "The wart is there and I can't do anything about it."

He also lodged objections to the activities of the CIA: "Subversion of other countries is hardly conducive to peaceful coexistence. Speaking in businessmen's terms, this is an enterprise which yields no profit." Khrushchev didn't offer to do away with his own KGB, however.

Senator Richard Russell replied, "I know of no appropriations anywhere for any subversive work in Russia—and I have been a member of the Appropriations Committee for twenty-five years." Russell then asked if the Russians had experienced any problems in launching their moon rockets—something Vice President Nixon had just hinted at in a speech.

"You had better ask Nixon. He answered your question when he said that the launching of our moon rocket miscarried three times. He knows how things are with us better than we do. Nixon said he was using information from a secret source. But of course, he didn't specify the source."[228]

A late arrival to the tea was Massachusetts Democrat John F. Kennedy, who had interrupted a "pulse-feeling" tour of Ohio as part of his quest for the Democratic presidential nomination, to be present for Khrushchev. While Kennedy waited for his Senate elders to complete their sessions with the Soviet leader, he recorded some impressions: "Tea—vodka—if we drank vodka all the time, we could not launch rockets to the moon. Tan suit— French cuffs—short, stocky, two red ribbons, two stars." When his turn to

[226] Beschloss, *Mayday*, 187–194.
[227] Weisberger, *Cold War, Cold Peace*, 191.
[228] Beschloss, *Mayday*, 195.

meet Khrushchev finally came, the Chairman told Kennedy that he looked too young to be a Senator: "I've heard a lot about you. People say you have a great future ahead of you." Walking back to his Senate office, Kennedy told Ohio Senator Mike Mansfield, "It was very important to see Khrushchev in the flesh."

Khrushchev himself remembered long afterward that he was "impressed with Kennedy. I remember liking his face, which was sometimes stern but which often broke into a good-natured smile." Soviet diplomat Georgi Kornienko remembered that when Khrushchev asked his ambassador to Washington and the Soviet Embassy staff about the Massachusetts senator, "I gave the most positive picture. I said that, while Kennedy was not yet another Roosevelt, he was independent and intelligent and could be counted on for new departures. Khrushchev listened."[229]

Tea with the Senate Foreign Relations Committee was followed, that evening, by a banquet for the Eisenhowers at the Soviet Embassy. In his toast, Khrushchev said, "My friends and I have had a fine day today. You are real exploiters, I must say, and have done a good job of exploiting us!" Once the laughter this remark produced died down, Khrushchev continued, "I feel sure—perhaps because I want it very badly—that our coming invitation, Mr. President, and your forthcoming visit to our country will help to thaw international relations. The ice of the Cold War has not only cracked, but had indeed begun to crumble."

The next day, Khrushchev began his cross-country tour of the United States.

Khrushchev was escorted on his trip by Henry Cabot Lodge, who twice daily kept President Eisenhower informed on events. The first stop was New York, which Khrushchev characterized as a "huge noisy city" with "vast quantities of exhaust fumes that were choking people." He had lunch with Mayor Robert Wagner and a thousand civic leaders and visited America's former wartime ambassador to Moscow Averell Harriman—the latter a longtime advocate of detente. That night, Khrushchev addressed a banquet of the New York Economic Club at the Waldorf-Astoria. It was at this occasion that he received a query as to why his people couldn't see American newspapers or hear the Voice of America. "I am here at President Eisenhower's invitation," Khrushchev answered. "We agreed that our talks would not concern third countries and that there would be no interference in the internal affairs of each other's nations."

"Answer the question!" someone shouted.

---

[229] Michael R. Beschloss, *The Crisis Years: Kennedy and Khrushchev 1960-1963* (New York: HarperCollins Publishers, 1991), 13, 15.

"If you don't want to listen, all right!" Khrushchev rejoined. "I am an old sparrow and you cannot muddle one with your cries. You should show enough hospitality not to interrupt. If there is no desire to listen to me, I can go." The room fell silent. "No cries can make the world forget the great achievements of the Soviet people. What our people hear on the radio is of no concern to other nations. Your great Negro singer Paul Robeson was denied the right to go abroad for some five to seven years. Why was *his* voice jammed?"[230]

Addressing the United Nations on September 18, Khrushchev dropped a major bombshell—one not even Eisenhower had known of: the complete abolition of nuclear and conventional weapons over the next four years, without any stipulation for inspection or supervision. If the West was unprepared for this course, Khrushchev was ready to seek a test-ban, which he declared was "acute and eminently ripe for solution."[231] The rest of Khrushchev's time in New York was spent riding to the top of the Empire State Building, touring the slums of Harlem, laying a wreath on FDR's grave at Hyde Park, and renewing his acquaintance with the state's recently installed Governor, Nelson Rockefeller.[232]

The next phase of the tour, California—specifically Los Angeles—went badly and almost sent Khrushchev packing his bags back to Moscow. The trouble began when he met his first local notable, Victor Carter. The head of Republic Studios and a California hospital, the City of Hope, Carter had fled the southern Russian community of Rostov years earlier. When Carter disclosed to Khrushchev the fact that he was a Jew, the Soviet Premier concluded that Carter was a class enemy as Jews, according to Czarist edict, were forbidden to live in Rostov unless they were well-to-do merchants. "Privately, Khrushchev wondered how to interpret the fact that the U. S. government had selected an emigrant from Russia to be beside him." Every inauspicious occurrence Khrushchev experienced during the Los Angeles portion of his trip, the Russian believed, had been hatched in Carter's mind.

Khrushchev and his party planned to visit Disneyland. The Khrushchevs had just started lunch when the Russian leader was informed that their visit had been canceled: in the opinion of the Los Angeles police the visit posed too great a risk. The Disneyland cancellation reinforced Khrushchev's suspicion that a wall was being deliberately erected between him and the American people during his tour. At a lunch in the Khrushchevs' honor at Twentieth Century-Fox, attended by numerous Hollywood celebrities, Khrushchev vented his rage: "Is there some kind of cholera or launching pad out there?

---

[230] Beschloss, *Mayday*, 196-198.
[231] Ambrose, *Eisenhower: Volume II*, 542.
[232] Beschloss, *Mayday*, 198.

You have policemen so tough they can lift a bull by the horns, yet they say it [Disneyland] cannot be securely guarded." When Madame Khrushcheva expressed her disappointment at not seeing Disneyland to David Niven, Frank Sinatra told Niven, "Screw the cops! Tell the old broad you and I'll take 'em down there this afternoon."[233]

The luncheon completed, the Khrushchev party was taken to the Stage 8 area, where they viewed the filming of a dance sequence from the studio's production *Can-Can*, which featured Sinatra, Louis Jourdan, and Shirley MacLaine. Finding can-can dancing not to his liking, Khrushchev believed the sequence had been contrived to humiliate him. His discomfiture was furthered when a studio publicity photographer sought to get two of the female can-can performers to pose with Khrushchev, with their skirts raised. The women declined to participate in the stunt. The Can-Can affair paled in comparison to Khrushchev's subsequent encounter that same day with Los Angeles mayor Norris Poulson. Characterized as "a conservative lightweight who seemed intent on having a highly public debate with Khrushchev," the mayor was a scheduled speaker at a dinner meeting of the Los Angeles world events forum. Looking over Poulson's remarks before the meeting, Lodge discovered it contained a reference to Khrushchev's celebrated declaration, "We will bury you."[234] During his earlier appearance before the National Press Club, Khrushchev had been asked to clarify those words, which he uttered in Moscow, before a group of Western diplomats, nearly three years earlier. A Russian adage, "We will bury you" meant, in effect, "I shall outlast you" or "I shall live so long that I shall be able to attend your funeral." What Khrushchev intended to express, his conviction that the Soviet system would prevail over capitalism, numerous Westerners saw as an expression of intention to bring about America's demise.[235] Now Lodge, who felt that Khrushchev had calmly explained the true meaning of his utterance, feared Khrushchev might erupt in rage were Poulson to resurrect the matter. When asked to delete this part of his prepared remarks, the mayor declined: "The speech has already been written and distributed. It is too late to change it."[236]

"Now, Mr. Chairman," Poulson said, "I want to make this statement in the friendliest fashion. We do not agree with your widely quoted phrase 'We shall bury you.' You shall not bury us and we shall not bury you. We are happy with our way of life. We recognize its shortcomings and are always trying to improve it. But if challenged, we shall fight to the death to preserve it. I tell you these things not to boast or to threaten, but to give you a picture of what

---

[233] Fursenko and Naftali, *Khrushchev's Cold War*, 232-233; Beschloss, *Mayday*, 199.
[234] Fursenko and Naftali, *Khrushchev's Cold War*, 233-234.
[235] *Ibid.*, 232.
[236] *Ibid.*, 234.

the people of Southern California feel in their hearts. . . . we are planning no funerals, yours *or* our own. There never will be a funeral for the free spirit that lives in every man."[237]

Just as Lodge feared, Khrushchev took offense to Poulson's remarks. Completing his prepared remarks, Khrushchev lifted his eyes from his text to vent his fury at Poulson.

"That was the end of my prepared speech, but the speaker that preceded me raised a number of points which I cannot fail to answer," he announced. "I turn to you, Mr. Mayor, my dear host. In your speech, you said that we want to bury you. You have shown wonderful hospitality towards me and my comrades and I thank you. I want to speak the truth. Can I do that here? I want to ask you: Why did you mention that? Already while I was here in the United States, I have had occasion to clarify that point. I trust that even mayors read the press. At least in our country, the chairmen of city councils read the press. If they don't, they risk not being elected next time."

These words evoked laughter from the audience. Khrushchev carried on.

"If you want to go on with the arms race, very well. We accept the challenge. As for the output of rockets—well, they are on the assembly line." By now, Khrushchev's face had turned its customary angry red hue and apparently was progressing to an angrier shade. "This is a most serious question. It is one of life or death, ladies and gentlemen, one of war and peace. If you don't understand . . ."

"We understand"! shouted someone in Russian.

Where, just mere moments earlier, the audience had been laughing, it was now in shock. "The audience gasped," wrote Associated Press correspondent Relman Morin. "It was not only the words but the manner in which they were spoken. Two large veins in Premier Khrushchev's forehead bulged as he said this, snarling at Mayor Poulson."

Khrushchev has yet to exhaust his wrath. "The unpleasant thought sometimes creeps up on me that perhaps Khrushchev was invited here to enable you to sort of rub him in your sauce and show him the might and strength of the United States so as to make him shake at the knees. If that is so—it took me about twelve hours to fly here, I guess it will take no more than ten and a half hours to fly back."

Commanding Alexei Tupolev, the son of the man who'd designed the plane that brought him to the United States, to stand up, Khrushchev asked, "Isn't that so?"

"Less than that," Tupolev answered.

---

[237] Parmet, *Eisenhower and the American Crusades*, 550.

"I am the first head of either Russia or the Soviet Union to visit the United States," Khrushchev said. "I can go, but I don't know when, if ever, another Soviet premier will visit your country." The dinner guests wondered if what they saw signaled either the conclusion of Khrushchev's visit or possibly the start of a war. "It was a terrible moment," wrote *New York Post* columnist Murray Kempton.

"His outburst seemed almost insane," recalled State Department chief of protocol Wiley Buchanan. "You could see the fuses of nuclear rockets sparking," wrote Harrison Salisbury of *The New York Times.* "Needless to say, this sent a tremor—*a tremor!*—through the assembled dignitaries," remembered State Department aide Richard Townsend Davies. "It was very threatening."

"Clearly," Lodge thought, "the Khrushchev visit to America is becoming a horrible failure."[238]

Back in his hotel, Khrushchev vented his full wrath to the entire Soviet delegation accompanying him: "How dare this man [Poulson] attack the guest of the president of the United States?" He gave serious thought to terminating the remainder of his trip. He would not proceed any further until he had received an apology from the American government. In reality he was merely blowing off steam for the benefit of the Americans accompanying him: "I was sure that there were listening devices in our room and that Mr. Lodge, who was staying in the same hotel, was sitting in front of a speaker with an interpreter and listening to our whole conversation." In the event the American eavesdroppers couldn't hear him, Gromyko presented a formal protest to Lodge, the main point of which dealt with a woman who had stood on a street corner, bearing a black flag and a sign proclaiming DEATH TO KHRUSHCHEV, THE BUTCHER OF HUNGARY. Khrushchev believed Eisenhower had been responsible for the protester's presence. Lodge endeavored to explain that, owing to America's nature, the protester was entitled to hold such opinions, however much embarrassment they might cause the American government. Moreover, Lodge conveyed his regrets for the ill-mannered conduct of some of the Americans Khrushchev had met during his visit. Gromyko took Lodge's explanation back to his room with him. With the trip at its lowest point, Lodge would have to take radical measures to rescue it.

The changes began the next morning. If Khrushchev gave his consent, Lodge would make it possible to allow the Premier closer contact with more average people. The idea was to treat Khrushchev in the manner of a political candidate. San Francisco was the next scheduled stop on Khrushchev's tour;

---

[238] Peter Carlson, *K Blows Top: A Cold War Comic Interlude Starring Nikita Khrushchev, America's Most Unlikely Tourist* (New York: PublicAffiars, 2009), pp.169-171.

Lodge believed that there were suitable places where Khrushchev could have the opportunity to meet the people. Lodge also decided to permit Khrushchev to meet reporters on the train.

The changes Lodge made proved the right tonic. "I felt that you had kept me under house arrest for six days," Khrushchev told him. He met the press corps aboard his train. During stops at Santa Barbara and San Luis Obispo, be avidly mingled with the crowds on hand to greet him. During one of these stops, an act of consideration on the part of one of his greeters greatly moved him. Mingling with the onlookers he lost his Lenin Peace Prize medal, which he wore on his jacket. Finding it, a member of the crowd gave it to Lodge, who returned it to the Premier before the latter had the opportunity to find he had lost it. "The incident pleased me very much," Khrushchev would remember, "the fact that the person returned it to me made me respect these people." The Soviet Premier's trip was becoming more agreeable.[239]

Then it was on to San Francisco. "You have charmed me," Khrushchev told the City by the Bay's residents; "But you have charmed my heart, not my mind. I still think our system is a good system." He met United Auto Workers head Walter Reuther, whom he scorned because he now sought the "extra nickel or dime" instead of the "victory of the working class." More to Khrushchev's liking was longshoreman's boss Harry Bridges, a "true progressive" who supported Soviet policies.

In Coon Rapids, Iowa, Khrushchev visited the farm of Roswell Garst, a hybrid-corn grower already acquainted with the Soviet leader.[240] The primary effect of the visit was to boost what Khrushchev felt he should do to improve the Soviet Union. Where Garst's farm was equipped with an extremely effective open pen system to feed livestock, in the Soviet Union, Khrushchev observed, "we provide each cow with a stall, each is allotted with a fork and a knife. . . . What kind of idiocy is this?"[241] During the visit to Garst's farm, Khrushchev ribbed Lodge about the latter's inexperience with barnyard odors. When shown imported Russian pigs, Khrushchev asked, "These Soviet and American pigs can coexist—why can't our nations?"[242] Another light moment involved host Garst's displeasure at the horde of journalists present at his farm. When photographers interfered with the Soviet Premier's look at how Garst's corn silage loading operation worked, an annoyed Garst pelted the photographers with corn cobs and kicked journalists in the shins. Khrushchev also posed for photographs, arms around shoulders,

[239] Fursenko and Naftali, *Khrushchev's Cold War*, 234–236.
[240] Beschloss, *Mayday*, 202.
[241] Fursenko and Naftali, *Khrushchev's Cold War*, 237.
[242] Weisberger, *Cold War, Cold Peace*, 192.

with Garst and Adlai Stevenson. Stevenson's willingness to pose with him, in Khrushchev's mind, was a "sign of tolerance toward the Soviet Union."

Because a strike had shut down the union steel mills of Pittsburgh, Khrushchev inspected a non-union machine works.[243] As he toured the facility, examining the machines, Khrushchev observed that the floor was covered with fresh spots of asphalt that were virtually still warm. Indicating them to the plant manager, Khrushchev said, "You know, in our country when the leadership goes to inspect a factory, the plant managers order all the cracks and holes in the floor to be patched up. I see you do the same here."

"Yes, we took care of that just before your arrival, Mr. Khrushchev."

As Khrushchev passed a machine, its operator switched it off to greet his foreign visitor and give him a cigar. Everyone present "obviously shared his sentiments. Perhaps he had been delegated to make a gesture on behalf of the collective. I gave him a friendly slap on the shoulder, took off my wristwatch and presented it to him .He smiled, obviously pleased, and then went back to work." When asked by an American journalist about the incident in relation to the charges in the Soviet press that Richard Nixon had sought to bribe a Moscow worker by offering him money, Khrushchev replied, "The worker I met had demonstrated his warm feelings toward me by giving me a cigar, and I was just repaying his kindness. There's a difference between mutual expressions of good will and bribery. My gesture had nothing in common with what Nixon was trying to accomplish by offering our worker money."[244]

While he was in Pittsburgh, Khrushchev received the key to the city from the mayor. Khrushchev accepted the gift as a sign of trust: "And you can rest assured—I *promise* you—that this key will never be used without the hosts' permission."

Contrary to reports he received from his ambassador in Washington, Khrushchev now saw for himself that the United States wasn't about to fall into the Soviet orbit. Despite his contention that he hadn't learned anything new from his trip, Khrushchev, in Lodge's words to Eisenhower, now saw America "quite differently."

> He is deeply impressed by . . . the conditions and attitudes of our people, our roads, our automobiles, our factories. He was struck by the vitality of our people. He probably does not now really think the Soviets are likely to surpass us—at least anytime soon. It is clear that he wants peace and thinks that Russia needs peace in order to do what he wants the nation to do.[245]

---

[243] Beschloss, *Mayday*, 202.

[244] Nikita Khrushchev, *Khrushchev Remembers: The Last Testament.* Translated and Edited by Strobe Talbott (Boston: Little, Brown and Company, 1974), 402-403.

[245] Beschloss, *Mayday*, 202-204.

On Friday, September 25, 1959, Khrushchev returned to Washington to begin his private talks with Eisenhower. The latter had promised de Gaulle and Macmillan that there would be no negotiations during these sessions; that would have to include France and Britain. For now, Eisenhower's objective was to determine if a summit meeting of the Big Four powers would produce real benefits. Berlin would be the central issue of the Eisenhower-Khrushchev talks. Should the Russian remove his ultimatum, Eisenhower in all likelihood would give his sanction to a summit: "This would then give us the opportunity to pursue other questions without a pistol at our head."[246]

Once the two leaders had adjourned to Camp David, Eisenhower, while intimating his opinion that FDR and Truman had made a mistake in placing the West in such an exposed position in the heart of East Germany, remained firm in his commitment to the current American policy on that area of the world. Despite this, Khrushchev decided to inform his host of his decision to abandon the concept of achieving diplomatic goals through issuing ultimatums; he acknowledged that he had attempted to force a resolution of the Berlin matter the preceding autumn because of what he felt was America's "high-handed" conduct. If Eisenhower now conceded that the United States opposed a permanent perpetuation of the current occupation of Berlin, the Soviet Union wouldn't hold firm to any deadline in the talks concerning the divided city. Considering that American policy was geared toward the ultimate goal of German reunification, Eisenhower had no objections toward Khrushchev's proposal.

After the Berlin ultimatum had been scrapped and Khrushchev had conceded that disarmament was the greater issue, Eisenhower gave his consent to a Big Four summit sometime before the end of the year.

Khrushchev, who received his government's permission to negotiate a settlement if this was possible during his meeting with Eisenhower, was disappointed in this regard. Eisenhower, when queried what his nation's stance was regarding disarmament, merely replied that his experts were examining Khrushchev's UN remarks on "general and complete" disarmament. Nor would the President reveal his own inclinations in this matter. Just the same, Aleksandr Fursenko and Timothy Naftali have written, Khrushchev "had learned what he needed, and he had been treated better by the U. S. government than he had expected to be treated." The American visit had another impact on the Soviet Premier: it encouraged him "to take ever-greater risks to achieve the Soviet society and international order that he dreamed about."[247]

---

[246] *Ibid.*, 204-205.
[247] Fursenko and Naftali, *Khrushchev's Cold War*, 238-239.

The Camp David summit was significant in another respect: it made meetings between American and Soviet leaders a more routine occurrence and put relations between their two countries on a more normal footing. Once again the popular standing Eisenhower had with the American people that previously had enabled him to end the Korean War on the identical terms Truman had sought without provoking the political furies of the kind that most certainly would have befallen Truman for doing so. As for meeting the Soviet leadership at Geneva in 1955 without being labeled an appeaser and being allowed him to receive Khrushchev in America; were Truman to have done the same with Joseph Stalin, the likely outcome might have been the former's impeachment.

One issue did not come up for discussion at Camp David: the U-2 overflights. A State Department official later noted that had Khrushchev informed Eisenhower how vexatious the flights were and of Russian hopes that they would be discontinued, Eisenhower in all likelihood would have agreed to do so. As it was, Khrushchev remained silent about the matter and the CIA continued planning additional U-2 missions.[248] The disastrous ultimate consequences of that action—including the revelation that the American government wasn't always candid with its people—lay eight months in the future. For now, "the spirit of Camp David" resonated as much as had the "spirit of Geneva" previously.[249] And, in the interim, the true, fraudulent nature of the quiz shows would finally be revealed to the American people.

---

[248] Beschloss, *Mayday*, 214, 215.

[249] William E. Leuchtenburg and the Editors of Time-Life Books, *The Life History of the United States. Volume 12: From 1945. The Age of Change* (Alexandria, Virginia: Time-Life Books, 1977, 1974, 1964), 106.

6. The Quiz Show Bubble Bursts (1958–1959)

The 1957–1958 television season was marked by the greatest number of quiz and game shows airing—many of them programs that partially owed their existence to the popularity of *The $64,000 Question* and the shows it inspired. By season's end the number of network quiz or game shows airing stood at twenty-two. They accounted for 18% of NBC's entire schedule, with forty-seven thirty minute time slots occupied by such broadcast fare. The new prize giveaway trend in game shows disturbed the majority of critics. One of them, Jack Gould, noting that money alone was no longer a sufficient enticement, continued:

> Viewers are weary of watching others win; they want something for themselves. After ten years the carnival concessionaires are descending on TV. . . . Television's creative bankruptcy in day to day programming could not be more vividly illustrated. . . . The renewed emphasis on giveaways, particularly with the added feature of giving money or prizes to home viewers rather studio participants, is symptomatic of the recession's influences on TV programming.[250]

As the number of quiz shows occupying the television schedules expanded, there was a decline in more serious journalistic and dramatic programs. In the wake of Louis Cowan's ascension to the presidency of the CBS television network in March 1958, *See It Now* faded from view. Some producers asserted that quiz shows represented a revival of live television; this line of reasoning argued that quiz shows had picked up the baton of live television drama from New York, which was dying out. To those critics lamenting the evident demise of TV's Golden Age, television executives contended that

---

[250] Anderson, Television Fraud, 105.

they were merely providing the public the kind of programs they wanted; quizzes and Westerns.

Still there was evidence that the quiz shows' heyday was drawing to a close. Ratings were dwindling. In part, this was due to overexposure as the public's enthusiasm for the quizzes waned. Of greater significance was the absence of new superstar quiz champions. Without the latter, "viewer attention focused on the all-too similar formats of each individual show, and the obvious weaknesses were exposed. By the middle of 1958," continued Harry Castleman and Walter J. Podrazik, "it became increasingly clear within the TV industry that quizzes were not a solid commodity, but a very unstable structure that needed just a slight push to collapse."[251] When that push came, television would be thrust into the greatest crisis in its history.

Dotto Breaks the Quiz Show Scandal

Following his graduation from the City College of New York in June 1957, Herbert Stempel once more approached Dan Enright for the purpose of giving him a job with Barry and Enright—only to be told that, since NBC now owed all Barry and Enright productions, there was nothing Enright could do to help Stempel. When he learned that Enright remained in charge of production he again approached him, only to be told that NBC had vetoed Stempel as a member of a rotating panel of contestants for the new quiz show *Hi-Lo*. These continued rebuffs merely swelled Stempel's rage. In early September he contacted *New York Journal-American* television critic Jack O'Brian, divulging his experience as a *Twenty-One* contestant. Fearing libel action, the paper decided not to print Stempel's allegations without additional corroborating evidence; nevertheless it queried Enright about the charges.

The New York Post, which Stempel had also contacted with his story, declined to publish his accusations as well, yet remained interested. Not long after the *Journal-American*'s query to Enright, the *Post* contacted Barry and Enright's Art Franklin. Franklin didn't deny its veracity, having learned from his PR experience that a denial could be viewed as acknowledging that there was substance to the story. To Paul Sand, the *Post* reporter who called him about the charges, Franklin said that both he and the *Journal-American* were informed of Stempel's accusation and that the paper had chosen not to publicize it.

Simultaneously, another *Journal-American* staffer learned that Stempel had contacted O'Brian and informed Ellis Moore, a press representative at NBC, to "prepare for the storm." Moore then assembled a meeting with the

---

[251] Castleman and Podrazik, *Watching TV*, 124-125.

vice-president in charge of press for the network—Sydney Eiges, along with Franklin, Al Davis, and Enright. When later asked if any discussion occurred at this meeting to undertake action to prevent the story from being publicized, Franklin said, "No; because NBC was so terrified about the possibility of this all being true that they sort of kept their hands as clean as possible by 'kicking it under the carpet.'" Regarding NBC's role at the initial sign a scandal was in the offing, Franklin further stated, "The meeting concluded with Franklin's recommendation that the best course was to do nothing.

This failed to appease another NBC official, Thomas Ervin, vice-president and general attorney for the network. At another meeting, Enright told Ervin he had secretly recorded his March 7, 1957 encounter with Stempel at which time the latter had threatened Enright with blackmail. He also produced a signed statement from Stempel that he had received absolutely no assistance from Enright during his *Twenty-One* appearances. This satisfied Ervin and the network. What remained to be determined was whether the press would be equally appeased. Eiges asked the *Journal-American* to talk with NBC prior to publishing any part of Stempel's allegation as there was "another side to it." The paper notified him that the *Journal-American* had decided not to publish the story without additional substantiating proof. Moreover, the *New York Post* also decided against publishing the story. NBC chose to believe Enright's version of events and put the matter out of its mind.

By the summer of 1958, Charles Van Doren, still viewed in the public eye as an intellectual superstar, had found his niche at NBC: Dave Garroway's summer replacement as host of *The Today Show*.

Rumblings also shook the EPI quizzes that same television season. The first involved a Tennessee clergyman, the Reverend Charles E. (Stoney) Jackson, Jr., who had initially appeared the previous season as an authority on great lovers on *The $64,000 Question*, winning $16,000. During that time, he had been screened in such a way during his pre-game warm-up session that, as he subsequently explained, he was genuinely unaware that the same information used in the rehearsal was actually used during his on-camera appearance. This led him to the conclusion that the quiz was a completely honest contest. Appearing on *The $64,000 Challenge* at the end of 1957 Jackson heard the very same question asked him before air time given to his opponent, who missed it. When the time came for Jackson to answer it, he was tempted to reveal he had already been supplied the answer but decided to answer the question, winning $4,000. Indignant at this development, Jackson declined to reappear on *Challenge* and at first refused to accept his check. *The New York Times* wanted additional evidence before publishing Jackson's story. If Jackson had known that the *New York Journal-American* and the *New York Post* were interested in his account, the story might have seen the light of day. Upon returning home, Jackson's frustration at getting the truth out continued: neither the *Nashville Tennessean* or his hometown twice-weekly paper (for which Jackson wrote the sports column) would publish his story. The indifference extended to his parishioners and fellow clergymen when he informed them of what had happened, and he dropped his crusade to bring the truth to light.

One of the most successful of the new quizzes that debuted during the '57-'58 television season, *Dotto*, initially aired as part of CBS' daytime schedule January 6, 1958. Based on the children's game where one connected dots, *Dotto* featured two rival players trying to connect dots that formed the face of a famous individual by answering questions. In finding contestants, *Dotto*, in contrast to other quizzes, drew players from its studio audience, always to appear on a broadcast a least one week later. The show also utilized the services of a contestant selection outfit to find suitable players.

So successful was *Dotto* that, beginning July 1, 1958, NBC began airing a nighttime version of the quiz. Both versions of *Dotto* featured the same sponsor, Colgate-Palmolive, and were produced by the same man, Edward Jurist, though one man served as associate producer for daytime *Dotto*, while another discharged the same function on the nighttime version. When it came to *Dotto's* fraudulent aspects, MC Jack Narz said he was completely unaware of such practices. All he knew was that, in addition to the three questions he possessed for connecting five, eight, and ten dots, there was a fourth. Known as the "kicker, this was used in place of the ten-dot question. Narz employed the "kicker" on those occasions when Jurist indicated him to. Narz knew the "kicker" was used to promote tie games and was seldom employed to eliminate contestants.[252]

The sequence of events that culminated in the public disclosure of quiz show rigging began May 20, 1958, when Ed Hilgemeier, a twenty-four-year-old part time butler and bit actor who was a standby contestant on daytime *Dotto*, discovered the presence backstage of a note book belonging to the woman who had been that day's winner. Examining the notebook's contents, Hilgemeier discovered the answers to the questions the winner had received. Now suspicious, Hilgemeier showed his discovery to the winning contestant's losing opponent and complained to *Dotto's* producers. After receiving a payoff in the amount of $1,500, Hilgemeier was content to leave the entire business at that—only to change his mind when he learned that the defeated contestant had received the same amount as that won by her rival, $4,400. On August 7, Hilgemeier lodged a complaint with Colgate-Palmolive. As all of this transpired away from public scrutiny, the sponsor's

---

[252] *Ibid.*, 107-110.

announcement, nine days later, that the plug had been pulled on both the day- and nighttime versions of *Dotto* was a totally unexpected development. An explanation for such drastic action wasn't forthcoming from either of the networks involved or the sponsor. The absence of such a clarification failed to quiet rumors that a discontented contestant had charged that *Dotto* was a fixed quiz and would present his case to the district attorney.[253]

Word that the latter had *Dotto* under scrutiny became a public fact on August 25. The next day Hubbell Robinson, Jr., executive vice-president in charge of television programming for CBS and the man who had brought $64,000 *Question* creator Louis Cowan to the network, disclosed that a probe on CBS' part had been unsuccessful in turning up any "improper procedures" of programs being televised—an announcement given credibility by the fact that *Dotto* was in its grave by this time. Robinson did make a valid point: the networks lacked the means to implement the kind of investigation necessary to ascertain the truth as virtually all quiz shows were produced independently of the networks.

Dotto's cancellation and the resulting scant publicity burst the dam open: people from other quiz shows were spurred to convince skeptical journalists that their tales of rigging were true. On August 28, 1958, the *New York Journal-American* and the *New York World-Telegram and Sun* printed Herb Stempel's allegations of rigging on *Twenty-One*, whereupon Barry and Enright retaliated with a civil suit against the *World-Telegram and Sun*, which was the first paper to cite specific names. They also requested a meeting with the district attorney. The day the story burst into the public's consciousness, NBC requested a meeting with the representatives of *Twenty-One*. One network bigwig present at the gathering, Ken Bilgy, believed the libel suit was a good course of action; NBC nevertheless declined to become a party to the suit. At the meeting, Enright produced two additional pieces of evidence in his defense: the bogus statement he had Stempel sign in March 1957 (a document NBC had already seen) and the revelation of the tape he recorded at the same March 1957 meeting with Stempel. As the tape was secured in a bank that happened to be closed, it was unavailable at present. Everyone concurred that this recording should be publicly disclosed as soon as possible. NBC, now convinced all was well, issued a public statement, expressing the belief that Stempel's accusations were groundless. The meeting also reached another decision: the tape should be given to the district attorney's office.

As Frank S. Hogan, the district attorney in overall charge of the quiz show investigation, was currently seeking a United States Senate seat, he assigned the genuine day-to-day probe to assistant district attorney Joseph Stone; the

---

[253] Castleman and Podrazik, *Watching TV*, 125.

latter, in turn, was assisted in this task by Melvin Stein and another attorney, and six other investigators. In the immediate aftermath of *Dotto's* cancellation, Hogan and Stone weren't certain if any criminal offense concerning the quiz shows had actually occurred. Larceny was a possibility in the event the quiz producers had rigged the contests using sponsor's money without the latter's knowledge. Enright's charge of extortion against Stempel would certainly warrant scrutiny. Even after the Stempel story came to light, Hogan declared, "It is unfair to say now that this is a burgeoning scandal."

In the initial stage of the district attorney's investigation, the only quiz shows under scrutiny were *Dotto* and *Twenty-One.* Art Franklin's attorney Edwin Slote offered Al Davis and Dan Enright some rather dubious legal counsel: the two should lie before the district attorney and perjure themselves before a grand jury should the latter be empaneled. Neither Davis or Enright jumped on these recommendations.

Meeting with Stone and executive assistant district attorney David Worgan on August 29, Enright showed them Stempel's alleged disclaimer and played the tape for them. This was followed, on September 2, by a press conference at which time Barry and Enright played the recording, which Enright thought would exonerate him. The tape revealed Enright directing Stempel to write the disclaimer that he (Enright) at no time assisted him, with Stempel complying, Enright telling Stempel to see a psychiatrist five days a week, with Enright covering the cost of these visits, and Enright telling Stempel that if the latter was a panelist on a future show, he'll appear once a show, every day on the air, and, toward that end, Stempel should lose weight.

For his part, Stempel, while conceding that part of the conversation had indeed occurred, strongly contended that Enright had changed the recording to make himself look better. Enright then revealed that he had advanced Stempel the $18,000 that the later hoped would add credibility to his story. The advance, Enright said, had been intended to appease an unsound mind. Stempel's credibility at this point was less than convincing. *Twenty-One* MC Jack Barry delivered what he believed was a truthful on-air rebuttal to Stempel before the start of the show's September 8 broadcast.

Then the tide turned in the quiz shows' accusers' favor. By the end of the first week in September Stone had summoned over thirty former *Dotto* contestants; several of them began saying they had received assistance. Then, on September 6, EPI fell under the taint of scandal when Stoney Jackson's story of assistance on *The $64,000 Challenge* finally received public airing. Before then, the people of EPI were being queried. After the emergence of the Stempel allegation and further developments in the developing scandal, Revlon convened a conference concerning the Cohn-Springer episode. By now the cosmetics company was no longer cosponsoring *Challenge*. It had previously been announced that the quiz show's final installment would air in September due to declining ratings. In his subsequent account of the meeting during his congressional testimony, EPI's Steve Carlin's statements revealed that either he believed Revlon was aware of his quiz shows' fraudulent nature or, more probably, that the producers continually camouflaged their controls and sought to ensnarl Revlon in the scandal when it became public.

Then the Stoney Jackson story emerged. The latest scandal involving *The $64,000 Challenge* was the last straw for its sponsor, P. Lorillard. Though *Challenge* aired as scheduled following a meeting about the quiz involving CBS, EPI, Revlon and P. Lorillard, is was *Challenge's* final broadcast: it was canceled September 12, 1958. NBC and a new sponsor decided against resurrecting it.

That same day district attorney Hogan announced that he would ask Judge Mitchell J. Schweitzer of the court of general sessions of New York County to empanel a grand jury to investigate the quiz shows to "determine whether the crime of conspiracy or other crimes have been committed." "The formal legal process had taken over."[254]

The Grand Jury Investigation

The grand jury probe of the quiz shows began September 18, 1958. Ed Hilgemeier was the lead-off witness. It didn't take very long, after one week, before the grand jury discovered a key witness: James Snodgrass. Unlike other former quiz contestants, who had voluntarily testified, Snodgrass had hoped he wouldn't have to do so. After Stempel's story became public knowledge and *Twenty-One* fell under the cloud of suspicion, Albert Freedman met with the reluctant potential witness to determine what his intentions were. At this time, Freedman sought to persuade Snodgrass that should he be summoned to the district attorney's office and not the grand jury, he should lie as no necessary legal oath would be involved. Snodgrass said he wasn't going to divulge anything about his experiences on *Twenty-One* but should he be subpoenaed he would have no other recourse but to tell the truth. Following Snodgrass' grand jury testimony, the public soon learned that, prior to his *Twenty-One* appearances, Snodgrass had mailed registered letters to himself containing the questions he would be asked on-air, along with the answers. For a time, Snodgrass refused to reveal that it was Freedman who gave him the information he had used on *Twenty-One*.

In addition to providing Stempel's story with great creditability, the Snodgrass letter was significant for another reason: it finally prompted NBC to

---

take a closer look at the workings of Barry and Enright. The network's effort to initiate its own wide reaching probe of *Twenty-One*, which would have included talks with Snodgrass and other ex-contestants, was dissuaded by the district attorney's office. NBC was successful in another way: the network disseminated nine affidavits to the Barry and Enright staff, including Freedman and the lower members of the staff totem pole, refuting the accusations of rigging, which every staff member signed. Within a week after the emergence of Snodgrass' evidence, NBC assumed production responsibilities of the above-the-line aspects of the Barry and Enright quiz shows it owned, one of which, *Concentration*, was a completely honest contest. Jack Barry continued as *Twenty-One's master* of ceremonies, while Bill Wendell assumed the same position on *Tic Tac Dough*. The production staff for the daytime programs was now directly answerable to the network's Roger Gimbel, the prime-time staff to Joe Cates, who had originally produced *The $64,000 Question*, and had since joined NBC.

The public explanation Enright provided for NBC's assumption of control of his organization was so that he could give more time to dispelling the accusations against his programs. It was evident that *Twenty-One's* days were numbered. At Joseph Stone's behest, the life of the grand jury's probe was extended to at least February 1959. On October 16, 1958, *Twenty-One* was replaced by *Concentration*. The explanation for *Twenty-One's* demise, according to Pharmaceuticals, Incorporated, was low ratings. While it was a fact that *Twenty-One's* ratings had tumbled, Pharmaceuticals, Incorporated offered no public explanation as to why this was so. *Twenty-One's* passing was followed, on November 4, by that of the show that had ignited television's quiz craze of the 1950s: *The $64,000 Question*. While its ratings, too, had declined, *Question* remained unblemished by the quiz show scandal at the time it left the air.[255]

Questioned before the grand jury by Joseph Stone on October 2, 1958, Albert Freedman denied under oath that he had given questions and answers to contestants on *Twenty-One* and *Tic Tac Dough*. Meeting with Stone several days later, Charles Van Doren characterized Stempel's allegations as "absurd." He concurred with *Time's* assessment that the main goal of his formal education wasn't memorizing information yet explained he had always possessed an excellent memory. His time as a standby contestant on *Twenty-One* provided the opportunity to learn what questions were utilized and he had studied various kinds of reference books. During his initial trip to the NBC studio to appear on *Twenty-One*, he had spent his time in a dressing room perusing a "World Almanac" before he was summoned.

---

[255] *Ibid.,* 130-132.

Stone believed Van Doren was lying. Van Doren denied meeting Freedman in the latter's office; the sole encounters between the two were in his dressing room prior to his on-air appearances. Van Doren also answered negatively to questions as to whether he had received assistance from Barry and Enright staffers, and whether he had been asked to kickback any likely winnings to remain on *Twenty-One.* He had provided gifts to those connected with the quiz during the Christmas season he was a contestant: a bottle of scotch to Barry, two bottles of champagne to Enright, a pewter pitcher to Freedman. When it came to the inconsistencies between Stempel and Snodgrass' version of events they had furnished the press and what he was now telling Stone, Van Doren merely said he was speaking for himself. He steadfastly adhered to his assertion that he had a good memory and had devoted considerable study when it came to answering the questions posed to him on *Twenty-One.*

Stone remained unconvinced of Van Doren's integrity. He informed the latter that he would be informed when the date for his testimony before the grand jury had been determined. Questioned by reporters afterward, Van Doren said he felt "surprise and disbelief" at Stempel's charges: "It's silly and distressing to think that people don't have more faith in quiz shows."[256]

The testimony of two teenagers, high school students at the time they were quiz show contestants, proved especially shocking to the grand jury. Francis Li and Kirsten Falke had both appeared on *Tic Tac Dough.* Li, now a freshman at Cornell University when she met with Stone's assistant Melvin Stein, had been a senior at the Bronx High School of Science when she made six appearances on the daytime edition of *Tic Tac Dough,* where she won $4,000. After being screened and acting as a standby contestant for one show, Li was informed that the quiz desired her as a contestant and was promised that she'd win $4,000—a sum that would pay a considerable portion of her college fees. Li gave her consent. Before each of her appearances, she was screened. She was totally familiar with every question posed to her on camera and, had it not been for the fact that she had to resume her high school classes, she may well have remained on the show. Li informed Stein that Howard Davis Felsher, the man who had coached her on *Tic Tac Dough,* had recently called her at Cornell with the news that the quiz was being scrutinized and that her name might become part of the probe. He exhorted her not to say she had received assistance, otherwise there'd be "repercussions all over the place." Should she be asked about such assistance, she should answer, to quote Felsher, "I didn't give you any assistance." That caused Li to wonder if Felsher was recording their conversation and to regard his words

---

[256] Stone and Yohn, *Prime Time and Misdemeanors,* 112-120.

as a kind of veiled warning. "I suppose he felt if I didn't tell you anything," she told Stein, "I wouldn't have to come before the grand jury." Because she had to return to college, Li went before the grand jury immediately.

An aspiring young singer, Kirsten Falke was a part time employee at a midtown Manhattan music store who lived with her mother. In December 1956, then sixteen-year-old Falke had answered a Barry and Enright call for musically gifted young people to apply to *Tic Tac Dough*. After successfully auditioning, she went through several screening sessions with Felsher, who told her she would make at least two appearances on the show, first to tie, then defeat the current daytime champion, Timothy Horan, who had by now denied knowledge of any fixing to Stein. On her first appearance, Falke tied Horan, answering questions she had studied on the screening cards. Prior to her second appearance, Felsher told her to select the categories in the first game in such a way as to tie Horan a second time, then defeat him the next day. However, when it came time to play the game, Falke erred in her assignment and emerged the winner. Horan was replaced and with the categories replaced instead of being rearranged, Falke was quickly defeated and left with merely $800. Felsher simply told her not to tell anyone the truth of what happened—an order Falke complied with. She only told her mother the truth when the reality of the quiz show scandal emerged. Felsher then called Falke, telling her the district attorney's office would question her and her mother, and that she should say she didn't receive any answers.

Falke's mother allowed the district attorney's office to eavesdrop on Felsher's next call to them. Again, he told Falke to say she hadn't received any form of assistance. "Yes, but I did."

"No, you didn't, Kirsten," Felsher said. Falke testified before the grand jury as scheduled. The Falke matter prompted Stone to put Felsher himself before the grand jury. Under Stein's questioning, he denied both revealing any questions or "answers" to any *Tic Tac Dough* contestant. After Felsher completed his testimony, Stone discovered him in the witness room conversing with an ex-contestant who was waiting to testify before the grand jury. Warned that such conduct might be viewed as interfering with the grand jury's labor, Felsher apologized and left.[257]

The cancellation of *The $64,000 Question* was quickly followed by the biggest bombshell to date in the unfolding quiz show scandal: the grand jury's indictment of Albert Freedman on two counts of perjury, both for having earlier denied that he had supplied contestants with answers. The maximum

---

[257] *Ibid.*, 124-127.

penalty for each count was five years' imprisonment and $5,000 fine. Freedman pled not guilty and was released on $1,500 bail.[258]

Testifying before the grand jury on November 12, 1958, Elfrida Von Nardroff denied receiving assistance. Vivienne Nearing, next to Von Nardroff - the most famous female contestant to appear on *Twenty-One* and the woman who dethroned Charles Van Doren, also denied both receiving help or being notified beforehand that she would beat Van Doren or lose to Bloomgarden. Reappearing before the grand jury in January 1959, Von Nardroff justified a series of phone calls she made to Freedman during her final weeks on *Twenty-One* as necessary to keep him apprised as to her location. She had met Freedman once after her quiz show run, when they lunched together after she received a subpoena, at which time the subject of what she would say to the grand jury went unmentioned. Subsequently, Freedman called her to sign an affidavit that she hadn't been coached while appearing on *Twenty-One*. Von Nardroff referred Freedman's request to a lawyer, but no action was taken regarding it. She had last spoken to Freedman soon after he was indicted, and then to convey her sympathy.

Appearing before the grand jury immediately after Von Nardroff's second appearance, Charles Van Doren again asserted, as he had in his meeting with Stone, that he hadn't received any kind of assistance during his *Twenty-One* appearances. He did disclose that, prior to his quiz show appearances, he had met Freedman at parties at Greenwich Village where both men were living at the time. While he was a *Twenty-One* contestant, Van Doren had met with Freedman in his office to organize such events as meetings with the press and picture-taking sessions.

Later that same month, Enright, Barry, and their executive producer, Robert Noah, appeared before the grand jury. Stone explained that the next move had already been prearranged:

> The jurors had heard Stempel's side of the story—in great detail, from a number of witnesses. Now Enright, the other principal in the affair, had arrived, presumably to tell his side of the story. In my role as their legal adviser, I previously had told the jurors that even if Enright was a complainant in the matter of the extortion attempt by Stempel, he, Barry, and Noah had become targets of the investigation. It was the jurors' decision to make, but I was advising them to have Enright, Barry, and Noah sign waivers of immunity before they would be heard, as Stempel himself had been required to do. I further advised the jurors that, according to the law, if Enright and company testified without waiving immunity, two things would happen: if they lied they would not be subject to perjury prosecution because, in the eyes of the law, as

---

[258] Anderson, *Television Fraud*, 132.

targets they would not have been legally sworn even though they took the oath; at the same time, they would be immune to prosecution for any wrongdoing they might admit to before the jury that came within the scope of the investigation. And so, at my request, the jury had voted not to hear Enright, Barry, and Noah unless they signed waivers of immunity.[259]

Meeting with Enright, Barry, Noah, and their attorney, Jacob Rosenblum, Stone explained the nature of the grand jury investigation and, because of the trio's connection to quiz shows and their prior announced willingness to cooperate with the probe, they would be afforded the chance to do so by appearing before the grand jury. Just the same, Stone continued, neither the district attorney nor the grand jury was ready to grant them immunity from prosecution in exchange for their testimony. To this, Rosenblum said that his clients were happy to testify, but couldn't sign waivers. Stone informed the grand jury members of this development, one they must have known would occur, then notified Enright and his companions that the jurors wouldn't hear their testimony at the present time. That ended the matter.[260]

On January 29, 1959, the members of the grand jury made the decision to suspend hearing testimony. Stone asked Judge Schweitzer for another extension of the grand jury to allow time for the presentment to be prepared and to put pressure on those who had committed perjury to recant and come clean. For his arguments, Stone received a one month's extension.[261]

It wasn't long before the perjurers began to come clean. Two former contestants from the daytime edition of *Tic Tac Dough* acknowledged that they were coached as well as having been in touch with Howard Felsher after the investigation commenced and, at Felsher's urging, had consulted attorney Sol Gelb, who counseled them that fundamentally no case against Felsher existed, hence it made no difference what they said about *Tic Tac Dough* to the investigation— a course that suggested that lying was no great matter.

The next to step forward and make amends was Felsher himself, who admitted coaching *Tic Tac Dough* contestants. Appearing before a quorum of grand jurors on April 2, 1959, Felsher explained that his motivation for lying rested on a pair of considerations: to keep *Tic Tac Dough* on the air and create a united front with those he had encouraged to lie after pledging he would inform the district attorney that he hadn't given any sort of assistance. Furthermore, Felsher had expected that, should they confess to having cheated on a quiz show, some contestants would suffer professional harm as a conse-

---

[259] Stone and Yohn, Prime Time and Misdemeanors, 172.
[260] Stone and Yohn, *Prime Time and Misdemeanors*, 159, 160, 170, 171-173.
[261] *Ibid.*, 184.

quence of telling the truth. For the jurors, Felsher's recantation was significant in that, in addition to augmenting a lesson they had previously learned from *Dotto*—that quiz show fixing was a frequent and commonplace, it revealed just how far quiz contestants had gone along with the rigging and their willingness to conceal the truth by committing perjury. Felsher testified that none of those he offered assistance to declined such help. "Out of twenty-six contestants" Felsher had named "as receiving assistance, fifteen had testified. Of these," Stone wrote, "more than two-thirds had denied receiving assistance. Two had returned in good faith to amend their testimony. That left only four out of fifteen who had testified truthfully to start with. The jurors had every reason to believe the ratio was similar for the twenty former contestants who had testified in connection with 'Twenty-One.'"[262]

The next to crack was Albert Freedman, who acknowledged aiding all the important *Twenty-One* contestants who appeared in the wake of Herbert Stempel's tenure as well as helping some twenty other contestants who were briefly champions or were defeated as challengers. Of these, three had testified before the grand jury that they hadn't been coached. Freedman explained that he had committed perjury out of his conviction that if he revealed the truth, it would have become known and that the resulting publicity would have harmed the contestants. \Calling them good citizens who would be "devastated" if it became public knowledge that they had gone along with the rigging, Freedman argued that it was they—not him—who requested his silence. After his initial appearance before the grand jury, Freedman met with Van Doren; the latter said the consequence of revealing the quiz show fraud would have calamitous consequences for his family, including the possibility that it might even kill his father.

By owning up, Freedman hoped it would result in the dismissal of the indictment and allow him to resume his broadcasting career. He conceded the fact that Enright was furnishing him financial assistance and was aware that he was now cooperating with the investigation. He asserted that the perjury he had committed was his own doing and hadn't originated with any imploring on Enright's part.

With Freedman's recantation, the grand jury had heard its final witness. Notified that the grand jury had heard its final witness and was concluding its labors, Judge Schweitzer scheduled June 10, 1959, as the date the jury would be formally discharged. Before then, on June 3, the judge summoned the committee of eight jurors responsible for the writing of the grand jury's presentment in the quiz show matter.[263] This wasn't the committee's first

---

[262] *Ibid.,* 186-187, 191, 192.
[263] *Ibid.,* 193, 196, 197, 199.

encounter with Schweitzer. At an earlier meeting with them, at the end of April, he had told them that, because he had decided that the presentment (a formal presentation of information to a court) wasn't legal, he couldn't accept it for filing and publication. For Stone, who had earlier head Schweitzer's concerns about the quiz show investigation's presentment, this was the first time the judge had formally conveyed his concerns to the jurors, "who were furious at the prospect of having the fruit of their long labor plucked from them. They saw no good reason for" Schweitzer, whose reputation was that of "a mechanic who kept the wheels of justice moving" instead of "as a guardian of the rights of citizens, to be suddenly climbing on a high horse."[264]

Now, at this second confrontation between Schweitzer and the committee of eight, the former virtually commanded the jury to discontinue its work without a report, reiterating his threats to expunge. Joining Hacker, Stone and Richard Denzer, chief of the Appeals Bureau "and our resident legal expert," argued that research had disclosed that in the history of New York County presentments, only one had been expunged and the action upheld on appeal. It was Denzer and Stone's contention that should anyone be affronted by the presentment, that individual could move to set aside part of or the report after the latter had been received, filed, and made public.

After he dismissed the jurors, Schweitzer focused his wrath on Stone, who argued there was nothing unfair about the report: it described conditions and offered suggestions for corrective action, not merely the private matters of businessmen. When Schweitzer finally requested to see the document, Stone presented a copy of the draft. It was later returned to Stone's office, absent of any comment on Schweitzer's part.

When, on the morning of June 10, 1959, Hacker, Richard Mangano, the assistant grand jury foreman, and Stone appeared in Schweitzer's courtroom to tender the presentment, Schweitzer, without giving the report a momentary look, declared, "The court's right to accept and make public this report has been challenged. Pending determination of the court's power to accept it, it is ordered impounded and sealed." Schweitzer continued that he was providing the district attorney "an opportunity to submit any law on my power to accept this report."

Anticipating such a move on Schweitzer's part, Hacker observed that neither the judge nor the district attorney had sought to restrict the investigation, nor had the judge charged the jury that it couldn't make a presentment. In the performance of its task, the jury was mindful of the latitude furnished by "the long and honorable tradition of the grand jury as an important Anglo-Saxon institution." The jury's report dealt with an issue that had drawn

---

[264] *Ibid.*, 197.

"universal attention" and concerned a significant public interest in that the manipulation of quiz shows involved moral, if not legal questions, and that the shows originated in New York and had a natural audience. "With this sense of responsibility, we have worked long, carefully and soberly, and we are hoping therefore that we shall be heard—and that our presentment shall be accepted."

Hacker's argument earned Schweitzer's response that he didn't indicate that the grand jury lacked the authority to make a report but was mainly concerned with felonies, such as larceny and extortion. Schweitzer then discharged the jurors with the court's thanks, terminating the grand jury, and directed the district attorney to make preparation to present its side of the presentment issue before him on June 26.[265]

In arguing for the presentment's release, district attorney Frank Hogan contended that the public had the right to know how far the quiz show producers had deceived them. Siding with Hogan was the Grand Jury Association of New York and the Citizens Union. NBC denied rumors that it was responsible for the presentment's impoundment, announcing it supported the document's issuance. Among those filing briefs favoring the impoundment were the Association of Lawyers of the Criminal Courts of Manhattan and the Kings County (Brooklyn) Criminal Courts Bar Association. As the wrangling continued, Hogan correctly surmised that a congressional hearing would be the sole means of laying bare the whole story before the public.[266]

"Congress in the Act"[267]

The beginning act of the congressional investigation of the quiz show rigging began on July 29, 1959, when Hogan received a letter from the chairman of the Senate Interstate and Foreign Commerce Committee, Senator Warren Magnuson who wanted a copy of the grand jury presentment. The senator would have to apply to Judge Schweitzer. The next day both Magnuson and his opposite number in the House of Representatives, Congressman Oren Harris, chairman of the House Interstate and Foreign Commerce Committee, announced their intention to subject the quiz shows to congressional scrutiny. This was followed, on July 31, by Harris' announcement that his committee's Subcommittee on Legislative Oversight would inquire into the quizzes—the latter he labeled a "national" problem and "a proper concern of the federal government."

---

[265] Ibid., 199, 200-201.
[266] Anderson, Television Fraud, 135-137.
[267] Title drawn from Stone and Yohn, Prime Time and Misdemeanors, 205.

An affidavit prepared by the Harris subcommittee's chief counsel Robert Lishman requesting the minutes of the testimony presented to the grand jury was presented in open court in New York on July 31. Schweitzer granted the request a few days later.

The Subcommittee on Legislative Oversight had been created as part of a postwar reorganization on congressional committees in 1946 to carry out an overall inquiry of those federal regulatory agencies that fell under the province of its parent committee. Not until over a decade later, when the subcommittee again scrutinized the regulatory agencies, especially the Federal Trade Commission (FTC), the Federal Communications Commission (FCC), and the Securities and Exchange Commission (SEC), did it achieve public attention.

Harris successfully asked that Joseph Stone serve as a special consultant to the subcommittee. Before leaving for Washington, Stone met with former *Twenty-One* contestant Hank Bloomgarden, who, at this time confessed to having lied both to Stone and the grand jury. During his confessional, Bloomgarden said he had stuck to his story of not receiving help out of loyalty to Freedman. After the latter recanted before the grand jury, Bloomgarden was summoned to Enright's office, where *Twenty-One*'s producer, emphasizing the harm the looming congressional probe could cause, asked Bloomgarden to see Senator John O. Pastore of Rhode Island, the second ranking Democrat on the Interstate and Foreign Commerce Committee, with the suggestion that the latter committee take action to head off the Harris committee's investigation. Such a tactic, Bloomgarden said, was impossible as was another recommendation: that Bloomgarden leave the country. Another idea that came up at this time was to bribe Pastore. Just before the hearings began, Bloomgarden had a visitor: Richard N. Goodwin, a figure who would play an important role in the congressional investigation. Asked by Goodwin if Freedman's statements about him before the grand jury were accurate, Bloomgarden realized his sole option was to admit the truth. When Goodwin asked Bloomgarden to voluntarily appear before the committee, Bloomgarden said that doing so would destroy him. Though he acknowledged that it was likely that Bloomgarden wouldn't be compelled to testify, Goodwin urged him to set the record straight before the district attorney. Bloomgarden's confession marked the first time an important *Twenty-One* contestant had admitted committing perjury.[268]

An investigator for the congressional committee, Goodwin had attended Tufts and Harvard Law School. Goodwin had obtained the grand jury presentment from Judge Schweitzer. Though he found the grand jury records

---

[268] *Ibid.*, 210-218.

contained contradictions, Goodwin found enough to convince him, like it had Stone, that the quizzes were a sham. As yet, the evidence failed to meet the standards of legal proof. "But," Goodwin wrote, "I knew. Now we must make the case." In his role as a special investigator, Goodwin spent the ensuing months in New York, with occasional trips to Hollywood, interviewing contestants and producers, making his way from that level to advertising agencies, sponsors, and the networks.

After meeting Charles Van Doren, Goodwin, who believed Van Doren was lying, began to doubt that he was. "He was so forcefully sincere. He seemed to believe, must believe, what he was saying. And perhaps he did. The depths of the human mind have hiding places for the most contradictory recollections and beliefs; desires whose powerful surge can overpower conscious knowledge and awareness."[269] What cinched the case for Goodwin was Freedman's testimony. When that happened, Goodwin called Van Doren to tell him where the investigation now stood. When the two men next met, Van Doren's lawyer accompanied him. Van Doren clung to his innocence, which drew Goodwin's telling comment that the only people not telling the truth were those who came from the best families—a reference to another quiz contestant who bore an outstanding pedigree. Convinced Van Doren was lying, Goodwin nevertheless saw no reason in having the committee publicly butcher him. The McCarthy hearings were fresh in memory, and Goodwin remembered those people for whom appearing before the investigating committees had produced devastating consequences. The real villains in the quiz show mess, in Goodwin's eyes, were the networks, the sponsors, and the producers. Stempel found Goodwin's reluctance to nail Van Doren galling. Stempel's repeated queries as to whether Goodwin was going to summon Van Doren finally prompted Goodwin to ask, "Herb, why do you hate him so much?" "I don't hate him," Stempel answered. It was then that Stempel recalled an occasion when he had tried to shake Van Doren's hand at a charity benefit but Van Doren, in Stempel's account of events, shunned him.

Speaking to the committee members in closed session, Goodwin said he possessed more than sufficient evidence as to the fraudulence of the quiz shows, but felt it wasn't necessary to publicly devastate Van Doren before the committee. Though the committee wouldn't be hearing from him, Goodwin cautioned Van Doren not to make any public utterance or do anything which the committee might regard as a challenge and might compel it to summon him. However, NBC upset this arrangement by directing Van

---

[269] Richard N. Goodwin, *Remembering America: A Voice from the Sixties* (Boston: Little, Brown and Company, 1988), 48-49.

Doren to telegram the committee that he had committed no wrongdoing or else he would be fired from *The Today Show*. His pride forcing him, Van Doren did as he was told and dispatched the telegram, with the inescapable result being that a subpoena calling him before the committee was issued. Goodwin consulted Supreme Court Justice Felix Frankfurter, for whom he had clerked after college. "A quiz-show investigation without Van Doren," the justice declared, "is like *Hamlet* without anyone playing Hamlet." Moreover, Van Doren had willingly participated in the scandal.[270]

At the outset of the Harris subcommittee's opening session on October 16 chairman Harris made it clear that body's only interest in the quiz show scandal was "whether commercial deceit has been practiced on a national scale by means of deliberate and willful holding out to the public as honest contests, performances which were rigged in advance." The first in the witness chair was Herbert Stempel, who appeared without a lawyer, and provided a complete account of his experience with *Twenty-One* and Dan Enright, supplemented with kinescope viewings of his important matches with Charles Van Doren. Then it was James Snodgrass' turn to testify. Snodgrass furnished the evidence establishing that Freedman had given questions and answers before his *Twenty-One* matches with the letters he had written—one of which, dated May 17, 1957, Snodgrass opened in the subcommittee's presence. "His testimony was followed by a kinescope of the following show, which demonstrated Snodgrass's deliberate intent not to" adhere to Freedman's orders "and correctly answer the Emily Dickinson question."

For his part, Dan Enright admitted that he had provided answers to Stempel and other contestants beforehand and said that, after the scandal became known, the network's main concern was "how to avoid having the story" revealed, no matter what the truth was. As to whether network executives knew that the quiz shows were fixed, "You would have to be very unsophisticated or very naive not to understand that certain controls have to be exercised."[271]

Another witness, Antoinette Dubarry Hillman, a contestant on *Dotto*, was quite candid in her assessment on appearing on a rigged quiz show: "I didn't have any moral qualms about it."[272] In characterizing how the quiz show operators conducted their business, a Democratic member of the subcommittee, John Moss of California, declared, "It is a perfect illustration of their lack of morality, a perfect illustration of their lack of ethics. They are perfectly willing to corrupt." "It was also clear," observed *Time* magazine, "that a great

[270] Halberstam, *The Fifties*, 661-663.
[271] www.pbs.org/wgbh/amex/quizshow/peopleevents/pande04.htl 5 November 2007.
[272] "A Make-Believe World': Contestants Testify to Deceptive Quiz Show Practices." Http://historymatters.gmu.edu/d/6555 30 October 2007.

many contestants, drawn from everyday America and tempted by small fortunes and big publicity, had been perfectly willing to be corrupted."[273]

NBC's directive to Van Doren that he telegram his innocence to the subcommittee came the evening the hearings began. But after complying, Van Doren began having second thoughts. After telling his lawyer the truth and requesting a temporary release from his teaching and television obligations, Van Doren and his wife drove through New England, while subcommittee chairman Harris sought to locate him. His whereabouts were untraceable. "Where's Charlie?" asked the *Washington Daily News*' headline. Having no option but adjournment, the Harris subcommittee subpoenaed the missing Columbia University instructor. When he rematerialized on October 13, he discovered that he was subpoenaed to appear the following day. He fraudulently declared that he didn't know the subcommittee wanted to hear from him. Shortly thereafter, Van Doren told the truth to his parents and to Hogan and Stone. He was to be the lead-off witness when the hearings resumed in November. As the date for his scheduled testimony drew near, his appearances at the district attorney's office fueled mounting rumination on the part of the press that his congressional statement might reverse his previous denials of receiving coaching.[274]

The next day, November 2, 1959, Charles Van Doren "folded himself uncomfortably into the witness chair, gulped some water, then stripped away the last layer of illusion separating him from the shills."[275]

> I would give almost anything I have to reverse the course of my life in the last three years. I cannot take back one word or action; the past does not change for anyone. But at least I can learn from the past.

> I have learned a lot in those three years, especially in the last three weeks. I've learned a lot about life. I've learned a lot about myself, and about good and evil. They are not always what they appear to be. I was involved, deeply involved in a deception. The fact that I, too, was very much deceived cannot keep me from being the principle victim of that deception, because I was its principle symbol. . . .[276]

Van Doren presented a history of his time as a *Twenty-One* contestant, then, after he had completed his testimony, subcommittee chair Harris praised him for telling the truth, which was followed by compliments from

---

[273] "The Big Fix," http://www.time.com/time/magazine/article/0,9171,869307,00.html 18 February 2008.

[274] Anderson, *Television Fraud*, 140-141.

[275] "Van Doren & Beyond," www.time.com/time/magazine/article/0,9171,811465,00.html 18 February 2008.

[276] Anderson, Television Fraud, 142.

the majority of the subcommittee's members—save for one. The dissenter was Congressman Steven Derounian of New York: "I don't think an adult of your intelligence ought to be commended for telling the truth." Dismissing the witness, Harris said:

> Mr. Van Doren, you have given a very dramatic, but in my humble judgment a very pathetic, presentation here today. . . . I think it was a great writer, you may remember, that said one time, "there is so much good in the worst of us and so much bad in the best of us, that it ill behooves any of us to talk about the rest of us.". . .

> I think I could end this session with you by saying what your attorney did say to you the other day; that is "God bless you." The subcommittee thanks you for your appearance here.[277]

Time magazine wasn't as impressed, characterizing the fallen idol's statement as filled with "phony arguments." Van Doren had wanted to leave *Twenty-One*, yet not one member of the subcommittee asked why he didn't retire, or deliberately miss a question to leave the quiz. Van Doren testified that he was telling all "for the benefit of his 'millions' of friends"—especially an "unnamed woman whose letter had moved him." The reality was that the Harris subcommittee's subpoena had forced him to come forward. "Furthermore, the evidence of fraud was overwhelming, and Van Doren had already admitted that he had perjured himself in his testimony before the grand jury in New York."

Present that day for Van Doren's testimony were Herbert Stempel and Joseph Stone. Speaking to Stone during the recess following Van Doren's statement, Stempel bitterly complained that the CCNY professors had rejected his proposal for his Ph.D. thesis. All the while he could see, out of the corner of his eyes, the mob surrounding Van Doren as he slowly made his way into the corridor where newsreel cameras were waiting to film him. Not even disgrace had diminished his celebrity. "Posterity would recall Van Doren as the symbol of a tawdry hoax that shook the nation," Stone would write of the moment, "while Stempel would be lost in the shuffle."[278]

The remainder of the hearings covered the EPI quizzes, with testimony from the Reverend Stoney Jackson and Arthur Cohn, Jr. describing their experiences on *The $64,000 Challenge*. John Ross, manager of child actress Patty Duke, testified that Bernstein supplied answers to Duke when she was a *Challenge* contestant.

---

[277] Anderson, *Television Fraud*, 142-143.
[278] Stone and Yohn, *Prime Time and Misdemeanors*, 251-252.

Koplin testified that 60 to 70% of the winners on *The $64,000 Question* and *Challenge* received assistance as did virtually every winner who climbed the $32,000 plateau. Koplin assigned responsibility for the fixing to Revlon, Inc., and the Revson brothers. The latter denied any involvement in the rigging, but this was disputed by Revlon's erstwhile advertising head, George Abrams, who believed the producers "were living between the mixed values of show business and advertising, and moral values were lost sight of."[279]

The hearings concluded with the appearance of NBC president Robert E. Kintner and CBS president Frank Stanton. Kintner contented that NBC, along with the public, had been duped "by a small group of people in the production field and the contestant field" but wouldn't "abdicate a program responsibility in the quiz, audience-participation, panel-show field." NBC had created a "standards and practices" investigatory unit, supported making quiz show rigging a crime, and offered to be the subcommittee's means of conveying to the public the results of its investigation. Though NBC favored laws criminalizing quiz show rigging, Kintner believed the public interest wouldn't be served if the networks were required to directly produce all programs, but neither should they be prevented from owning and producing their own programs. Under this line of reasoning, broadcasting content should be the province of the broadcaster; government regulation would "inject the government into the program process itself," which would be both contrary to the "whole concept" of American broadcasting and ineffectual when it came to quiz shows, as it couldn't deter a producer from colluding with a contestant.

When it came to knowing about dishonesty pertaining to his network's quiz shows, Stanton asserted ignorance in this regard until August 8, 1958, and the *Dotto* affair. Conceding CBS' accountability for what it aired, including those productions produced by outsiders, Stanton cited his decision to eliminate all big-money quizzes from CBS as a measure toward making CBS "the masters of our own house." Stanton pledged that the next move would be the issuance of regulations "to assure that programs will be exactly what they appear to be." CBS was studying the utilization of a new code of standards that would "eliminate legitimate complaints" concerning commercials because "in the long run it is as much to the advantage of the advertiser as to the broadcaster that there is public confidence in the medium of television and public support for its practices." Stanton supported a law criminalizing the employment of "deceitful practices in any game or contest or in any advertising medium" and expressed confidence that the subcommittee "would

[279] "How It Was Done," www.time.com/time/magazine/article/0,9171,811467,00.html 18 February 2008.

not recommend legislation which would invade the areas of programming or result in censorship."

When asked about *Time* and *Look* magazines' 1957 articles about the possibility of quiz rigging, Stanton noted that the motivations of the publications had to be taken into account, as they were competing with the networks for advertising money and information. "This isn't to excuse us for not knowing more, but I say we weren't triggered and perhaps shouldn't have been" by the magazine pieces. Moreover, the magazine companies were rivals who also owned television stations, which continued airing the quiz shows without any objection being raised. CBS had taken "affirmative action" against the quiz shows without waiting for "someone in Washington" to say something about them.[280]

The Aftermath

For Van Doren, the consequences of his finally owning up to the truth weren't long in coming. In quick succession, the trustees of Columbia University accepted his resignation and NBC fired him. Van Doren wasn't without his supporters at Columbia. Two students obtained 650 signatures on a petition advocating his continuance as a Columbia instructor and 500 students flocked to a pro-Van Doren rally on the Columbia quad. Columbia's president Grayson Kirk declined to reverse the trustees' decision to terminate Van Doren. In Hallock, Minnesota, a write-in campaign elected Van Doren the town constable. Officials representing several colleges put out the word that they would be happy to hire him. *Leisure*, a newly created, Manhattan based publication, invited him to pen a column, "The Intellect at Leisure."[281]

Appearing on *The Today Show*, where Van Doren had proclaimed his innocence in 1958, host Dave Garroway emotionally declared that he was "still a friend of Charles Van Doren. . . . I can only say I am heartbroken. He was one of our family. We are a little family on this show, strange as it may seem. Whatever Charles did was wrong of course. I cannot condone or defend it. But we will never forget the non-Euclidean geometry essays or the poetry of Sir John Suckley which Charles left us with." Ironically, it was subsequently learned that Garroway's breakdown, while authentic, had actually been prerecorded before it was aired.[282]

---

[280] Anderson, Television Fraud, 143; Stone and Yohn, Prime Time and Misdemeanors, 265-268.

[281] Anderson, *Television Fraud,* 147; "Van Doren & Beyond," www.time.com/time/magazine/article/0,9171,811465,00. html 18 February 2008.

[282] Stone and Yohn, *Prime Time and Misdemeanors,* 258.

For his part, Van Doren felt no animus toward Richard Goodwin, as evinced by a letter he wrote Goodwin after his congressional testimony:

> Dear Dick:
>
> There are a number of things I'd like to talk to you about—none of them having to do with quiz shows. I made the mistake of reading the papers. I should have taken your advice. I wish the next six months were already over.
>
> There have been many hard things. But I am trying to tell you that we will live and thrive, I think—I mean I know we will live and I think we will thrive—and that you must never, in any way, feel any regret for your part in this. Perhaps it is nonsense to say that, but I thought it might be just possible that you would.
>
> Charlie[283]

Other voices were raised concerning the state of television specifically, and, in the final analysis, the overall condition of American society. Television's true fraud, *Saturday Review* editor Norman Cousins believed, was its extravagant use of crime and violence in most of its programs. The *Reporter* observed that the struggle between the network and the sponsor—with the latter's advertising agency in the sponsor's corner—for the final word regarding programming had long been a fact of life in television: "The one commands the dollars, the other the time on the air, and the balance of power has oscillated between them roughly according to the laws of supply and demand." What truly disturbed the *New Yorker* wasn't the hoaxers who put the quiz shows on the air but the contestants, "almost all of whom must have applied in good faith," who were corrupted into going along with the deception. The viewing audience watched for years, suspecting nothing amiss about what they saw. What finally broke the scandal out into the open was a winner, "disgruntled because he had not won more," who blew the whistle. "We are fascinated by the unimaginably tactful and delicate process whereby the housewife next door was transfigured into a paid cheat." One of America's most eminent journalists, James Reston of the *New York Times*, drew a connection between the quiz show scandal and a steel strike then gripping the nation:

> There is an overwhelming feeling here that somehow we have lost our way. Nobody seems to know just how or why, but everybody feels that something's wrong. It is not only the TV quiz scandal but the steel

---

[283] Goodwin, *Remembering America*, 57-58.

strike that has given the impression of haphazard greed, and a system debased and out of balance.[284]

Reston was one of several journalists who raised the quiz show matter with President Eisenhower at the latter's press conference two days after Van Doren's subcommittee appearance. "I think I share the American general reaction of almost bewilderment that people could conspire to confuse and deceive the American people," said the President. "Selfishness and greed are occasionally, at least—get the ascendancy over those things that we like to think of as the ennobling virtues of man, his capacity for self-sacrifice, his readiness to help others, and so I would say this: the kind of things that you talk about do remind us that man is made up of two kinds of qualities." "Whether the president clarified the national feeling over the scandal is, or course, debatable," historian Kent Anderson would write from the perspective of the 1970s, "but he did maintain firmly that there was no national indifference to questions of morality as exemplified by the Van Doren story."[285]

Television wasn't without its apologists—one of whom, Albert Freedman, asserted that the rigged quiz shows wrought no financial injury upon any one, including the public, who watched television free of charge. "Our only error," Freedman declared, "was that we were too successful. The stakes were too high and the quiz winners fused themselves into the home life and the hopes and aspirations of the viewers." Freedman believed the clamor regarding ethics beside the point - quizzes were entertainment after all. "It is about time the television industry stopped apologizing for its existence and begin to fight back. It should insist that sponsored programs be recognized and judged as entertainment and entertainment only."[286]

Utilizing a sample of 2,289 households and projecting the results into the tens of millions to denote the all of the American adult population, the polling firm of Sindlinger and Company discovered 46,170,000 (42.8%) supported the Harris subcommittee probe; 32,962,000 (30.6%) did not; 18,790,000 (17.4%) had no opinion; 9,985,000 (9.2%) furnished evasive or qualified answers. When Sindlinger further inquired, "Even though contestants on quiz shows" received assistance, "have you found the quiz programs" sufficiently educational and entertaining "to want to see them on TV again?" 39.9% answered affirmatively.

---

[284] Anderson, Television Fraud, 152.

[285] Anderson, *Television Fraud*, 148-153.

[286] "Years later, Freedman noticed that while the press greatly emphasized the quiz show scandal, television's contribution to real-life violence passes without comment: "On television every form of violence is okay in this country, but nudity and sexuality is forbidden. Wal-Marts refuse to sell a video of cars and pretty girls in bathing suits. Yet they sell thousands of copies of *The Texas Chainsaw Massacre*. What can I say? Welcome to America." Kisseloff, *The Box*, 498.

An Elmo Roper poll revealed the following: "These disclosures show just how bad television is": 4%; "These practices are very wrong and should be stopped immediately, but you can't condemn all of television because of them": 65%; "No one can really be in favor of this kind of thing, but there's nothing very wrong about it either": 7%; "What happened is a normal part of show business and is perfectly all right": 7%. Taking his survey out into the streets of New York City, an inquiring photographer from the *New York Daily News* asked, "Would you have any qualms about appearing on a TV quiz show if it were rigged and you knew you would win a large sum of money?" Four out of every six of those replying answered yes, they would do so.[287]

In the immediate aftermath of the scandal, the ax fell on numerous quizzes—honest and dishonest alike, with CBS, acting under Frank Stanton's orders, taking greater action in this regard. Banished from the Tiffany Network's schedule were *Name That Tune* (despite CBS' placement of an announcement that contestants had been "prepared" by listening to melodies), *Top Dollar* and *The Big Payoff.* Less drastic than CBS, NBC cancelled some but not all of its quiz and game shows, though it had to scrap Enright's *Tic Tac Dough* and replaced it with the ironically named *Truth or Consequences.* Both networks also created departments of "fair practices." In his capacity as head of that unit at NBC, Ernest Lee Jahncke, Jr. went so far as to censor what he deemed a risqué joke on *The Tonight Show,* prompting host Jack Parr to walk off the show and briefly retire from show business.

The Parr episode demonstrated that television's newfound rectitude could assume extreme forms. This was especially true at CBS, where canned laughter and applause was eliminated from all programs unless it was announced that such devices were in use. Musical and variety programs presenting entertainers who lip-synched previously recorded songs now had to say: "Certain portions of this program were pre-recorded."

Another to leave CBS in the wake of the quiz show scandal was Louis Cowan. During the Harris subcommittee probe, Cowan had been unable to testify in his capacity as CBS Television Network president due to his hospitalization for phlebitis in his left leg. A few critics found his inability to testify convenient and his absence from the congressional hearings raised questions about his part in the rigged quizzes, though Mert Koplin's testimony absolved him of knowing anything about how EPI operated the quiz show he created after he moved on to the executive wing at CBS. "To the careful observer, there was no question that Cowan was blameless, and few network presidents of CBS had been more committed to the News Division than" Cowan, "once he had joined forces with Murrow and Friendly."

---

[287] Anderson, *Television Fraud,* 153-156.

As Stanton told the story, in June 1959 Cowan notified the former of his intention to depart CBS in approximately a year. In the wake of the hearings, Stanton expedited Cowan's departure. In resigning, Cowan told Stanton:

> During recent weeks you have expressed, both publicly and privately, your complete confidence in me and in the fact that I had nothing to do with the rigging of quiz shows. Nevertheless, in spite of my record and your confidence in my integrity, you have suggested repeatedly, directly and indirectly, that I should resign. I have asked you explicitly whether the real reason you did not want me as president of CBS television network is that, at this particular moment, you do not want a man who has had an association with quiz shows, even though his association was completely honest and honorable. But you have told me emphatically that this is not the reason for your desiring my resignation.[288]

In Stanton's view, the fact that Cowan, the man who had birthed *The $64,000 Question,* was also the president of the CBS Television network at the time that television was subject to intense scrutiny was injurious to both the network's and the industry's image, regardless of Cowan's innocence in the scandal.[289] "The quiz thing," in the view of CBS counsel Ralph Colin, didn't lead to the firing of Lou Cowan. It might have been the match to set off the flash of powder. It was, rather, Lou's lack of executive training and lack of decision-making capability. He was a wonderful person—intellectual, cultured, but absolutely impossible as an executive."

As was the case with the majority of programmers who lost their executive positions as a result of a disastrous occurrence, Cowan never held another position of power. In 1976 both he and his wife Pauline lost their lives in a fire that devastated their duplex apartment in New York's Westbury Hotel.[290]

Self-regulation on the part of the television industry was, in the view of the Harris subcommittee, an insufficient remedy for the quiz show scandal. In the wake of the hearings, the subcommittee readied a report on legislative remedies covering the technically noncriminal methods of the quiz producers. Before then, President Eisenhower ordered Attorney General William Rogers to conduct and ready a report by the first day of January 1960. Though it preceded the Harris subcommittee's interim report by a few months, the Rogers report presented basically the same proposals as those forwarded by the Harris subcommittee's report. In the view of the Rogers report, the FCC

---

[288] Anderson, Television Fraud, 161-162.
[289] Anderson, *Television Fraud,* 161-162.
[290] Bergreen, *Look Now, Pay Later,* 199.

possessed the authority "to take appropriate measures" to ensure the honesty of quiz shows. Though such measures were already at hand, the report additionally advocated further legislation. Moreover, the report advocated the licensing of networks by the FCC. For its part, the interim report filed by the Harris subcommittee proposed the addition of criminal penalties for programmatic fraudulence on television and a brief suspension of stations found to have aired such fraudulent programs."

In late March 1960 Harris submitted two pieces of legislation for the House of Representatives' consideration: the first would allow the direct licensing of networks; the second would criminalize the airing of deceptive quiz shows. By late June Representative John Bennett's clause licensing the networks went down to defeat by a vote of 149-35, while Harris won enactment of an amendment proscribing the conferring of honoraria and gifts to members of the FCC—the latter resulting from FCC chairman Doerfer's presence on a yacht belonging to a friend who also owned a number of radio and television stations. The episode led to Doerfer's resignation in March 1960. Another section of the initial amendments, that which stipulated a $10,000 fine and a ten-day license suspension for stations guilty of violating FCC regulations, made the FCC responsible for establishing that the station was indeed guilty of an offense. Most congressmen apparently believed that the restrictions were too severe and made it clear that such disciplinary measures be applied solely in the event the transgression arose from "negligent or intentional" conduct.

When the United States Senate got around to considering the legislation, the chair of the Commerce Subcommittee on Communications, Democratic Senator John Pastore (RI) eliminated the suspension clause, leaving the fine intact. Doerfer's successor as FCC chairman, Frederick Ford, supported the House incarnation of the legislation but was unsuccessful in persuading the Senate to go along. Under the provisions of the legislation Eisenhower signed on September 13, 1960, the FCC could require license renewals of less than the lawfully mandated three years should the agency feel such action was in the public interest; barred gifts to FCC members; and made unlawful any contest or game meant to perpetrate deception on the audience.[291]

Postscript: The "Payola" Scandal

The revelation of quiz show rigging wasn't the only instance of broadcasting misconduct to come to light during this period. The quiz show scandal was immediately followed by the "payola" scandal in which disc jockeys

---

[291] Anderson, *Television Fraud*, 163-165.

received favors for promoting records on-air. The term "payola" was coined by *Variety* in 1938 to define gifts, favors, or money secretly bestowed for the purpose of getting orchestra leaders and disc jockeys to play songs.[292] Though the payola investigations disclosed the fact that the practice had been part of the music industry for at least a century, this failed to alter the opinions of those congressmen conducting the probe; in their view, the root of payola was rock'n'roll. The real issue in the payola investigation, some observers appreciated, was the old guard's resentment at its growing popularity. The principle targets of the inquiry were Dick Clark and Alan Freed. The host of television's *American Bandstand*, Clark was of great interest to the congressional investigators. In the words of Michigan's John Burnett, "I think it is pretty convincing that Clark was involved with payola as all other disc jockeys, but on a much larger scale." Clark, in Illinois U.S. Representative Peter Mack's characterization, was "the top dog in the payola field," while California's John Moss called the probe "Clarkola." Testifying before the congressmen in the spring of 1960, the neatly attired Clark declared that he had never consented to "play a record in return for payment of cash or any other consideration." Questioned about playing records by performers who recorded for those companies he had an interest in, Clark answered that he didn't "consciously favor such records. Maybe I did so without realizing it." When Clark wrapped up his testimony, subcommittee chair Harris told him, "You're not the inventor of the system or even its architect. You're a product of it." Harris called Clark "a fine young man."[293]

On the other hand, the payola investigation destroyed Alan Freed's career. A classically trained musician, Freed initially became famous while working as a pop music disc jockey in Akron, Ohio. He went on to a late-night classical music show at Cleveland's WJW in 1951. From a record store owner, Freed learned that local white adolescents wanted to hear R&B records.. Captivated by music where "the beat is so strong that anyone can dance to it without a lesson," Freed began his program in June 1951. *The Moondog Show* featured a wailing sax solo transmitted over WJW's powerful 50,000-watt signal. (He then moved on to the coveted WINS 1010AM in New York City.) Numerous disc jockeys believed they had the actual say in which records would in fact be played on radio. Formula programming meant a loss to them of both their creative control and a good portion of their likely earnings. It was here that payola came into play and afforded rock's enemies the opportunity to declare war on the music they deemed a menace to society.

---

[292] Glenn C. Altschuler, *All Shook Up: How Rock'n'Roll Changed America* (New York: Oxford University Press, 2003), 142.

[293] David P. Szatmary, *Rockin' In Time: A Social History of Rock-and-Roll* (Englewood Cliffs, New Jersey: Prentice Hall, 1991, 1987), Second Edition, 66-67.

As the payola investigation wound down, the now jobless Freed faced charges of commercial bribery in connection with payola lodged by a New York grand jury. In December 1962, Freed, now a pariah within the music industry, stood trial and pleaded guilty to two counts of commercial bribery, for which he received a $300 fine and a six-month suspended sentence. His legal woes continued when, on March 16, 1964, another grand jury charged him with income tax evasion during the period 1957 to 1959 and directed him to pay nearly $38,000 in back taxes to the IRS. Freed's ordeal finally exacted their price from him: later in 1964 he entered a California hospital, suffering the effects of alcoholism. The forty-three-year old Freed died on January 20, 1965.[294]

Charles Van Doren and Herbert Stempel compete on Twenty-One. Far left: Van Doren. Third from left: host Jack Barry. Far right: Stempel. Credit: NBC/Photofest.

Elvis Presley's entry into the Army removed him as a target just as the anti-rock backlash was gathering steam. The singer's departure from the rock'n'roll scene was part of a strategy conceived by his manager, Colonel Tom Parker, to sustain his entertainment career. Believing that "the very controversy that had originally fueled Elvis's fame was now" having the opposite effort of restricting it, Parker opted to "remove Elvis from the fray. In the aftermath of the quiz show scandal, Elvis Presley loyally doing his duty for his country rendered him a far more attractive figure, compared to the now disgraced Charles Van Doren.[295]

[294] Szatmary, Rockin' In Time, 67.
[295] Marling, As Seen on TV, 183.

7. The U-2 Bubble Bursts (1960)

While the American public reeled from the revelations of the rigged quiz shows, hopes for the betterment of Soviet-American relations soared. For his part, President Eisenhower hoped that the forthcoming gathering in Paris and his subsequent visit to the Soviet Union would lead to an accord curbing the arms race. In his state of the union message for 1960, he observed that Khrushchev now appeared truly prepared to collaborate in "diminishing the intensity of past rivalry." Eisenhower also desired the lessening of Cold War tensions, and was resolved to sign a nuclear test ban accord before exiting the White House. At the negotiating table in Geneva, Soviet, British, and American representatives were making progress in narrowing points of disagreement concerning such an accord. Occasionally, Eisenhower rejected the arguments against concessions on the part of Atomic Energy Commission chief John A. McCone, saying he would "probe in every way the sincerity and intent of the Soviet declaration on disarmament." The attainment of an agreement on nuclear testing wasn't a favor to the Soviets, Ike declared, but a "vital" American advantage furnishing "a ray of light in a world that is bound to be weary of the tensions brought about by mutual suspicion, distrust and arms races."

Khrushchev returned from Camp David lauding Soviet-American friendship and excited about the Paris conclave and Eisenhower's Soviet visit. Successful East-West talks were, in Khrushchev's eyes, a way of enhancing his standing as an international statesman. Moreover, Khrushchev sought collaboration in precluding the attainment by West Germany and China of atomic weapons. In the case of Germany, Khrushchev was motivated by traditional concerns. His anxieties were such that he might have been ready to drop his insistence on Western recognition of East German sovereignty if Eisenhower consented not to permit the placement of atomic weapons on German territory. When it came to China, Khrushchev worried about Chinese challenges to Soviet leadership and distrusted the Communist Chinese leader Mao Tse-tung. Both of these issues alarmed Khrushchev about the possibility that China would join the nuclear club. Hence, Khrushchev viewed detente as a means of enhancing Soviet security.[296]

Yet detente with the West wasn't without its risks for Khrushchev. Domestically, he wanted to strengthen his position without employing Stalinist purges; loosen the grip of the police state without inciting domestic revolts or alienating the KGB; reduce military spending without incurring the displeasure of the Army; lessen Moscow's hold on its satellites without letting them separate from Moscow's control. Internationally, he desired better relations with the West, but sought to take advantage of the liberation of the Third World from colonial rule, weaken NATO and sustain Lenin's gospel that Communism would ultimately prevail over capitalism.

Quite possibly by the fall of 1957, Khrushchev had already alienated those elements within the Soviet Union necessary to his political survival: the KGB and Moscow apparatchiks "whose wings he had clipped"; those upset over his failure to meet the needs of the Soviet people, to subdue Yugoslavia and his unorthodox conduct on the world stage. Before his trip to the United States, a few Party leaders had objected to the idea of international Communism's leader journeying to Washington as if he were a traveling salesman. Ideologues supposedly objected that peaceful coexistence deviated from the Marxist line, Foreign Ministry officials that this new policy would estrange Soviet allies—China in particular. As was true in America, the leaders of the Soviet military-industrial complex undoubtedly believed that diminished Cold War tensions wouldn't benefit their interests.

Another stumbling block to Khrushchev's goals was France's Charles de Gaulle, who sought to delay the Big Four summit until France had regained its position as a world power. This feeling arose in part from the wartime indignities he experienced from Roosevelt and Churchill which fomented concerns regarding an Anglo-Saxon scheme to thwart French destiny. Also by the time the summit finally convened, France would be more of an equal partner of the Americans, Russians, and British as she would by then possess her own atomic bomb. In the end, de Gaulle had his way. In December 1959, the United States, Great Britain, and France extended a formal invitation to Khrushchev to attend a Big Four summit gathering, scheduled to begin May 16, 1960, in Paris.[297]

---

[296] Pach and Richardson, *The Presidency of Dwight D. Eisenhower*, Revised Edition, 214-215.
[297] Beschloss, *Mayday*, 219-222.

Khrushchev took another gamble when, in January 1960, he announced that he was reducing the Soviet military by 1.2 million men—a decision motivated by the lessening of "the clouds of war" owing to his "historic" American visit, the obsolescence of large standing armies, surface navies and bomber fleets in the nuclear age, and the accuracy of Soviet missiles—so unerring they could hit a "fly in outer space." The savings acquired from military reductions would benefit Soviet workers as they would improve their opportunity to own apartments and television sets.

That same January, Khrushchev informed Thompson that Eisenhower could go "anyplace in the Soviet Union"—even places like Vladivostok and the Sevastopol naval installation, "despite the fact that as a military man, the President is an especially dangerous person." Eisenhower's reception would be "friendly in the extreme" and security measures would be unnecessary. During his American visit, Khrushchev had invited Eisenhower's grandchildren to visit Russia. Much to Eisenhower's displeasure, their father refused to allow them to accompany their grandfather on his Russian trip. Under the agreed upon itinerary, the Eisenhowers would arrive in Moscow on June 10, 1960. In Moscow, they would among other events attend a state dinner at the Kremlin, attend the Bolshoi Ballet, and lunch with the Khrushchevs at their country dacha. This would be followed by a trip to Leningrad, where Eisenhower would deliver a brief radio and television address to the Soviet people. In Kiev, Eisenhower would lay a wreath at the Tomb of the Unknown Soldier, make another broadcast address, and attend a concert. Returning to Moscow, he would receive an honorary degree from Moscow University, receive Khrushchev for dinner and make yet another broadcast address.

Eisenhower requested Khrushchev's authorization to allow him to use his own plane within Soviet territory. Once permission was granted Eisenhower authorized the transformation of his plane into a spy in the sky: high-resolution cameras were being installed in the belly of the aircraft to snap photographs of places of interest to the Air Force and the CIA during Ike's visit. Richard Bissell would later explain:

> I think Ike would have taken the position, "All right, if you can put some equipment on my aircraft unobtrusively and take what you get, that's all right." But I think he would have drawn the line at not altering the flight path in any shape or manner. . . . It would have been very unwise to let it be thought that his trip was being made in any sense or conditioned by intelligence.[298]

Then there was the matter of the U-2. By 1958 Eisenhower had begun diminishing the number of U-2 missions. The President was aware of their

---
[298] *Ibid.*, 223-224, 226-227, 228-229.

provocativeness and made it clear that nothing would incite America to war more rapidly than for it to know that the Soviets were doing the same thing to it that the we were doing to the Soviets with the U-2. Eisenhower's caution increased as he began reaching out to Khrushchev. The CIA, on the other hand, invariably appeared to want additional U-2 missions. This gave rise to a ritual: the agency requesting additional flights, and Eisenhower seeking to hold the line and give the agency less than it desired and more than he desired.

Eisenhower wasn't the only one feeling uneasy about the U-2 flights; so were the U-2 pilots. By the fall of 1958 evidence existed that the Soviets were both tracking the U-2s on radar and firing SAMs (surface-to-air missiles) that were coming, as Francis Gary Powers characterized it, uncomfortably close. Powers observed that the pilots were aware that the Soviets were experiencing problems with their guidance systems, but by 1960 new SAM-2 missiles were positioned all through the Soviet Union. Unlike their precursors, these new missiles possessed a far greater range; according to CIA calculations, they were capable of striking a target seventy thousand feet high. Concurrent with this advancement in Soviet weaponry, the U-2s were becoming heavier, owing to the addition of further equipment.

The diminished number of U-2 missions increased the difficulty of each flight. An added complication arose: there was evidence that the U-2 program wasn't as secret as it used to be. An article about the aircraft, accompanied by drawings, had appeared in the March 1958 edition of a model-airplane magazine. Moreover, there was word that the official paper of the Soviet air force had reported on the U-2 missions, dubbed the spy plane "the black lady of espionage." Both CIA chief Allen Dulles and Richard Bissell were evidently stunned by the news from an American mole within Soviet intelligence that the latter possessed considerable information regarding the U-2. While he was in West Germany during the summer of 1958, Hanson Baldwin, military writer for *The New York Times*, saw a U-2 on the tarmac and instantly appreciated its mission. When Baldwin informed one of Allen Dulles' top associates, Robert Amory, of his intention to do a story on the plane, Amory was aghast: such a story would ruin the United States' greatest intelligence operation. Amory's boss discussed the matter with *Times* publisher Arthur Hays Sulzberger, who decided not to publish the story. Still Sulzberger informed Dulles that the story was ready to go in the event that someone like Drew Pearson got wind of it, also. Slowly, top Washington journalists also became aware of the U-2's existence but declined to publicize the fact. As presidential historian Michael Beschloss noted, "knowing about the U-2 became something of a status symbol on the Washington din-ner-party circuit."[299]

For his part, Bissell had no excuse for pleading ignorance that there exist-ed a real likelihood that the Soviets could down a U-2. A report issued by the Air Technical Intelligence Center (ATIC) of the Air Force on March 14, 1960, warned Bissell that the Soviets' SA-2 Guideline missile had a good chance of downing the plane. A subsequent report, a CIA National Intelligence Esti-mate on the range and precision of Soviet SAMs, sounded the same warning. That same March, Eisenhower, who had been urged to resume U-2 flights, authorized another mission by the end of the month. When clearance from Pakistan to launch the mission from their soil wasn't immediately forthcom-ing, Eisenhower approved an extension to April 10 and also sanctioned Bis-sell's request for a second mission, setting a deadline of April 19. Numerous obstacles, disagreeable weather among them, ultimately pushed that date to May 1.

The April 9 mission, flown by Bob Ericson, covered the nuclear test site at Semipalatinsk, the missile test base at Tyura-Tam, and the missile test range and a radar facility elsewhere. The notion that Ericson's flight could enter Soviet airspace from the south unnoticed by taking off from Peshawar, Pakistan, and crossing Afghanistan was dashed during this flight. Ericson's U-2 carried electronic apparatus that indicated that the Russians located the craft shortly after its penetration of Soviet territory. During the time Ericson was aloft—six hours—he was chased by myriad Soviet jet fighters, some of which were armed with air-to-air missiles; none however succeeded in getting within the range necessary to fire on Ericson. Cognizant of the breakthroughs the Soviets has made in aeronautics, Kelly Johnson, the U-2's creator, had begun outfitting a new generation of U-2s—called the U-2C—with the more powerful Pratt & Whitney J75-P13 engine. It was this new generation of U-2 that Ericson was piloting that April day in 1960. Though it weighed more than its predecessor, the Pratt & Whitney J57, this new engine enabled the U-2 to ascend at a faster rate, diminishing the interval when contrails were likely to be produced, and furnished a greater cruising altitude: 74,600 feet. All of these factors may have enabled Ericson to escape Soviet interception but the primary element that saved him was incompe-tence on the Soviets' part. By the time Soviet pilots received authorization to pursue Ericson, the latter's U-2 most of the time was already beyond range as the Soviet pilots took-off in pursuit.

Yet, the fact remained that if the Russians possessed both the capability of tracking Ericson's flight in its entirety and new missiles capable of knock-

---

[299] Halberstam, *The Fifties*, 706-707, 708-709.

ing it out of the sky, then Ericson's U-2 mission should have been the last one to fly over Soviet territory. Khrushchev appreciated this, but neither Bissell or Eisenhower did. Indeed the President evidently thought that since the Russians lodged no protest over the April 9 U-2 incursion it meant that they had decided to accept the flights as a fact of life. This prompted George Kistiakowsky, Killian's successor as Eisenhower's science adviser, to wonder if the Russians' silence was intended as a stratagem to lure the United States into sending another U-2 aloft so that the Russians might shoot it down. Their silence, Kistiakowsky wrote, was "virtually inviting us to repeat the sortie."

At the time Bissell had a full plate handling other projects: test launchings of a spy satellite and various secret operations directed at unfriendly foreign regimes—of the latter the prime target being Fidel Castro. Given all this, Bissell was in no position to recommend cancellation of further U-2 incursions; rather he requested presidential extension of the deadline for the second U-2 flight scheduled for April to May 1. Permission was granted.

In agreeing to this extension, Eisenhower may not have fully grasped the significance of the mounting risk the Soviets posed to the U-2. The President believed that scant chance existed that a U-2 and its pilot would survive a successful attack. Both the CIA and the Joint Chiefs maintained the plane would "virtually disintegrate," leaving insufficient proof substantiating American penetration of Russian airspace. Asked long after the fact if Eisenhower knew of the Air Force warning and other information concerning the reality of the Soviet threat prior to sanctioning Power's ill-fated mission, presidential aide Andrew Goodpaster replied:

> I don't think so. Not in a specific way. We had the general view that over time the risks were going to become greater and greater, and they would finally gain the capability of shooting it down. But I think I would remember if we had had that kind of notice during the discussion in the president's office, and I don't remember such a thing.[300]

Apparently no one informed Eisenhower that, in Philip Taubman's words, "a red line had been crossed and that the probability of a successful Soviet attack on the plane had been established and was now an immediate danger." Given the imminence of the Paris summit, "Eisenhower would likely have been especially sensitive to the possibility of a diplomatic furor" in the event one of the planes was downed.[301]

---

[300] Taubman, Secret Empire, 304.
[301] Taubman, *Secret Empire*, 298-305.

Shoot Down

The U-2 mission of May 1, 1960, flown by Francis Gary Powers, was slated to be the first to fly all the way across the Soviet Union. It was to take off from Peshawar, Pakistan, and, nine hours and 3,800 miles later, conclude with Powers' landing in Bodo, Norway. The prelude to the flight didn't argue well for its success. Powers wasn't happy with the plane he was to fly this time out, believing it to be a lemon, always experiencing mechanical problems. Powers himself violated regulations by carrying his regular identification along with him that day—an indication that the U-2 pilots were becoming smug about the hazards they faced in flying. Also in Powers' possession that day was a silver dollar equipped with a pin. Should they fall into Soviet hands, the pilots were to insert the pin into a groove, which would emit a poison. The pilots had decided among themselves that, even in a worst case scenario, they wouldn't utilize the pin.

Wearing his sealed flight suit, Powers seated himself inside the cockpit of his U-2 at 5:20 A.M. and waited for presidential authorization for the take-off to come through. As he perspired while waiting for clearance, a friend outside removed his shirt and held it over the cockpit to screen Powers from the sun. Just over an hour after boarding the plane, the clearance for take-off finally arrived and Powers took to the sky. The time was 6:26 A.M.[302]

An hour into the flight, Powers neared Soviet airspace. He transmitted two clicks to Pakistan and received one click in reply—the signal he was to proceed as planned.

A telephone call from Khrushchev's Defense Minister, Marshal Rodion Malinovsky, roused the Russian Premier from his sleep: an unidentified plane had crossed the Afghan frontier into the airspace of the Soviet Union. There was no question as to who was responsible for this latest incursion. To send a spy flight over Soviet territory on a national holiday, with the Big Four summit in Paris only fifteen days away, was, in Khrushchev's view, outrageous. Malinovsky had already issued the order to down the intruder: "If our anti-aircraft units can just keep their eyes open and stop yawning long enough, I'm sure we'll knock the plane down."[303]

After covering his initial target within the Soviet Union, the Baikonur missile test facility, Powers proceeded to Chelyabinsk, just south of Sverdlovsk. His planned course would take Powers over Dushanbe (formerly Stalinabad), Baikonur/Tyura-Tam, the Sverdlovsk industrial center, northwest to Kirov (now Vyatka), north over the ICBM base at Plesetk, followed by the submarine construction facility at Severodvinsk, northwest to Kanda-

[302] Halberstam, *The Fifties*, 709.
[303] Beschloss, *Mayday*, 22, 23-24.

laksha, north to the naval base as Murmansk, after which he would proceed west to the terminus of his flight, Norway. The lengthy period of time Powers would be in the air would provide the Russians sufficient time to track him and launch their latest antiaircraft missiles.[304]

May 1, 1960, was May Day, an important Russian holiday. Consequently, the absence of the usual volume of Soviet civil and military air traffic allowed Soviet air-search radars to locate and follow Powers' flight more easily. Moreover, the U-2's penetration of Soviet airspace prompted the Soviets to halt civilian flights in a large area of the USSR. Soviet radar detected Powers when he was fifteen-miles south of the Soviet-Afghan border and continued following him as he flew over the Central Asian republics. Powers followed a northward course, periodically activating his photographic and electronic recording gear in compliance with the instructions provided for him on his charts.

When Powers reached the Tashkent region as many as 13 Soviet fighters had been dispatched to try to intercept him. One of these intercept missions was flown by Captain Igor Mentyukov in a Sukoi Su-9 Fishpot-B, a Mach 1.8 fighter-interceptor that had only recently been added to the Soviet Air Forces. Credited with a service ceiling of 55,700 feet, an unarmed, modified prototype had reached 94,659 feet. Mentyukov's plane was incapable of attaining this altitude, but that fact did not deter his superiors from ordering him to down Powers' U-2. As Powers continued his flight, MiG-19 and Su-9 fighters at Perm, located some 175 miles northwest of Sverdlovsk, were being readied for take-off. Yet, as this was a holiday, no Su-9 pilots could be found. When Mentyukov was, he explained that time was required for him to suit up and ready the plane for battle. He was ordered to take-off immediately - and ram the U-2.

Guided by ground controllers, Mentyukov took off. In flight, he encountered electronic interference— rendering his radar ineffective. Registering both aircraft on radar, the ground controllers guided Mentyukov toward his target. Flying on afterburner for optimum speed, he approached Powers' craft but was unable to make visual contact. Mentyukov overflew Powers and, as he had expended the lion's share of his fuel flying on afterburner for much of his time aloft, was ordered back to the base.[305]

After he had photographed the Tyura-Tam Cosmodrome and proceeded to Chelyabinsk, Powers began experiencing problems with the U-2's autopilot. Switching it off, the flew manually for a few minutes, restarted the autopilot, only to have it malfunction again. He tried again, then cut it off for

---

[304] Polmar, *Spyplane*, 134; Taubman, *Secret Empire*, 305.
[305] Polmar, *Spyplane*, 135.

good. If he continued the flight, he would have to fly manually—all the while attending to his other tasks. In the event the U-2's nose pitched too high, his airspeed would decline, possibly flaming out his engine. Should the latter happen, he might have to plunge the U-2 to 30,000 feet to restart the engine. Such an altitude would place him in easy range of Soviet missiles. Instead of aborting the mission, Powers decided to continue the flight.

Sverdlovsk, his next objective, was guarded by the SA-2 Guideline missiles. In Powers' subsequent account, he activated his cameras and additional equipment, and made a ninety-degree turn toward the city's southwestern periphery. He noted the location, speed, altitude and time. In Washington, the clock read 1:53 A.M. Sunday; in Moscow 8:53 A.M. As *Pravda* later reported, the anti-aircraft unit guarding Sverdlovsk hastened to its duty: "The fighting men in charge of the grim machinery for defending our airspace were ready in an instant." So high an altitude was the "pirate plane" flying, it barely registered on the radar screen. A target mark was fixed to the intruder. In *Pravda's* account, the commander now ordered: *"Destroy the enemy plane!"*

In Powers' subsequent recollection, he heard a dull "thump." The U-2 convulsed and an orange flash illuminated both the cockpit and sky. Powers now cried, *"My God, I've had it now!"*[306]

Powers had been downed by an SA-2 missile that exploded just aft of the U-2, rendering the latter inoperable. The CIA concluded that, at the time of the incident, the U-2's altitude above the Sverdlovsk region was 70,500 feet. Out of control, the doomed plane began a downward spiral. Owing to centrifugal force, Powers was thrown up against the canopy; he was unable to utilize his ejection seat. Discharging the canopy, he prepared to bail out of the stricken craft, waiting until the last moment to activate the mechanism that would destroy the camera so it wouldn't explode while he remained aboard. Unfastening his seatbelt, Powers was instantly sucked out into space; the only thing still securing him to the plane was his oxygen hose. In this manner, he couldn't reach the destruct mechanism. When the oxygen hose did sever, Powers descended from the plane at an altitude of approximately 25,000 feet. When he reached 15,000 feet, his parachute automatically unfurled.

Powers' decent came to an end near a village. Nearing earth he saw an automobile following his downward plunge. When he hit the ground, he was instantly surrounded by farmers and presently schoolchildren. When the farmers pointed to his parachute, signifying that they'd viewed a second one, Powers gestured that he was alone. The second chute belonged to the pilot

---

[306] Beschloss, *Mayday*, 24-26.

of a MiG-19 that had been downed by the same missile salvo responsible for bringing the U-2 down; unlike Powers, the MiG's pilot was killed.

The car transported Powers to a nearby town. His "captors" were neither antagonistic toward him or frightened. His pistol and survival knife were confiscated. During his parachute descent, Powers had removed his poison-tipped needle in its sheath from its silver dollar container, and placed the lethal device in his flight suit pocket, discarding the coin. Once the car had delivered Powers to the town, he was searched by security officials, received a perfunctory medical examination, and was taken, under guard, to Sverdlovsk.

Reviewing the May Day parade in Moscow, Khrushchev was informed of the U-2's downing and Powers' capture.

After being searched in Sverdlovsk, with his poison needle being discovered this time, Powers was flown aboard a civil airliner to Moscow, where he was taken straightaway to the Lubyanka prison complex. During the ensuing two months, he was subjected to almost daily questioning. "We were totally unprepared for the crash possibility," Powers later wrote:

> I could not speak Russian, had no one to contact. In the four years I had worked for the agency, only once had I received instructions on what to do in the event of capture. And that, brought on by my own questioning, had been the single remark of the intelligence officer: "You may as well tell them everything because they're going to get it out of you anyway."[307]

Though he experienced neither torture or abuse at the hands of his captors, Powers was told again and again that could be imprisoned for 7 to 15 years—or executed. The Russians were always concerned about his health and, incredibly, he was taken on a brief automobile tour of Moscow. Powers' U-2 had survived its downing, and the Soviets could identify much of its equipment when the craft went on exhibition shortly thereafter. Nor would the planes' destruct mechanism—even had Powers been able to switch it on—have obliterated it. The sole purpose of the tiny explosive charge was to destroy the camera. Viewing the wreckage himself, Powers was shocked by how many pieces of it were clearly identifiable. The Soviets had also developed the U-2's mostly undamaged film.

During his interrogation, Powers sought to keep the Russians in the dark about some of the things he knew. He did not mention his prior missions over the Soviet Union and China or the identities of fellow U-2 pilots; he

---

[307] Polmar, Spyplane, 136.

continually declared that when he was downed, he had been flying at the U-2's optimum altitude—68,000 feet.[308]

On the afternoon of May 1, 1960, President Eisenhower's aide, General Goodpaster, telephoned him with the word that the U-2 was "overdue and possibly lost." Assuming that both the pilot and plane hadn't survived, Eisenhower thanked Goodpaster for notifying him and attended to other matters. The next afternoon, Goodpaster had additional information for the President: the CIA had informed him that the U-2 was still missing. "The pilot reported an engine flameout at a position about thirteen hundred miles inside Russia and has not been heard from since. With the amount of fuel he had on board, there is not a chance of his still being aloft." If the pilot wasn't still in the air, he was dead, and his plane destroyed as well. Eisenhower decided to take no action, leaving responsibility for the next move in Khrushchev's hands. The latter, it was assumed (or hoped) would take no action. "Having shot down a U-2," Eisenhower's biographer Stephen E. Ambrose wrote, "the Russians had made their point." If Khrushchev really wanted the summit meeting to be a success, "he would either downplay the event or ignore it altogether, contenting himself with a private remark or two to Eisenhower in Paris." The President continued with plans for the Paris conclave.[309]

Now that he had downed the U-2 and had captured its pilot alive, Khrushchev pondered his next move. If he concealed the incident, both the summit and Eisenhower's visit might continue. Yet this option would provide Khrushchev's opposition the opportunity to contend that the Soviet Chairman had been so taken in by the American President that he was prepared to ignore such a violation of Soviet sovereignty at a time when Soviet-American relations were presumably improving. Such a course was the only thing one could expect from one who desired to reduce the military and gamble on further "reckless" policies involving the security of the Soviet Union. By contrast, disclosing the U-2 incident and unleashing a propaganda assault on the United States would have two advantages: it would mollify Khrushchev's critics and place the United States on the defensive. Still such an option wasn't without its hazards: "the spirit of Camp David" would be extinguished and the anger "of Soviet outer circles and the Soviet people" might jeopardize the summit conference in Paris and force renewal of Cold War tensions.

Khrushchev opted to tell the Supreme Soviet that an American spy plane had entered Soviet territory and been shot down, but would not disclose that the pilot was in Russian custody. In pursuing this strategy, Khrushchev

---

[308] Polmar, *Spyplane*, 135-137.
[309] Ambrose, *Eisenhower: The President*, 571.

intended to confuse the American government into thinking the pilot was dead, so it would adhere to its story that the plane had accidentally entered Soviet airspace. Subsequently, Khrushchev would reveal that the pilot had survived and that the Soviets could prove that he had been on a spy mission. Khrushchev's strategy could demonstrate that he commanded the forces that had defended the Soviet Union by shooting down the U-2. When the Americans persisted in their story that the U-2 was a weather plane that had veered off-course and Khrushchev sprang his surprise, he could show they'd lied about the plane's true purpose. Khrushchev might then charitably accept Eisenhower's apology and proceed to the Paris summit on the tide of a propaganda triumph.

After initially addressing domestic matters in his remarks before the Supreme Soviet on May 5, Khrushchev took up international concerns. Success in Paris was "essential if a solid basis is to be laid for peaceful coexistence between states with different social systems." Yet "certain ruling circles in the United States have at present not reached the conclusion that a relaxation of tension and the solution of controversial problems through negotiation is necessary. Lately influential forces—imperialist and militarist circles, whose stronghold is the Pentagon—have become noticeably more active in the United States. These aggressive forces stand for the continuation of the Cold War and the arms race. And they have been going in for downright provocation." As instructed by the Soviet government, Khrushchev was reporting on recent "aggressive actions against the Soviet Union . . . by the United States of America."

The latter "has been sending aircraft that have been crossing our state frontiers and intruding upon" Soviet airspace. Despite numerous prior protests of these "aggressive acts" to the Americans and the UN Security Council, the United States , "as a rule offered excuses and tried in every possible way to deny the facts of aggression—even when the proof was irrefutable." After citing the April 9 intrusion, Khrushchev declared, "The American military apparently found this impunity to their liking and decided to repeat their aggressive act." For this, they selected "the most festive day of the working peoples of all countries—*May Day!*" When Khrushchev announced that the May Day incursion had been shot down, the audience erupted: "Shame to the aggressor! Shame to the aggressor!" When Khrushchev said that the initial investigation revealed that the offending aircraft was American, this elicited another outburst.

"Outright banditry!" someone shrieked—or so *Pravda* subsequently reported. "How can this be squared with Eisenhower's pious speeches?" "Just imagine what would have happened had a *Soviet* aircraft appeared over New

York, Chicago or Detroit," Khrushchev continued. "How would the *United States* have reacted?" Turning his head to view one of his listeners, American Ambassador Thompson, Khrushchev asked, "What *was* this? A *May Day* greeting?"

After these words generated another uproarious audience reaction, Khrushchev addressed the matter of who was responsible for ordering the U-2 into Soviet airspace: Eisenhower or "Pentagon militarists" without the former's knowledge. "If American military men can take such actions on their own, the world should be greatly concerned. American aggressive circles sought to torpedo the Paris summit or, at any rate, prevent an agreement for which the whole world is waiting."

While the "American military provocations" had produced "feelings of indignation," said Kruschev, that, "must not guide our actions: .

> We address the American people: in spite of these aggressive acts against our country, we have not forgotten the friendly encounters we had during our visit to America. Even now, I profoundly believe that the American people—except for certain imperialist and monopolist circles—want peace and friendship with the Soviet Union. I do not doubt President Eisenhower's sincere desire for peace.[310]

In the wake of Khrushchev's speech, Eisenhower authorized a statement. "One of NASA's U-2 research airplanes, in use since 1956 in a continuing program to study meteorological conditions found at high altitude, has been missing since May 1, when its pilot reported he was having oxygen difficulties over the Lake Van, Turkey, area." Apparently, the plane in question had veered off course, possible entering Russian airspace. "The unstated assumption was that Powers' weather plane was the one the Russians had shot down."

The next act belonged to Khrushchev: on May 6, he revealed a photograph he said was that of the downed U-2. In reality, the plane in the photograph wasn't Powers' but another aircraft. It was part of Khrushchev's strategy: he wanted Eisenhower to continue believing that Powers had expired and his plane had been destroyed, so that America would adhere to the "weather research" story it had promulgated. American obliged him.[311]

The same day Khrushchev revealed his photograph, the American Embassy in Moscow identified Francis Gary Powers as piloting the missing "unarmed weather research plane" and requested "full facts" concerning the fate of the aircraft and Powers from the Soviet Foreign Ministry. Speaking to reporters, State Department spokesman Lincoln White said, "The gentle-

---

[310] Beschloss, *Mayday*, 40-41, 43-44.
[311] Ambrose, *Eisenhower: The President*, 573-574.

man informed us that he was having difficulty with his oxygen equipment. Now our assumption is that the man blacked out. There was absolutely no— NO—no deliberate attempt to violate Soviet airspace. There never has been." The United States had now given Khrushchev the pretext he needed.

Speaking once again to the Supreme Soviet on May 7, Khrushchev informed his audience that he must let them in on a secret: when he had spoken two days earlier, he "deliberately refrained from mentioning that we have the remnants of the plane—*and we also have the pilot, who is quite alive and kicking!*" Khrushchev announced that Powers was in Moscow and revealed his name. Powers had stated that he experienced neither dizziness or malfunction with his oxygen equipment, and was on a spy mission "until the very moment his pirate flight into this country was cut short." Holding aloft a picture of Powers' poison pin, Khrushchev said, "Here it is! The latest achievement of American technology for killing their own people!" Cries of "Shame! Shame! Shame! Shame!" emanated from the audience.

Khrushchev also disclosed other items in Powers' possession at the time of his capture. There was a pistol with a silencer: "Why a noiseless pistol? Not to take air samples, but to blow out someone's brains!" There was the foreign currency—rubles and French gold francs: "I have seen them with my eyes and you can see them here in this photograph. They are covered with cellophane on both sides—done in a *cultured, American* way." Finally, there were two gold watches and seven gold ladies' rings: "Perhaps he was supposed to have flown still higher, to Mars, and seduced the Martian ladies!"

Khrushchev went on to warn those nations that allowed U-2 flights to take-off from their soil: *"Do not play with fire, gentlemen!"* As for Powers, "I think it will be proper to prosecute this flier so that world opinion can see what actions the Americans are taking to provoke the Soviet Union and heat up the atmosphere, thus reversing those successes which have been achieved in relieving international tensions." As for Eisenhower, "I am quite willing to grant that the President knew nothing about the fact such a plane was sent into the Soviet Union. . . . But this should put us even more on guard." When the military began running things, "the results can be disastrous. Such a pirate, prone to dizziness, may in fact drop a hydrogen bomb on foreign soil." That meant "that the peoples of the land where this pirate was born will unavoidably and immediately get a more destructive hydrogen bomb in return."[312]

"Unbelievable" was Eisenhower's reaction upon learning that what the CIA had always pledged wouldn't happen had indeed come to pass. What was even more astonishing was Ike's decision to continue lying. Secretary of

---

[312] Beschloss, *Mayday*, 55, 58-61.

State Christian Herter oversaw the preparation of a statement meant to get the President "off the hook." After securing Eisenhower's approval, the State Department revealed that U-2 flights had been made along the Soviet border for intelligence collection purposes and were necessary owing to Soviet secrecy that hindered valid American efforts to guard against surprise attack. Despite the fact that such flights had been conducted for four years, the State Department still maintained that permission for the ill-fated Powers flight had not originated in Washington. This statement was significant for two reasons: it acknowledged for the first time that the United States practiced foreign espionage but didn't acknowledge that Eisenhower sanctioned—or was even cognizant of—such intelligence operations.

Eisenhower's intuition told him that the statement might be an error—a feeling borne out by the press reaction it generated. If the authorization for the overflight didn't originate with the President, where did it come from? If Eisenhower indeed hadn't sanctioned the flight, had he handed over his authority to CIA director Dulles or Secretary of State Herter or was it because he was just too wrapped up in his passion for golf? Had Eisenhower or his aides set up a system whereby a local commander or pilot could conduct overflights of the USSR at his own discretion? Finally, if such an operation could be executed without Washington's permission, could a B-52 pilot undertake a nuclear strike in the same manner? The public response diminished Eisenhower's spirits to the point that he informed his secretary, Ann C. Whitman, "I would like to resign."

Instead of choosing so drastic a course, Eisenhower decided to assume responsibility for the U-2 crisis. As he told his son John on May 9, "We're going to take a beating on this. And I'm the one, rightly, who is going to take the brunt." This was followed, that afternoon, by another State Department utterance on the matter which defended aerial surveillance on the grounds that it prevented the Soviet Union from making "secret preparations" that might leave the Free World with the option of "abject surrender or nuclear destruction." In this latest declaration, the State Department now disclosed that the President had sanctioned the U-2 operations but, as before, didn't go so far as making a total admission so as to protect Eisenhower. "Specific missions . . . have not been subject to Presidential authorization." To critics who divined that the Paris summit would fold, the statement concluded that the U-2 affair "should serve to underline the importance to the world of an earnest attempt to achieve agreed and effective safeguards against surprise attack and aggression."[313]

---

[313] Pach and Richardson, *The Presidency of Dwight D. Eisenhower*, Revised Edition, 217-218; Beschloss, *Mayday*, 257.

This latest State Department release suggested that U-2 flights over Russia might continue—something Eisenhower privately believed improbable, as the program had been exposed. Leaving the overflight option open, however, allowed him a bargaining chip: if promising Khrushchev that the U-2 would abstain from violating Soviet airspace was a necessary prerequisite to rescue the summit conference, then Eisenhower could formally make such a guarantee. For Khrushchev, who had gone to great effort to exonerate Eisenhower from culpability in dispatching the spy flight, the latest State Department announcement was earthshattering; it appeared "as though Eisenhower was boasting arrogantly about what the United States could do and would do. Here was the President of the United States defending outrageous, inadmissible actions!" Once more the Americans were merely pursuing "their selfish goals. They wanted to dictate to us their conditions from a position of power."[314]

Eisenhower himself made his first comments on the U-2 incident in a prepared statement at a White House press conference on May 11. "No one wants another Pearl Harbor." This necessitated "knowledge of military forces and preparations around the world." Intelligence gathering was "special and secret," separate from the recognizable agencies of government and supervised under broad directives:

> It is a distasteful but vital necessity. We prefer and work for a different kind of world and a different way of obtaining the information essential to confidence and effective deterrence. . . . This was the reason for my Open Skies proposal in 1955. . . . I shall bring up the Open Skies proposal again at Paris, since it is a means of ending concealment and suspicion. . . .

> We must not be distracted from the real issues of the day by what is an incident or a symptom of the world situation today. This incident has been given great propaganda exploitation. The emphasis given to a flight of an unarmed, nonmilitary plane can only reflect a fetish of secrecy. The *real* issues are the ones we will be working on at the Summit—disarmament, search for solutions affecting Germany and Berlin and the whole range of East–West relations.[315]

Despite his prior warnings that the U-2 incursions over Russia were almost tantamount to an act of war, Eisenhower now told the assembled journalists, "I'll tell you *this*: the United States and all of its allies that I know of have engaged in nothing that could be considered honestly provocative.

---

[314] Beschloss, *Mayday*, 258, 259.
[315] Ibid., 264, 265-266.

We are looking to our own security and our defense and we have no idea of promoting any kind of conflict or war. It's absolutely *ridiculous* and they *know* it is."[316]

Three days later, Eisenhower left for Paris. In his arrival statement there the next morning, he said, "The hopes of humanity call on the four of us to purge our minds of prejudice and our hearts of rancor. For too much is at stake to indulge in profitless bickering. The issues that divide the Free World from the Soviet bloc are grave and not subject to easy solution. But if goodwill exists on both sides, at least a beginning can be made. The West, I am sure, will meet Mr. Khrushchev halfway in every honest effort in this direction. America will go every foot that pride and honor permit." Eisenhower concluded his remarks by saying that it would be "a pleasure to meet again" with his "old friends" de Gaulle and Macmillan. The fact that Khrushchev's name was absent from Eisenhower's list of "old friends" didn't escape journalists' attention.

Khrushchev had already arrived in Paris the preceding day, promising his delegation to "exert all effort to make the conference a success" despite the "influential circles trying to revive the Cold War." Khrushchev had secured his associates' permission to go to Paris and go there early, conceivably to see Eisenhower privately for the purpose of determining whether both the summit conference and Eisenhower's Russian visit could still move forward—provided that Ike publicly expressed regrets for the U-2 incursion and there be an acknowledgment that the United States hadn't the right to violate Soviet territory.

"With our relations falling to pieces, we couldn't possibly offer our hospitality to someone who had already, so to speak, made a mess at his host's table," Khrushchev subsequently observed. "To receive Eisenhower without first hearing him apologize would be an intolerable insult to the leadership of our country."

On Sunday, Khrushchev paid his respects to de Gaulle. Accompanying the Soviet Chairman was the man who had awakened him that May Day morning with the news that Francis Gary Powers' U-2 had entered Soviet airspace, Defense Minister Malinovsky, who, it was observed, clung to Khrushchev "like a leech." Malinovsky, it was believed, was in Paris to keep an eye on Khrushchev and make certain the latter wasn't duped by the Western leaders. Khrushchev himself may also have desired Malinovsky's presence so that he could prove to the Kremlin that the leader of the Soviet Union was acting in the latter's best interests.

---

[316] *Ibid.,* 265-266.

De Gaulle listened as his visitor vented his rage against Eisenhower. Why did the latter concede his knowledge of the U-2 flights? To Khrushchev, such candor on the Americans' part revealed, not forthrightness, but disdain for the U.S.S.R. He then presented de Gaulle a six-page document setting forth his conditions for the continuance of the Summit: all four leaders must promise not to transgress the sovereignty of other countries; America must regret its prior deeds of "inadmissible provocation"; punish those guilty of such actions; and forswear additional such offenses. Should these stipulations be fulfilled, Khrushchev would do all in his power to make the conference successful. If not, he couldn't meet with the head of a nation "which had made perfidy the basis of its policy toward the Soviet Union." For Khrushchev, relying on type-written papers to convey his sentiments to foreign heads of state wasn't his normal procedure, so why, on this occasion, had he taken this course? Had the Kremlin prepared the document and Khrushchev pledged to present it to de Gaulle? If such were the case, this approach wouldn't allow Khrushchev the opportunity to make rash concessions. If he planned to negotiate with Eisenhower over his conditions for attending the Summit, Khrushchev might have believed that presenting his proviso in written form might reinforce his position.

After studying the document, de Gaulle informed his guest that he "could not seriously expect" an apology on Eisenhower's part. Responsible heads of state didn't do such things.

Eisenhower had been driven to the official residence of the American ambassador to France after arriving in Paris. After a nap and lunch, the President met with de Gaulle, Macmillan and Adenauer—the latter in town to keep an eye on Allied negotiations concerning Germany. Observing that he and his summit partners had had a long association, Eisenhower said, "I don't know about anybody else, but I myself am getting older."

"You don't look it," de Gaulle replied. "I hope that no one is under the illusion that I'm going to crawl on my knees to Khrushchev," said Eisenhower. "No one is under that illusion," replied the French President, who mentioned the Soviet Chairman's threat to attack U-2 bases in other countries. This elicited Eisenhower's observation that "rockets can travel in two directions." Before the meeting broke up, de Gaulle told Ike, "With us it is easy. You and I are tied together by history."

Returning to the American ambassador's residence, Eisenhower called a meeting to assess Khrushchev's threat: "We must consider whether it would be better to break the conference off ourselves." If this was to be the decision, opined Ambassador Thompson, then it should be done concerning a matter other than spy flights: "Khrushchev may be taking a reading with our allies to test our resolution on this." Because Khrushchev was "vulnerable at home over his impulsiveness," America could argue that it "could not negotiate with a man who uses language of this kind in a serious conference."

The President wondered why Khrushchev hadn't issued his warning before anyone had traveled to Paris. If all Khrushchev desired was a four-power document denouncing espionage, that would be fine. "We will not go beyond that to forswear specific activities unilaterally, however."

The State Department's Livingston Merchant felt it would be better if Khrushchev, not Eisenhower, walked out of the Summit. Chip Bohlen counseled immediately informing the Russians that the United States was aware of Khrushchev's threat and in the event it was presented, America would have to adhere to its position: "The Russians are trying to get us to grovel—or to assert a legal right to overfly, which they will challenge as untenable."

While noting that espionage had been practiced all through history and that it was the responsibility of "the affronted country" to foil spies acting against them, Eisenhower nevertheless lamented the failure on the CIA's part to appreciate the "emotional, even pathological reaction of the Russians" to territorial violations against them.

Eisenhower wanted to make an opening statement when the Summit convened the next day: "It could be quite simple. Everybody knows there has been espionage throughout history. For the Russians to demand that we forswear espionage while knowing that we are the victim of their espionage is completely unacceptable." Given the "right circumstances," the President was agreeable to relinquish sending the U-2 into Russia again. Such flights were a thing of the past now in any event. Meeting with Eisenhower and Macmillan that evening, de Gaulle told the President that should Khrushchev open the conference with an angry outburst, Eisenhower should say that everyone practiced espionage—including the Soviets: "obviously you cannot apologize, but you must decide how you wish to handle this. I will do everything I can to be helpful without being partisan." At the opening session of the Summit, de Gaulle's first order of business would be to call on Eisenhower; the latter then would respond to Khrushchev's written complaints.[317]

However, when the Big Four leaders seated themselves at the conference table for the initial session of the Summit on May 16, 1960, the carefully laid plans to have Eisenhower speak first were quickly dashed. De Gaulle had hardly finished calling the proceedings to order when Khrushchev stood up and insisted on speaking first. De Gaulle looked at Ike, who consented, whereupon the Soviet leader unleashed an anti-Eisenhower and anti-Amer-

---

[317] *Ibid.*, 270, 273, 274-280.

ican diatribe. When Khrushchev began shouting, de Gaulle cut him off, turned to the Soviet interpreter: "The acoustics in this room are excellent. We can hear the chairman. There is no need for him to raise his voice." When the interpreter hesitantly began translating de Gaulle's remarks, the latter stopped the former and gestured to his own interpreter, who unflinchingly conveyed the French President's words to Khrushchev. Giving de Gaulle an irate look, Khrushchev continued his remarks, his tone subdued this time.

But not for long. Pointing above him, Khrushchev yelled, "I have been overflown!" Once more, de Gaulle cut in, this time to say he had been overflown as well. "By your American allies?" Khrushchev queried. "No," said de Gaulle, "by you. Yesterday that satellite you launched just before you left Moscow to impress us overflew the sky of France eighteen times without my permission. How do I know you do not have cameras aboard which are taking pictures of my country?" Catching de Gaulle's notice, Eisenhower grinned. Raising both hands above his heads, Khrushchev said, "As God is my witness, my hands are clean. You don't think I would do a thing like that?"[318] At this, de Gaulle grunted.

After resuming his statement, Khrushchev asked, "What devil made the Americans do this?" De Gaulle noted the presence of devils on both sides and that such a subject wasn't worth the attention of world leaders to whom the world sought indications of peace from.[319]

Khrushchev ended his statement with word that Eisenhower's visit to the Soviet Union had been canceled. Eisenhower now finally had his opportunity to speak: Khrushchev needn't have gone so far as to cancel his invitation, that his purpose in journeying to Paris had been in the hope of participating in serious talks, and that it was his desire for the summit to now take up substantive issues. The Russians walked out of the room. Eisenhower rose to take his leave when de Gaulle took him aside: "I do not know what Khrushchev is going to do nor what is going to happen, but whatever he does, or whatever happens, I want you to know that I am with you to the end."[320]

None of the Western leaders were able to convince Khrushchev to soften his position. Eisenhower announced that there would be no further U-2 missions and revived a version of his Open Skies proposal for aerial surveillance flights conducted by UN aircraft. For his part, Macmillan, who implored Khrushchev to face the reality that all nations conducted spying, believed that the American President's action in halting the U-2 flights did much to redress Soviet demands. In addition of pointing out to Khrushchev that his

[318] Ambrose, *Eisenhower: The President*, 578-579.
[319] Ambrose, *Ike's Spies*, 289.
[320] Ambrose, *Eisenhower: The President*, 579.

latest space satellite had overflown France numerous time daily, de Gaulle asked the Soviet Chairman why, if his anger was such that it precluded negotiations, had he permitted everyone to come to Paris under false pretenses and, in so doing, waste everyone's time. Unmoved by any of these arguments, Khrushchev boycotted the Summit when it conveyed the following day.[321]

His verbal bombast wasn't finished, however. Appearing at the Palais de Chaillot before he left Paris, Khrushchev was asked why, during his Camp David talks with Eisenhower, he hadn't asked the President to end the U-2 flights.

> "I will answer that question with pleasure. When I was at Camp David with President Eisenhower, I almost opened my mouth to make that statement. The atmosphere was so convivial, with the President telling me to call him 'my friend' in English and calling me '*moi drug*' in Russian. Like a brother he was. It was then that I wanted to tell my friend that it was not nice to fly over a friend's territory without his permission.
>
> But then I thought better of it and decided, 'No, I am not going to tell him. There is something stinky about this friend of mine.' I did not broach the subject. And it turned out that I was right in my doubts, because we caught the American spy—like a thief, red-handed! We told the Americans that they act like thieves and they say, 'No, this is our policy. We have flown and will keep flying over your territory.' It's their *thief-like policy*, that's all! How could a summit conference be started under these conditions?"[322]

Waving his fists, Khrushchev continued, "To hear President Eisenhower, it would seem that the question of whether U.S. military planes will or will not fly over the U.S.S.R. depends on him and him alone. Just think—*what presumption!* Now he says they will not overfly—*what magnanimity!* This to be decided by us and us alone. We shall shoot such planes down. We shall deal shattering blows to the bases where they came from—and at those who set up the bases!"

As shocking as Khrushchev's words were to Westerners, their true significance lay in what the one uttering them didn't say: there was no threat to sign an immediate German peace treaty; there would be no halt to the test ban talks in Geneva; another summit meeting should occur following Eisenhower's retirement. The spy flight "has affected relations between the U.S.S.R. and the United States. But in the end, it will be necessary to overcome its consequences and digest all of this. Relations must be normalized

---

[321] Pach and Richardson, *The Presidency of Dwight D. Eisenhower*, Revised Edition, 219.
[322] Beschloss, Mayday, 299-300.

so the American and Soviet peoples can live not only in peace but friendship." At the end of his oration, a spent Khrushchev hoisted a glass of mineral
water: "*Vive la paix!*"323

With the summit conference irretrievably shattered, Eisenhower's scheduled state visit to Lisbon, Portugal, was moved up to May 19. The reception
Eisenhower received upon his arrival there greatly cheered him: I'm sure glad
to be *here* and away from *there!*" Ironically, the failure of the Paris Summit in
no way dampened the President's popularity with his countrymen; polls in
America showed it soaring. Similarly, when, the next year, the Bay of Pigs
failed to dampen the popular standing of Ike's newly installed successor, the
latter [Kennedy] commented, "It's just like Eisenhower. The worse I do, the
more popular I get." Disembarking at Andrews Air Force Base upon his return to the United States, Eisenhower had an emotional reunion with First
Lady Mamie Eisenhower. "After a trip of this kind," Ike told those who had
turned out to welcome him home, "you can well understand what it means
to me to have this kind of welcome." As returned by car to the White House,
Eisenhower was greeted by fireboats spraying their salute, well-wishers
standing along his motorcade route, and an enormous banner on Pennsylvania Avenue bearing the words: THANK YOU, MR. PRESIDENT. Such a reception accorded a President in the aftermath of a major diplomatic blunder
would undoubtedly strike later, more cynical generations as unbelievable,
yet it was an indication of the confidence Americans of that time had in their
government. After reaching the White House, Eisenhower acknowledged
the presence of those present at the Executive Mansion's black iron fence,
then stepped inside.324

Why did the Summit fail? Officials, American and Russian, and historians have weighed in on that question with their own assessments. Eisenhower himself came to the conclusion that Khrushchev had likely gathered
that he wouldn't get what he wanted in the matter of Berlin. Possibly he had
faced enormous pressure from the Soviet military or the Chinese to renounce
improved relations with the United States. He may also have become uneasy
that his own countrymen might accord Eisenhower too warm a welcome.
To Eisenhower's mind, the ultimatum Khrushchev gave de Gaulle indicated
that, whatever lay in back of Khrushchev's actions, the Soviet Premier had
seized upon the U-2 overflights as a basis for torpedoing the summit conference and persuading the world the responsibility for the Summit failure
lay with the United States. Eisenhower wasn't the only one to think that
Khrushchev had misgivings about the presidential visit to the Soviet Union.

---

323 Beschloss, *Mayday*, 300.
324 *Ibid.*, 297-298, 303, 304.

Meeting with his Cabinet following his return to the U.S. from Paris, the President disclosed de Gaulle's and Macmillan's belief that Khrushchev had "seized upon the U-2" as a way to renege on Eisenhower's visit out of his anxiety over the Soviet people's reception for him. Chip Bohlen expressed the opinion that, earlier in the year, Khrushchev had determined that he "would not get at the Summit what he wanted regarding Berlin." As a result, he employed the U-2 as an instrument to sink the Summit.[325]

From the Soviet side came the assessment of Arkady Shevchenko. A former member of the arms control division of the Soviet Foreign Ministry, who later defected, becoming a U.S. intelligence consultant, Shevchenko said:

> I never at that time understood why Khrushchev reacted in that way—such an absolutely incredible reaction, canceling the Paris summit, canceling something on which I myself had been personally involved in preparing the instructions for the Soviet Foreign Ministry. We thought that it would be going on as serious negotiations on arms control and on many other things. All the things had been prepared in the Foreign Ministry, went to the Politburo, approved by the Politburo. And, all of a sudden, because of the incident, which, you know, was not unusual because there were flights going on all the time—why had it happened?
>
> Only later, when I had more access to the more important people in the Soviet Union and talked within the circles of the leadership of the Soviet Union or looked at some of the documents, did I find the answer.
>
> The answer was that at this period of time Khrushchev had antagonized the military by reducing very substantially the armed forces of the Soviet Union and by reducing the production of the conventional weapons like tanks, placing everything on the strategic force. Before that, he had antagonized the KGB by downgrading the ... security apparatus of the Soviet Union.
>
> [The U-2 incident] was an internal political move in which Khrushchev wanted to show that he was really defending the interests of the Soviet Union in the military field.[326]

In addition to his foes in the Kremlin, Communist China disapproved of Khrushchev's detente policies. China was vying for dominance of the Communist movement and had long accused Khrushchev of propitiating

---

[325] Ibid., 277, 309-310.
[326] John Sharnik, Inside the Cold War: An Oral History (New York: Arbor House, 1987), 114, 119-120.

the West. 1959 witnessed a serious worsening of Russian-Chinese relations. That summer Khrushchev declined to share information concerning atomic and nuclear weapons with the Chinese and, when the downward spiral in relations between the two Communist powers worsened even more that winter, Khrushchev ceased Russian technical assistance to China. In light of all this, Khrushchev's actions in scuttling the Paris Summit may have stemmed, not only from inflaming the U-2 incident to win a propaganda triumph at the West's expense, but, in J. Ronald Oakley's words, "to assure his colleagues, the Chinese, and communist leaders" the world over "that he was not an appeaser" and was every bit an anti-imperialist and Communist as they were. Just the same, the U-2 incident failed to rectify Soviet-Chinese differences, nor did it end the fragmentation of the international communist movement.[327]

The conclusions of Eisenhower and others who believed Khrushchev's motivation in scuttling the Summit rested on the Chairman's realization that he wouldn't obtain his objectives on Berlin notwithstanding, the fact is that Khrushchev had wanted the Summit to succeed. He believed, as Eisenhower did, that an interval of lessened international tensions would result from the conference. Toward that end, both leaders had invested elements of political assets and personal prestige. Until Khrushchev had presented his ultimatum of Soviet conditions for continuing the Summit, he had been unwilling to relinquish his efforts till then to make detente a reality.

More than just the downing of Francis Gary Powers was responsible for the failed summit. An analysis of what America and the Soviet Union intended to say to each other at the Paris conference table reveals that significant progress on Berlin and disarmament was improbable. The West was reluctant to relinquish its protection of West Berlin, and Khrushchev's opinions on that city remained unchanged since November 1958. When it came to the disarmament issue, where Khrushchev's opinions were more malleable, he seemed worried about American might and agreements yielding to Eisenhower's request for a verification system of on-site and aerial surveys that would calm official American suspicions of the Russians. Aleksandr Fursenko and Timothy Naftali have written that, "the dynamics of a summit where the Soviet Union would have been treated as an equal might have alleviated" Khrushchev's anxieties. What the U-2 incident did disclose, Fursenko and Naftali continue, was the immense part reputation played in the Soviet-American standoff over the spy flights. In making their most important decisions during the affair, both Eisenhower and Khrushchev were guided by issues of personal prestige. At significant junctures, neither man

---

[327] Oakley, *God's Country*, 389, 391.

could put aside his pride when such a course would have rendered the U-2 missions less of an issue. In this instance neither grandeur or vanity were the reasons. In a struggle, the essence of which was more psychological than military, where a superpower's greatest defense was preventing an enemy attack from occurring in the first place, "the credibility of each leader carried enormous" weight.[328]

Aftershocks

While the Summit had failed, the aftershocks it produced continued to reverberate. In a televised report to the American people on "the remarkable events" in Paris, Eisenhower placed the responsibility for the summit's collapse solely on Khrushchev. Soviet complaints about the U-2 were merely hypocrisy. At Camp David, Khrushchev had been silent about the matter. Soviet agents continued their efforts to acquire U.S. defense secrets. Eisenhower reiterated his assertion that sending the U-2 over the Soviet Union, even doing so at a time so close to the summit, had been an appropriate action on his part. Once more he said, "From Pearl Harbor we learned that even negotiation itself can be used to conceal preparations for a surprise attack."

Privately, however, Eisenhower was disconsolate over the summit's failure, telling Kistiakowsky that "the stupid U-2 mess" had ruined all his hopes of "ending the cold war." "No temporary rise in the polls," Chester J. Pach, Jr. and Elmo Richardson have written, "could compensate for the evaporation of his dreams of leaving a legacy of detente as his greatest achievement." He told Kistiakowsky that "he saw nothing worthwhile ... to do now until the end of his presidency."[329]

Since Khrushchev's first words about the U-2, the Russians had promised to lay the matter before the United Nations. Immediately after he had returned to the White House from Paris, Eisenhower had summoned Henry Cabot Lodge to map out the argument America would present to the UN Security Council. Lodge should emphasize the cessation of the U-2 overflights over Russia and that Washington was prepared to negotiate an Open Skies plan. Though Eisenhower didn't want the U-2 flights judged as "aggressive," he was prepared to admit they were "illegal and, in fact, immoral."

No less a Soviet representative than Foreign Minister Andrei Gromyko attended the Security Council session to present the Soviet side of the argument: the U-2 must be branded as aggression. Merely one plane was necessary to drop a nuclear weapon. At Paris, Khrushchev had done "everything

---

[328] Fursenko and Naftali, *Khrushchev's Cold War*, 289-290.
[329] Beschloss, *Mayday*, 308; Pach and Richardson, *The Presidency of Dwight D. Eisenhower*, Revised Edition, 220.

possible" to rescue the summit conference but Eisenhower had simply argued again the "espionage and sabotage which is allegedly necessary for American security." Ike's "perfidy" in devising U-2 flights during Khrushchev's stay at Camp David was akin to the Japanese envoys "smiling in Washington before Pearl Harbor."

France's Armand Bernard asked if there wasn't "a flagrant lack of proportion between the May first incident" and the actions on the part of the Soviets resulting in the Summit's collapse and the dashing of humanity's hopes for the advent of detente. Britain's representative reminded Gromyko that they were no longer in the eighteenth century: the U-2 must be viewed as a "symptom of the fear of surprise attack." The problem giving rise to such a fear had to be eliminated.

In his turn, Lodge explained that the purpose of the U-2 missions was to guard the Free World against surprise attack on the part of a nation that frequently boasted that it could destroy other countries with nuclear missiles. Open Skies would "obviate forever the necessity of such measures of self-protection." Evidently Khrushchev didn't think the U-2 flights were a sufficiently serious matter to warrant raising it to Eisenhower during the Camp David talks. Why were the Russians protesting now at the UN? Where was Soviet solicitude for international law when they "forcibly and brutally snuffed out" Hungary's freedom in 1956? Lodge had one final card to lay on the table. Eight years earlier, a British radio expert in Moscow had picked up America's ambassador to Moscow George Kennan dictating correspondence in the Ambassador's residence. American counterintelligence eventually discovered a listening device inside a U.S. Seal on the wall. The U.S. government had uncovered over a hundred such mechanisms in its embassies in recent years. Lodge then displayed the compromised seal, complete with its bugging device, to the delegates. Gromyko scoffed at Lodge's evidence as being a CIA forgery. "The Soviet motion was defeated seven to two (the Soviet Union and Poland), with two abstentions."[330]

The U-2 also came before another official body during this period: the Senate Foreign Relations Committee, chaired by J. William Fulbright of Arkansas. Among those testifying before the committee were Secretary of State Christian Herter (aided by the State Department's Douglas Dillion) and CIA chief Allen Dulles. Asked what the lesson of the U-2 was, Herter replied, "Not to have accidents." Had the government considered the danger Power's flight might have posed to the summit conference? "That was a risk that we were running in connection with every one of them. Call it bad luck, if you will. But if we had tried to adjust these things to particular meetings, it

---

[330] Beschloss, *Mayday*, 310-313.

would have been almost impossible for the program to succeed." Some of the answers Herter provided to the committee placed him in real danger of being charged with perjury. Asked if the President authorized every U-2 mission, Herter lied: "It has never come up to the President." Had there been flights in the interval between April 9 and May Day? "I can't tell you, quite honestly." As for the route the flight of April 9 followed, "I am ashamed to say I can't remember." Herter's answers, Dillion admitted long afterward, were "one of the most embarrassing things I ever went through, because we didn't want to tell a falsehood. On the other hand our testimony was not totally frank because we were ... trying to hide the White House responsibility for this." Another official present at the hearings, Richard Helms, who was acting in the capacity as a censor for the CIA, went even further: Herter and the others who testified untruthfully before the committee could have been charged with perjury.

In his turn before the committee, Dulles called the U-2 "one of the most valuable intelligence collection operations that any country has ever mounted at any time." It had made the Russians "far less cocky." When queried as to why Eisenhower had assumed responsibility, Dulles, though he privately disagreed with the decision, still defended Ike: "The fact that I was going ahead on my own authority to do something of this magnitude may not have been widely believed, even if I had asserted and stuck to it." Why was the U-2 flown on May Day? "I don't discuss what the President says to me or I say to the President." The CIA was interested in those targets "that we were afraid we would not be able easily to get at a later time and which we thought were of great value to our national security." Dulles ridiculed the notion that Powers might have defected to the Russians: "He loved flying, was making good money and was very happy. If you are going to defect, you don't fly into the heart of Russia, where you may be shot down anywhere before you got there." None of the committee members raised the issue of whether any actions on the CIA's part might have been a factor in Powers' downing or the events culminating in the summit collapse. Future CIA chiefs wouldn't be accorded such passes.

Speaking to journalists following Dulles' testimony, Fulbright publicly exonerated the CIA of "questionable decisions" in the U-2 incident: "political officers" bore the responsibility. The committee's final report did not lay blame for the events of the May Day flight to either Powers or CIA preparations for the mission: it was a case of "just plain bad luck." The senators nevertheless were of the opinion that insufficient consideration had been given to the flight's possible impact on the summit meeting. The cover stories, according to Michael Beschloss, "should have been more careful and the government better coordinated." With the exception of one senator, all the committee members signed the final report. The lone dissenter, Homer Capehart of Indiana, had been outraged by the timing of Powers' flight ("They had been doing it for four years and they had all the information they possibly needed"). Two other senators attached their own addendums censuring Khrushchev for shattering the conference and lauding both the U-2 program and Eisenhower's conduct.

For his part, Fulbright remained skeptical that the committee ever heard the full story: "I have often wondered why, in the midst of these efforts by President Eisenhower and Khrushchev to come to some understanding, the U-2 incident was allowed to take place. No one will ever know whether it was accidental or intentional."[331]

Another diplomatic reversal was in store for Eisenhower following the summit failure and the cancellation of the President's visit to Russia. In an effort to recover from the Paris fiasco, the White House scheduled a goodwill tour of the Western Pacific: in addition to his trip to Japan, Eisenhower would visit the Philippines, Taiwan, Okinawa, and Korea. When the ratification of a Japanese-American mutual defense treaty and the use of a Japanese base for U-2 flights incited violent anti-American demonstrations within Japan—at one point presidential press secretary Jim Hagerty and his party were attacked, necessitating the use of a helicopter to rescue them—the Japanese prime minister called off Eisenhower's visit. "Viewed from any angle," Eisenhower reflected, "this was a Communist victory."[332]

The bad news kept coming. On June 27, the Soviets exited the test ban negotiations in Geneva. On July 1, another American reconnaissance plane, an RB-47 flying along the Soviet Union's northern coast, disappeared over the Barents Sea. The flight had originated from a British base. The Soviets, in Khrushchev's words, had downed the plane to end another "gross violation" of their airspace. Two survivors had been rescued. This "new act of American perfidy" demonstrated that Eisenhower's promise to halt spy flights was "not worth a busted penny." The British should be aware that permitting the use of their installations for "aggressive actions" would place their people in great danger.

American intelligence showed that at the time it was downed, the RB-47 had been more than thirty miles outside Soviet territory. The most likely explanation for the Soviet military's action in this instance was that, after the embarrassment it suffered from the disclosure that it had permitted U-2 incursions over Soviet territory for such a long period, it had downed the

---

[331] *Ibid.*, 313-317.
[332] Beschloss, *Mayday*, 319; Pach and Richardson, *The Presidency of Dwight D. Eisenhower*, Revised Edition, 221.

plane as an image-enhancing measure. When the Russians learned that they had shot down the aircraft over international waters, Khrushchev, to save face, had sought to transform the RB-47 episode into another U-2 incident.

Eisenhower informed Secretary of State Herter that he now didn't trust the Russians in any way. Should America be able to demonstrate that this latest downing had occurred over international waters, it should sever relations with the Soviets. Such action, however, wasn't without risk, as it could jeopardize U.S. tracking stations. The Soviets, Dulles told Eisenhower, were seeking to frighten U.S. allies into refusing to let the United States utilize their bases. As was the case earlier with the U-2, this latest instance of an American aircraft being downed by the Russian military came before the UN Security for consideration. The council declined to condemn, in the Russians' words, the "American provocation."

The flight of Western aircraft through international airspace bordering Soviet territory was a daily occurrence. To his aides, Eisenhower said if the Russians continued shooting at them, he would take retaliatory action, with the possibility that the later might trigger an international conflict. During the UN debate, yet another incident involving the Russians and an American aircraft occurred when a C-47 strayed over the Kurile Islands and the Russians sought, unsuccessfully, to down it.

Later that summer, a presidential aide secretly recommended that the Pentagon trick a Soviet aircraft, submarine or trawler toward American waters. The craft would be seized without force: "We would then claim a violation of territorial waters, whether absolutely technically true or not." This would enable the President to once again take the lead in the global propaganda war by calling attention to an instance of Soviet espionage—and prove that America treated violators of her sovereignty in a more civilized fashion than Moscow did. Eisenhower vetoed the idea.[333]

In the midst of this gloomy season, a ray of light finally broke through. Two years earlier, Bissell and Dulles obtained Congressional sanction for the clandestine financing of CORONA, America's initial spy satellite. In February 1959, Eisenhower informed the CIA that, pending the satellite's availability, the number of U-2 flights should be kept to a minimum. By the time Francis Gary Powers flew on May 1, 1960, the CIA and Air Force had tried eleven times to launch a satellite but, in each case, equipment malfunctions had thwarted a successful outcome.[334] Finally, on August 18, Discoverer XIV was successfully launched from California's Vandenberg Air Force Base. The satellite attained an orbit bearing an apogee of 500 miles and a perigee of

---

[333] Beschloss, *Mayday*, 321-322.
[334] *Ibid.*, 323.

120 miles. The following day, the capsule, which had ejected over Alaska on its seventeenth pass, was retrieved in midair at an altitude of 8,500 feet by a C-119 Flying Boxcar assigned to recover it. The satellite's mission had been a success, providing coverage of the Soviet Union in excess of one million square miles: more coverage than all the four years of U-2 overflights had yielded together.[335]

The day before Discoverer XIV's successful launch, Francis Gary Powers went on trial. The Soviets staged the proceedings as a show trial for the utmost propaganda value. During the trial, Powers continued withholding as much information as he could, yet, acting on the recommendation of his Soviet defense counsel, declared remorse for what he had done. He drew a sentence of 10 years' "deprivation of liberty" from the Soviet military court; the initial three years were to be spent in Vladimir prison. Powers spent the ensuing eighteen months there, 150 miles east of Moscow. During his confinement, Powers was well treated and, at his request, was provided a cell mate in the form of an English-speaking Latvian dissident.[336] Powers' "cooperation" with his captors and his professed remorse brought blood to the eyes of numerous Americans. After conversing with Allen Dulles, *The New York Times'* C.L. Sulzberger noted that the CIA director gave him "the impression that Powers should somehow have knocked himself off. He said that Powers had been brainwashed prior to the trial. I gather Dulles is unhappy with Powers' behavior, but doesn't like to say so." Powers wasn't without his supporters, however, who cited his refusal to condemn the United States. One Powers' champion, Red River Dave, a country-and-western singer, recorded a song, "The Trial of Francis Gary Powers" to the tune of "The Battle Hymn of the Republic":

> In the stately Hall of Columns, 1960 was the year
> When young Francis Gary Powers stood before the Russian bear.
> They were trying him for spying, o'er the Soviets he flew
> In the famous plane, U-2.
>
> Glory, glory, he's a hero! Glory, glory, he's a hero!
> Glory, glory, he's a hero who flew for Uncle Sam.[337]

Upon viewing televised coverage of the Powers trial, Khrushchev decided to carry the Soviet propaganda assault directly to the United Nations by attending that fall's session of the UN General Assembly. In so doing, he had three objectives: to heave verbal invective at the West, court the Third

[335] Brugioni, *Eyeball to Eyeball*, 53.
[336] Polmar, *Spyplane*, 142.
[337] Beschloss, *Mayday*, 335-336.

World, and seek to sway the American presidential campaign. Because the plane he had flown to America the year before was out of commission and because he didn't want to employ an aircraft of smaller size, Khrushchev sailed to America aboard the Soviet passenger ship *Baltika*. In his memoirs, he recalled an incident during his sea voyage when he received word that visual contact had been made with a submarine on the surface:

> The sub had been sighted on the surface so close to our ship that I could see it clearly through my binoculars. It was huge, and the waves were rolling over it. The submarine was not flying a flag, but there was no doubt to whom it belonged: the United States. Here we were going about our own business. So why did this submarine have to come to the surface and keep us company? It was undoubtedly a military demonstration of some sort, an unfriendly show of force. I think the Americans wanted to splash cold water in our faces. The submarine tailed us for a while; then, after it had its presence felt, it submerged. That's all there was to it. But the point had been made.[338]

At the UN, Khrushchev would charge that the submarine had followed his ship, looking for an opportunity to sink it.[339]

When the *Baltika* reached the Port of New York, longshoremen showed their displeasure at the Russians' presence by refusing to berth the vessel; Russian diplomats supposedly secured it themselves. Informed of possible assassination plots, Eisenhower limited the movements of Khrushchev, Castro and Hungary's Janos Kadar solely to Manhattan Island. The General Assembly session began on September 22. Opening day witnessed an appearance by Eisenhower. The President, in the words of the *Economist*, "let himself be whisked on and off the podium, like a piece of property on a revolving stage, lest he come into physical contact with Mr. Khrushchev." The latter's turn to speak came the following day. During a three-hour harangue in which he blasted Western governments, the Soviet leader called for the removal of UN Secretary-General Dag Hammarskjold and his replacement with an East-West troika. When Third World leaders called for a new summit meeting between Eisenhower and Khrushchev, Chip Bohlen counseled Ike not to agree to such an encounter unless some indication of good faith on Khrushchev's part—such as the release of the RB-47 fliers—was forthcoming. If not, the world would conclude that the Soviets were so powerful that they could treat the United States disdainfully, then resume the Spirit of Camp David the next minute.

---

[338] Khrushchev, Khrushchev Remembers: The Last Testament, 465.
[339] Beschloss, *Mayday*, 337-338.

For his part, Khrushchev declared the only way he would see Eisenhower was if the latter apologized for the U-2 and RB-47 incidents. He unsuccessfully sought a General Assembly debate on the U-2 and immediate liberation for all colonial territories. He branded the Security Council a "spittoon" and censured Eisenhower for "lying" in regard to spy flights. America was a "disgrace to civilization."[340]

Speaking to Herter by telephone, Eisenhower said that "he was a rather long sufferer, but one day he was going to call Khrushchev the 'Murderer of Hungary.'" Eisenhower expressed the view that "Khrushchev is trying to promote chaos and bewilderment in the world to find out which nations are weakening under this attack and to pick what he can by fishing in troubled waters." Ike also said that if he were a dictator, he would "launch an attack on Russia while Khrushchev is in New York."[341]

When British Prime Minister Macmillan cited Khrushchev's wrecking of the summit conference, Khrushchev bellowed from the audience, "Yes, let us talk about Powers. Don't send your spy planes to our country!" This prompted Macmillan's deadpan response, "I should like it translated, if you would." Khrushchev subsequently provided the best remembered image to come out of that season's General Assembly session by striking his fist and shoe on his desk. Trying to restore order, the presiding officer broke his gavel. Macmillan, *Pravda* declared, was the captive of antiquated views which filled the air "with the musty odor of the Victorian Age."[342]

Naturally the U-2 incident and the change of fortunes it occasioned became an issue in the 1960 presidential campaign. Addressing the Democratic convention in Los Angeles that July, Texas Democratic Congressman and Speaker of the House Sam Rayburn thundered, "would you have thought that Truman or Roosevelt or Woodrow Wilson would have had the debacle that Eisenhower had at Paris?" In his acceptance speech, John F. Kennedy reminded the convention delegates that the President "who began his career by going to Korea ends it by staying away from Japan." On the Republican side, Nelson Rockefeller, Vice President Nixon's rival for the top spot on the GOP's ticket, had publicly come out for $3 billion more per year for defense, bewailed the Missile Gap, announced that he would accede to a presidential draft, and threatened a floor fight against a GOP platform that endorsed Eisenhower's policies.

In an attempt to quell such a floor fight, Nixon met secretly with Rockefeller in New York just before the beginning of the Republican convention. The "Compact of Fifth Avenue," as the document that emerged from their

[340] Beschloss, *Mayday*, 338.
[341] Ambrose, *Eisenhower: The President*, 590.
[342] Beschloss, *Mayday*, 338-339.

get-together was called, implied that the Vice President had ratified important elements of Rockefeller's criticism of Eisenhower's policies. This prompted Eisenhower to inform Nixon that it would be hard for him to endorse a platform lacking "respect for the record of the Republican administration." Platform language satisfactory to everyone was formulated, but after speaking to the Republican convention, Eisenhower left without sticking around for Nixon's nomination.[343]

Once the campaign swung into high gear, the Democratic nominee observed that the Khrushchev who had been limited to Manhattan was the same man who had been invited to Camp David: "The Spirit of Camp David is gone. The Soviets have made a spectacle before the world of the U-2 flight and the trial of our pilot and have treated this nation with hostility and contempt." Lumping the Missile Gap and the U-2 with other American reversals on the international stage, Kennedy portrayed the America under Republican rule as country with weakening political and military power.

Through a series of briefings Kennedy received from Allen Dulles, SAC, and General Earle Wheeler (the latter representing the Joint Chiefs), Eisenhower sought to persuade Kennedy to dampen his disparagement of American defense policies. The briefings, however, lacked adequate classified information that could convincingly refute the existence of a Missile Gap; hence Kennedy wouldn't drop the issue. During the campaign he spoke of the Soviet missile "advantage," without employing exact dates and figures, mentioning nonpartisan authorities: "I say only that the evidence is strong . . . that we cannot be certain of our security in the future any more than we can be certain of disaster." Several times during the campaign Kennedy called the opposition "the party which gave us the Missile Gap."

Before the downing of Francis Gary Powers, Nixon had anticipated using Eisenhower's foreign policy record to his advantage but now found himself on the defensive. Kennedy, Nixon charged, was "the kind of man Mr. Khrushchev will make mincemeat of." When it came to repeated queries about how Eisenhower managed the U-2 incident, Nixon said diplomatically that, "any of us as Sunday morning quarterbacks might have done things differently."

When it came to whether Kennedy had asked Eisenhower to "express regrets" to Khrushchev, "That shows such a naive attitude. An apology or expressing regrets without getting something in return wouldn't have satisfied him. It wouldn't have saved the Conference. It would only have whetted [Khrushchev's] appetite." There was another reason too why the President of the United States could not and should not have done that. No President

---

[343] *Ibid.*, 327-328.

of this country must ever apologize or express regrets for attempting to defend the security of the United States against attack by somebody else!"

This elicited Kennedy's observation that an earlier episode in 1958, in
which a plane digressed across southern Russia, prompted the Administration to convey regrets: "That is the accepted practice between nations. If that
would have kept the Summit going, in my judgment, it was a proper action.
It's not appeasement. It's not soft. It would have been far better for us to
follow the common diplomatic procedure of expressing regrets and then try
to move on."

Publicly, Nikita Khrushchev found no difference between Kennedy and
Nixon. Yet in private he described Nixon as "a typical product of McCar-
thyism, a puppet of the most reactionary circles in the United States. We'll
never be able to find a common language with him." Kennedy, on the other
hand, seemed more promising. For now, Khrushchev would do nothing that
might adversely affect the choice of an American President, insofar as the
latter's ability to do business with the Soviet Union.

Still there was something Khrushchev could do to sway the American
electorate: the matter of when to release Francis Gary Powers from Soviet
custody. The Eisenhower government was seeking freedom for both Powers
and the RB-47 fliers. The Soviets, Khrushchev subsequently said, weren't opposed to this. "There was no need to keep Powers in prison. But the question
was, when?" To free Powers now, said Khrushchev, would work in Nixon's
favor. "Judging from the press, I think the two candidates are at a stalemate.
If we give the slightest boost to Nixon, it will be interpreted as an expression
of our willingness to see him in the White House." Khrushchev kept Powers
in custody and, as he subsequently crowed, cast the "deciding ballot" in Kennedy's November 1960 electoral triumph.[344]

The failure of the Paris Summit—and, with that, the dashing of his hopes
for a true dawn of peace—meant for Eisenhower that his Presidency would
conclude in much the same way it had begun—without any substantial
headway. His goal, he explained shortly before his death, had been "to give
the United States and the world a lasting peace." Instead he "was able only to
contribute to a stalemate." In reality, Eisenhower did accomplish something
significant during his White House tenure: he prevented nuclear war from
erupting, despite the fact that during his administration, both the United
States and the Soviet Union developed the hydrogen bomb and the intercontinental delivery systems that could carry such weapons to each other's
homelands. Eisenhower's fundamental decency and the respect of his fellow
Americans enabled him to calm the Cold War crises of the 1950s and, in so

---

[344] *Ibid,.* 339-341.

doing, "permit a relatively safe passage through" that tense era.[345] The U-2 contributed to that success. In his memoirs, Eisenhower wrote: "When I have been questioned about the wisdom of the U-2 flights, I have replied with a question of my own: 'Would you be ready to give back all of the information we secured from our U-2 flights over Russia if there had been no disaster to one of our planes?'

"I have never received an affirmative response."[346]

Holding a model of a U-2 in his hand, Francis Gary Powers testifies before the Senate Armed Services Committee in 1962. Credit: Photofest.

---

[345] Halberstam, *The Fifties*, 712.
[346] Eisenhower, *The White House Years: Waging Peace*, 559.

8. Tying Up the Loose Ends (1960–1962)

The day following John F. Kennedy's inauguration as President of the United States, Khrushchev informed Ambassador Thompson that, as a measure toward improving Soviet-American relations, he was releasing the RB-47 fliers. Upon their return to the United States, they were welcomed by President Kennedy himself. Francis Gary Powers heard about their release from Radio Moscow and, while he was "happy for the RB-47 boys," couldn't help thinking that were it not for the fact that they had been downed, he might have been released instead.

In February 1961, the Soviet Ambassador to the United States, Mikhail Menshikov, lodged an appeal with the new Under Secretary of States, Chester Bowles, for the release of Igor Melekh. A Russian in the UN Secretariat, Melekh had been arrested the previous October for espionage. In response to Menshikov's appeal, Bowles said that Melekh might be freed if Powers was released. To this, Menshikov contended that Melekh should be released unconditionally, as was the case with the RB-47 fliers.

Melekh was given his freedom. The State Department believed that Powers' release might be the next move toward improving relations. However when Thompson raised the subject in Moscow, Gromyko merely replied that he was "glad" Thompson appreciated that the Melekh and Powers cases were "entirely different."

According to President Kennedy, the matter of Powers' release wasn't discussed during his meeting with Khrushchev at Vienna in June 1961. In his diary, Powers wrote: "I don't expect him to go out of his way to help me, but I feel that I would have been released long before now if he had made the slightest effort when he met with Khrushchev."

What Powers did not know was that the CIA was seeking his freedom in exchange for a Soviet spy in American custody—Rudolf Abel. Taking up residence in Brooklyn in 1950, where he passed himself off as a painter and photographer using the moniker Emil Goldfus, Abel carried out trivial duties for the KGB apparently while waiting for the recruitment of an American spy important enough to be placed under his supervision. In 1957, Abel's assistant, Reino Hayhayen, defected and put the finger on him. While in American custody, Abel refused to break, going so far as declining to acknowledge that he was a Soviet citizen. His defense attorney, James Donovan, formerly an OSS general counsel and architect of the Nuremberg trials, contended that his client's room had been the object of an unlawful search. True to form, Abel remained silent during his trial and received a thirty-year sentence in federal prison in Atlanta. Donovan unsuccessful argued his case right up to the Supreme Court.

It was Powers' father Oliver who proposed that Abel be exchanged for his son. Upon receiving Oliver Powers' proposal, Abel, who maintained that he was East German, asked Donovan to contact his "wife" in Leipzig. "Hellen Abel" wrote in the summer of 1961 that she had visited the Soviet Embassy in East Berlin and found the Soviets receptive to the notion of releasing Powers for Abel. Both Donovan and Lawrence Houston of the CIA were of the opinion that Abel's "wife" was in fact a KGB operative; in all likelihood fearful that Abel, given the fact the he wouldn't be a free man again until 1987, might crack and reveal all that he knew. The Russians were eager to get him back. His return would serve two purposes: it would bolster KGB morale worldwide and Abel might be a valuable asset to the American section in Moscow.

Donovan wrote Mrs. Abel that Powers' release should be unilateral in nature, the same as with Melekh's. She should then ask for clemency on her husband's behalf from President Kennedy. In response, Mrs. Abel said that the Embassy in East Berlin wanted a simultaneous release.

The CIA approved the idea in November 1961, informing Secretary of State Dean Rusk that while the Russians may have concluded that they had obtained all the most valuable information from Powers, the latter hadn't disclosed anything injurious to American interests. The Agency wanted to know the "precise events" that precipitated Powers' capture and how he had been treated and questioned. Powers' letters from captivity indicated his concern about his wife and Washington's failure to obtain his release. Presently he might break down and reveal information he had been withholding. Once he was back with the Russians, Abel would always be viewed with suspicion. Any American secrets he brought back to Russia with him would be obsolete by at least five years.

Summoned to Washington in January 1962, Donovan was informed that an exchange had received authorization at the "highest level." Donovan notified Mrs. Abel of "significant developments" and suggested a meeting at the Soviet Embassy in East Berlin at noon February 3. The reply she delivered—"HAPPY NEW YEAR"—signified her agreement to Donovan's proposal. Donovan also learned about two other Americans who were in East German custody: Frederick Pryor, a Yale graduate student arrested for spying while researching a dissertation, and Marvin Makinen, a Fulbright scholar imprisoned for photographing Soviet military facilities. While he should seek the release of all three Americans, Donovan's primary mission was Powers' freedom.

When the meeting at the Embassy occurred, Donovan met a woman who said she was Mrs. Abel and Ivan Schischkin, whose official position was the Embassy's second secretary, but whom the CIA knew as head of Soviet espionage in Western Europe. Wolfgang Vogel, Mrs. Abel's attorney, had informed the U.S. mission in West Berlin that she was "confident" that freedom for Pryor and Makinen would occur in the event the United States released Abel in return for Powers. Yet, when Donovan raised the subject of the other Americans' freedom at his meeting with Mrs. Abel and Schischkin, the latter declared his ignorance of them. Donovan said that if Schischkin wouldn't discuss their release, he would have returned home. Nonetheless, a document commuting Abel's sentence, bearing JFK's signature, was ready should the exchange take place. In the event an agreement was struck, Abel could be in East Berlin within forty-eight hours.

After four days of negotiations, Donovan and Schischkin reached an accord: Powers would be exchanged for Abel. Simultaneously, at another location, Pryor would be freed from East German custody. Should Soviet-American relations improve, there was "every expectation" that the third detainee, Makinen, would be released. Emphatically determined not to acknowledge that the Soviets engaged in spying, Schischkin insisted that Abel not be publicly tied to the Soviet government.

On February 10, 1962, Powers and Abel crossed the Glienicker Bridge that separated East Germany and West Berlin. True to the CIA's prediction, the KGB never trusted Abel. Following his death from lung cancer, the KGB disclosed the truth of Abel's origins: he had been born in Britain, the son of Russian emigres. Shown his grave, Western journalists learned his true identity: William Fischer.

Powers was secretly flown to Delaware, then taken to a safe house in Maryland for breakfast, a meeting with a CIA psychiatrist, and a reunion with his parents and wife. When reporters discovered the safe house, he was relocated to a place, ironically, near the Eisenhower farm in Gettysburg. While there, Powers had a visitor: U-2 creator Kelly Johnson, who informed him that whatever the outcome of the investigation, should he ever need a job, he could have one at Lockheed, then asked, "What happened to my plane?" There followed an extensive debriefing by the CIA. During this time, relocation to another safe house near CIA headquarters in Langley, Virginia, became necessary when reporters again discovered Powers' location. The freed U-2 pilot wasn't happy with the questions he was being asked, as he explained sometime afterward: "I couldn't help discerning an obvious pattern behind them—that the Agency was not really interested in what I had to tell them. Their primary concern was to get the CIA off the hook."[347]

Powers' debriefing was conducted by the Damage Assessment Team. The same body had earlier convened in the summer of 1960 to appraise both the extent of Powers' knowledge of the U-2 program and what he could have told the Soviets about it. Considering the length of time Powers had been part of the program, the team's initial judgment was that his knowledge was quite broad and that he likely had disclosed the majority of it to his captors. Now, two years later, after debriefing Powers, the team reversed its initial finding and was quite satisfied with Powers' conduct. So was Allen Dulles: "We are proud of what you have done," he told Powers.

But by the time Dulles uttered those words, he was no longer CIA director and his successor, John A. McCone, wasn't satisfied with Powers' conduct, empaneling a new board of inquiry under retired federal judge F. Barrett Prettyman. After eight days of hearings and deliberations, the Prettyman Board submitted its findings on February 27, 1962: Powers had conducted himself in line with the instructions he had received and had "complied with his obligations as an American citizen during this period." The board recommended he be given his pay back. In reaching its decision, the Prettyman panel drew upon an enormous bulk of evidence indicating Powers' veracity regarding his doomed flight: the testimony of the experts who debriefed him following his release; a complete examination of Powers' background, featuring testimony from doctors, psychiatrists, onetime Air Force associates, and his superiors at Adana; the testimony Powers himself presented to the board; the findings of a voluntary polygraph test; and photographs of the remnants of his U-2--the latter Kelly Johnson studied and found consistent with Powers' account.

The Prettyman Board's conclusion favorable to Powers failed to convince McCone. He requested an Air Force examination to appraise Johnson's assessment of the U-2 photographs. The Air Force inquiry supported John-

---

[347] Beschloss, *Mayday*, 343-350.

son's conclusions. "McCone," writes Norman Polmar, "then seized upon the one piece of evidence that contradicted Powers' testimony"—a National Security Agency (NSA) report *suggesting* "that Powers may have descended to a lower altitude and turned back in a broad curve toward Sverdlovsk before" he was shot down—"and ordered the Prettyman Board to reconvene" on March 1 to reexamine this evidence. The NSA evidence failed to alter the board's initial judgment.[348]

Testifying before the Senate Armed Services Committee on March 6, 1962, Powers recounted the events surrounding his downing:

> "My first reaction was to reach for the destruct switches but I thought that I had better see if I can get out of here before using this. I was being thrown forward, and if I had used the ejection seat at that time, I would have probably lost both legs. . . .

> "I kept glancing at the altimeter as the aircraft was falling and it was going around very fast. I tried to get back into the aircraft so that I could activate these destructor switches. I couldn't get back in the airplane. I didn't know whether I could get those oxygen hoses loose or not. I couldn't activate the destruct switches, so then I decided to try and get out."[349]

Powers described his poison pen, his capture, imprisonment and apology in Moscow—the latter he had made at the recommendation of his defense counsel. Powers' "main sorrow was that the mission failed."

Massachusetts Senator Leverett Saltonstall inquired about the parachute and survival kit and extolled Powers as a "courageous, fine, young American citizen." Save for Allen Dulles' comments, Saltonstall's were the first endorsement a top member of the American government had given him. Mississippi's John Stennis observed that Powers had been "exonerated by the men who must know how to judge what you did. I know it makes you feel mighty good." Powers: "There was one thing that I always remembered while I was there—and that was that I am an American."

The room burst into applause; at that moment, observed a journalist, Powers seemed nearly as much a national hero as John Glenn, who had just become the first American to orbit the Earth. Other senators haled Powers, yet Barry Goldwater remained silent: during the hearing, the Conservative Republican Senator from Arizona sent Powers a handwritten message,

---

[348] Polmar, *Spyplane*, 143.
[349] Beschloss, Mayday, 353-354.

thanking him for his service to his country. Still Goldwater didn't believe Powers' account of his downing.[350]

Despite the fact that Powers was cleared of improper conduct by the various probes of his actions while in Soviet captivity, few of these investigations' conclusions were publicized; the public's view of Powers had been fashioned by sensational press accounts and statements on the part of public officials who were ignorant of (or chose to disregard) the facts pertaining to Powers' conduct during his incarceration. One figure who spoke up in Powers' behalf was Delaware GOP Senator John J. Williams. A member of the Foreign Relations Committee, Williams posed the question to CIA Director McCone: "Don't you think he is being left with just a little bit of a cloud hanging over him? If he did everything he is supposed to do, why leave it hanging?"[351] The answer to Williams' question may well be that the official clearance Powers received notwithstanding, the fact that he survived the downing of his U-2 and chose not to kill himself to avoid Soviet capture both embarrassed and enraged the CIA.

Because Powers received no public acknowledgment of his attempts to conceal information from the Soviets, a cloud continued to hang over his actions and loyalties. Unlike the RB-47 fliers, he received no personal welcome from President Kennedy. McCone, who remained antagonistic toward Powers, conferred the CIA Intelligence Star on all U-2 pilots, except Powers, in 1963. This rebuff was rectified when, on April 25, 1965—two days before McCone's resignation took effect—Powers was awarded the Intelligence Star (bearing the date 1963 on its reverse side) from deputy CIA director Marshall S. Carter.

There was also the issue of Powers' return to the Air Force. Despite resistance to this, the Air Force on April 4, 1962, consented to Powers' reinstatement. This decision received CIA, State Department, and White House clearance. However, the beginning of Powers' divorce proceedings caused the Air Force to delay his reinstatement, lest the divorce generate unfavorable notice. In the interim, Powers found another job as a U-2 test pilot at Lockheed, ultimately choosing to remain there until U-2 testing ended in September 1969. With no other work for him available at Lockheed, Johnson had no choice but to discharge him.[352]

In 1970, Powers published his story in *Operation Overflight*. Though he eliminated certain pieces of sensitive information from the book as a courtesy to the CIA, Powers still faulted the Agency for failing to prepare U-2 pilots for the possibility that they could be captured, the inadequate cover story, the

[350] Beschloss, *Mayday*, 354.
[351] Polmar, *Spyplane*, 144.
[352] *Ibid.*, 144-145.

failure to refute the public notion that he violated orders by not committing suicide and by talking to the Russians. He began giving lectures. He sought employment with the aerospace industry but, despite what his second wife termed "first-class treatment all the way" from companies he had applied to, no one hired him. In 1972, he asked his lawyer and friend Gregory Anderson for assistance in convincing Congress to reopen its U-2 investigation and exonerate him, but their efforts in this endeavor proved fruitless.

Finally Powers landed a job as an aerial traffic reporter from KGIL Radio in Los Angeles. This was followed by a job with Los Angeles television station KNBC covering news events from a helicopter. On August 1, 1977, Powers and his cameraman took off to cover a blaze in Santa Barbara. After completing that assignment, Powers requested another. Fifteen minutes later, they were hovering above a field where a softball game was in progress.

Once again fate intervened in Francis Gary Powers' life. One of the ball players heard a popping sound and recalled, "I looked up and saw the helicopter swaying in the air and making all sorts of dips and then it kind of conked out. Then he looked as if he got it going again. Then it just conked out again and dipped down and hit the ground really hard and everything flew everywhere." Some of the boys were certain that the pilot had deviated his helicopter so as not to hit them. In the words of a police sergeant, "We found no evidence of fuel on board and the craft didn't burn, so from all appearances, it would seem he ran out of gas. That's the unforgivable pilot error." Anderson remembered that shortly before Powers' death, the former U-2 pilot had been photographing a moving train on fire when the reading on his fuel gauge indicated he was low: checking his fuel supply after he returned from his assignment, he discovered he still had sufficient fuel remaining for an additional half-hour, "so it really bothered him that he'd missed some great footage." According to Anderson, Powers hadn't been informed that the gauge had been repaired the evening before his last flight ever.

Powers' wife Sue didn't buy this story: "Frank was just too good a pilot to run out of fuel." Though no evidence was at hand to support them, conspiracy theorists took note of the presence of both the CIA and Lockheed at Van Nuys Airport, the staging area of Powers' flight that fateful August 1, and maintained that his demise had resulted from the sabotage of his helicopter for the purpose of silencing him to prevent the disclosure of injurious classified information or as retribution for criticizing the CIA.

Believing that, if he should die before his wife did, the latter would seek to have him interred at Arlington National Cemetery, Powers had instructed Anderson to dissuade her from so doing. But Sue Powers wouldn't be stopped. Anderson contacted everyone he could think of in Washington.

The issue was finally decided by President Carter who, acting upon the CIA's recommendation, authorized Powers' burial in Arlington.[353] Further vindication for Powers would follow ten years later, when he posthumously received the Distinguished Flying Cross from the United States Air Force.[354]

Final Act in the Quiz Show Scandal

Shortly before Powers' release, the final act in the quiz show scandal played itself out. The beginning of the end could be said to have started in late 1959 with a pair of events: Charles Van Doren's appearance before the Harris subcommittee and district attorney Frank Hogan's subsequent revelation that, in his opinion, out of the 150 witnesses who had appeared before the grand jury during the latter's probe of the quiz show matter, only 50 had been truthful. Now, approximately 30 former witnesses contacted Hogan, expressing their desire to change their testimony.[355]

By the end of December 1959, Hogan's office had talked to some two dozen ex-quiz show contestants who conceded lying to the grand jury. Most had been cited by under oath, while others, who hadn't testified before the grand jury, admitted lying during office interviews. The belated revelations helped resolve the question of why so great a number of upright, normally principled people had committed perjury en masse, yet raised the possibility, in Joseph Stone's words, "of extensive subornation of perjury by lawyers, inducing grand jury witnesses to lie under oath."

One instance involved contestant Timothy Horan. The latter, a friend of Felsher, had received help from the producer of the daytime version of *Tic Tac Dough* and went on to become a prime time champion. Recanting his original grand jury testimony, Horan acknowledged receiving assistance as a quiz contestant and having numerous contacts involving himself, Felsher and attorney Sol Gelb, prior to and after his appearance before the grand jury, which followed by two days Felsher's initial grand jury appearance in October 1958. In Horan's account, it was during these gatherings that Gelb counseled him that, since Felsher had just testified under oath that he hadn't helped anyone he would be in trouble should Horan fail to sustain his testimony. Other former contestants on *Tic Tac Dough* provided equivalent stories. Each acknowledged meeting, at Felsher's direction, with Gelb at least once before testifying.

Given these developments, Stone wanted to reexamine everything with Felsher again, since in prior recantation he hadn't mentioned Gelb's actions.

---

[353] Beschloss, *Mayday*, 398-401.
[354] Polmar, *Spyplane*, 145.
[355] Anderson, *Television Fraud*, 167-168.

Felsher, however, wanted no further dealings with Stone: he was upset because he had no job—a development he attributed to the Harris subcommittee's acquisition of his recantation, and he felt betrayed. His new attorney, Maurice Nessen, a partner of Van Doren's lawyer, notified Stone that the only way his client would answer any further questions would be in the event he was subpoenaed.

Stone decided not to employ the latter course until he and his office had completed the picture with evidence provided by former *Twenty-One* contestants who were now changing their stories. One such individual, James Bowser, acknowledged Dan Enright's personal assistance and provided information regarding encounters with Enright during the probe. Before his scheduled meeting with Stone in September 1958, Bowser asserted, Enright told him he didn't require legal counsel and implored him to merely tell Stone that he hadn't been assisted in any way while appearing on *Twenty-One*. After seeing Stone, Bowser reported on the meeting to Enright, then wrote the latter, warning him he would sue for damages should it be demonstrated that the contestant he lost to on *Twenty-One* had been helped. Bowser had been moved to write the letter on the advice of friends and was meant to divert suspicions on their and his employer's part that he had been involved in the rigging. He also mailed Enright a postcard, which featured the message "Dan—Disregards, MYERS." The latter term "Myers" was a code name both Bowser and Enright devised for communicating with each other. Bowser also contended that, when Enright received both the letter and postcard, he called to say that he comprehended their meaning.

Bowser's account both enhanced Stone's knowledge of how far Enright had gone to arrange the mass perjury on the contestants' part and discredited his Washington testimony that Freedman and Felsher were responsible for the subornation. As to why he had committed perjury, Bowser maintained he had done so out of "self-pride," not wanting to look as though he was guilty of misconduct and the desire to assist Enright who was in trouble.

Stone now felt that, with further assistance from Felsher and Freedman,

> We could make a case for a conspiracy against Enright, Gelb, and Myron Greene to suborn perjury by various contestants. Freedman had more explaining to do as well: we had new statements from two former "Tic Tac Dough" contestants handled by him when he was that program's producer; he had named only one of them in his recantation of May 1959. The other, Terry Curtis, had won $2,800 on daytime "Tic Tac Dough," then later won $78,000 on the short-lived "High Low," which Freedman had also produced and Bloomgarden indicated was rigged. She had denied receiving assistance on either show to the Third

September 1958 Grand Jury; now she was telling us that Freedman had assisted her on both.[356]

Accompanied by her attorney, Vivienne Nearing appeared at Stone's office June 3, 1960, to confess to perjury. Glorianne Rader conceded that, in her capacity as Freedman's assistant, she was aware that he was assisting contestants and that the majority of *Twenty-One* contests were fixed; additionally, she had personally helped two contestants on *Tic Tac Dough*, one of whom had testified before the original grand jury that he hadn't been assisted. On July 1, 1960, a grand jury indicted Bernard Martin and Arthur Roberts, both formerly associated with *Treasure Hunt*, for misdemeanors of requesting and accepting gifts and gratuities, as agent and employee of another, and conspiracy. The pair were charged with seeking monetary kickbacks from ten contestants appearing on the show during the period of October 1958 to October 1959. Stone and his staff had interviewed half of the 250 contestants who had been on *Treasure Hunt* since it debuted in the fall of 1957, and discovered that some 30% of those had been chosen to appear on the show with the help of Martin and Roberts. The key to the scheme was that winners could choose to take cash in place of merchandise as prizes. Roberts and Martin entered the accords with potential contestants, many of the latter friends and acquaintances of the pair, promising them that they would win on the show in return for a 50-50 split of the cash value of the prizes after 25% of the value had been subtracted for income tax purposes. Arrested and arraigned on July 8, the pair were released on their own recognizance pending trial.[357]

With Freedman returning to New York, Hogan sanctioned the seating of a new grand jury to hear the perjury cases and other issues involving the initial probe. On July 5, 1960, the day after Freedman took up residence in a hotel after his arrival at the airport, the Fourth Grand Jury of the July 1960 term was seated to consider accusations of perjury, subornation of perjury, obstruction of justice, and conspiracy in connection with the 1958 quiz investigation. For almost two weeks, Freedman, under a grant of immunity, testified almost every day. The cases were presented on an individual basis, and each time Freedman had to restate the essential facts of the quiz shows and how he was involved. When it came to the matter of how Enright's attorneys conducted themselves in the affair, Freedman wasn't so candid. Stone threatened him with a contempt action to compel him to talk.

After Freedman completed his testimony, the grand jury heard from erstwhile *Twenty-One* contestants who had formally asked for permission to testify on their own behalf. After verifying that they had waived immuni-

---

[356] Stone and Yohn, *Prime Time and Misdemeanors*, 276-278.
[357] *Ibid.*, 286-287, 289-290.

ty to come before the grand jury, Paul Bain, Ruth Miller, David Mayer, and Richard Klein, along with Von Nardroff, Bloomgarden, and Van Doren, were notified that they were defendants and were being given the chance to testify in relation to the charges against them. The first four defendants were comparatively unknown figures as far as the public was concerned; now, before the grand jury, they explained that they had perjured themselves for fear that telling the truth about Freedman would be injurious to him and lamented their error in doing so. "All had good backgrounds, were highly educated and model citizens in all aspects of their lives, and the jurors were inclined to pity them." The same didn't hold for Von Nardroff, Bloomgarden, and Van Doren.[358]

Obtaining an extension of the grand jury's life for three months, Stone set to work on preparing a presentation against the *Tic Tac Dough* perjurers. This phase of the hearings would include testimony on the part of Felsher who presented his story during numerous appearances and the testimony under waiver of immunity from twelve ex-contestants, ten of whom had received help from Felsher, while the remaining two were tutored by Freedman. Upon learning from Stone that the district attorney's indictment against him couldn't be dismissed. Freedman was understandably angry. Should any of the cases involving the *Twenty-One* contestants be tried, he would have to appear to testify in open court.

As a result of the new grand jury's investigation, on October 7, 1960, misdemeanor charges were brought against *Twenty-One* contestants Bain, Bloomgarden, Klein, Mayer, Miller, Nearing, Van Doren, and Von Nardroff and *Tic Tac Dough* contestants Terry Curtis, Henrietta Dudley, Charles Gilliam, Morton Harelik, Timothy Horan, Ruth Klein, Patricia Nance, Joseph Rosner, Patricia Sullivan, Michael Truppin, and Neil Wolfe. In the weeks to come, the defendants turned themselves in. Two immediately pled not guilty to the charges and were releases on their own recognizance; the others were released as well but were given delays in filing their pleas. It should be noted that the defendants were charged, not for appearing on rigged quiz shows, but for committing perjury for lying to the original grand jury. Before the enactment of the 1960 legislation resulting from the Harris subcommittee's investigation, quiz show rigging wasn't a crime.[359] The notion that the big fish were escaping unpunished greatly influenced the grand jury to return misdemeanor charges against the defendants.

Stone wanted to pursue the lawyers, whose part in the arranging the perjury had come to light during the new grand jury hearings. As October

---

[358] *Ibid.*, 292.
[359] Anderson, *Television Fraud*, 167.

came to an end, Stone secured another extension, and the grand jury panel continued taking testimony until December. They were resolved to go deeper with their inquiry and perhaps proceed against Greene, Gelb, and Slote. With this in mind, Stone told Hogan they might consider the option of presenting Enright the offer of immunity. Enright had doled out considerable sums of money to different lawyers and no longer had any genuine motive to protect them. The evidence indicated that it wasn't Enright, but the lawyers who appreciated his financial worth, who suborned the perjury and placed impediments in the way of Stone's investigation from the beginning. Should Enright be given a reason to talk, it could open the door to nailing those lawyers involved. Even if the evidence failed to warrant criminal charges, it could at best permit the grand jury to recommend submitting its findings to the Bar Association for possible action.

Hogan vetoed the idea. Enright, more than any other person, bore the responsibility for the quiz show fixing, and to grant him immunity for the purpose of taking the investigation down a new course would be a PR disaster. What trial jury would countenance the word of Enright and those contestants who perjured themselves before the grand jury against lawyers like Gelb and Greene? Stone had no choice but to comply.[360]

On November 8, 1960, Stone met with Dr. Joyce Brothers, telling her his office had evidence that she hadn't been completely forthcoming when she testified before the old grand jury more than a year earlier, on January 7, 1959. Specifically, she had been pretested before going on the air, asked a series of thirty to forty questions meant to prep her, and that within these questions was material that was to be utilized during the broadcast. Stone's assertion that he had evidence that Brothers had received assistance, her denials to the contrary notwithstanding, distressed her. Speaking to Stone, she said she dreaded her quiz show appearances and loathed the studying and tension associated with them. The only times she was happy was when the shows were over, when she could enjoy a good meal. But then her anxieties returned when she had to get ready for the next quiz show appearance. She had continued her ordeal because of her and her husband's financial situation: at the time of her quiz show appearances, her husband drew a salary of $50 a month as a hospital intern and, between that and her college teaching, they made a mere $4,000 a year. "Their financial dependence on her parents," Stone wrote, "had become degrading, but then she gave me no clear answer as to why she had gone on to become a 'Challenge' contestant after winning $64,000 on the 'Question.'"

---

[360] Stone and Yohn, *Prime Time and Misdemeanors*, 296-299.

It was after reading the Washington testimony of Steve Carlin and Merton Koplin that Brothers finally understood that the producers and sponsors called the shots on the shows. While she didn't know anything about her fellow contestants, her own success on the quiz had been due to her own efforts. Now she felt she way being persecuted for the latter. After being grilled by NBC executives, she was absolved and permitted to remain on her weekly psychological advice program.

When it came to the punishment for second degree perjury, the offender faced up to a year's imprisonment and/or a fine of up to $500; as the erstwhile quiz show contestants were charged with first offenses and had acknowledged their misdeeds under oath with varying degrees of contrition, it was highly improbable that they would face serious consequences. For both private and professional reasons, and because they felt betrayed in the expectation that the charges would be dropped during the course of the investigation, the contestants were all resolved to fight. Appearing in the Court of Special Sessions on November 7, 1960, three of the defendants requested and received delays before entering pleas. The others had entered not guilty at their arraignments.

On November 14 Nearing, Von Nardroff, and others moved to dismiss on account of several technical grounds. On December 2 Van Doren and six others who hadn't participated in the prior motions pled not guilty. While it was true that Van Doren had acknowledged committing perjury before the Harris subcommittee, his attorney Carl Rubino said he couldn't pled guilty while the issue of the charges' authenticity was disputed. Pending a judgment on the motions filed November 14, all cases were adjourned until the following January.

The defendants maintained that they couldn't be charged with perjury in the matter of being assisted on the quiz shows as the original grand jury had no right to ask them about something that wasn't illegal. Thus the grand jury, in the defendants' opinion, hadn't been legally authorized to put them under oath—meaning that an essential element of perjury was absent and mandated the dismissal of the charges.[361]

The defendants learned the outcome of their motion when, on April 7, 1961, Judge Gerald Culkin of New York County's Court of General Sessions ruled against them. Dismissing the line of reasoning that the September 1958 Grand Jury was simply examining the content of TV programs, the judge asserted that the grand jury was set up for a legal purpose, meaning that the oaths the defendants took were legally given. As there was no evidence before the initial grand jury that the defendants had perpetuated crimes, this

---

[361] *Ibid.*, 302-303.

meant they weren't "targets" of prosecution whose right against self-incrimination had been violated; the grand jury, just the same, had the authority to investigate the conduct of other people who might have been legitimate targets.

Culkin also held the district attorney's office guilty of insufficiently informing the defendants of their rights as they related to immunity and of the outcome of committing perjury. That admonition notwithstanding, the path was now open for trials to begin; they were slated to commence in the Court of Special Sessions on May 8, 1961.

On that date Nearing entered a guilty plea and drew a suspended sentence. This was followed by the filing of thirteen additional motions to dismiss on behalf of the remaining defendants. Each one had to be rebutted by the district attorney's office, meaning a postponement to the ultimate outcome.

In the period encompassing June and the end of December 1961, Dudley, Horan, Miller, Rosner, and Truppin pleaded guilty and received suspended sentences. As the new year of 1962 dawned, there remained the cases of the thirteen of the initial twenty contestants. Their saga came to a conclusion on January 17, when Van Doren, Von Nardroff, Bloomgarden, and the others plead guilty. Stone explained to Judge Breslin that he had been involved with the cases for quite some time and could tell how sorry the defendants were. They had suffered sufficient punishment already. Breslin felt the same way, too: he suspended the defendants' sentences without levying probation.[362]

Other former quiz show contestants sued producers, networks, sponsors, and advertising agencies on the grounds they suffered damages resulting from appearing on rigged shows. The decisions rendered in these cases suggest that none of them ever went to trial. Nor are indications of cash payments that might have been made evident, since, as allowed by law, such payments could have been concealed as a stipulation of the settlement.

In the period between October 1958 and September 1961 numerous contestants who had appeared on *Tic Tac Dough* and *Twenty-One* sued for damages against Barry and Enright, NBC, sponsors, and other contestants. The suits covered such issues as defamation, damage to credit rating and reputation and ensuing financial losses, and breach of contract.

Each of the suits that made it to the higher court level because of actions by one side of the dispute or other were eventually dismissed. The plaintiffs had to demonstrate specific financial losses resulting from having appeared on the quiz shows—something the courts found they hadn't done.

---

[362] *Ibid.*, 307–309.

The courts, additionally, didn't accept the argument that they deserved to recover sums they might have won had the quizzes been fixed against them. Not until May 1967 was the last judgment in these cases handed down.

Charles Van Doren quickly withdrew from public life. Relocating to Chicago, he obtained, with the help of Mortimer Adler, editor of the Great Books series, an editorial position with the Encyclopedia Britannica. He maintained a largely low profile in the Windy City, where he and his wife raised their two children. He never wrote or commented about the events relating to the quiz show affair, shunning requests for interviews from journalists. Among the compilations he edited were *The Great Treasury of Western Thought* and *The Joy of Reading*, yet his ability to promote such works, which would have elevated their sales and his standing as well, was circumscribed by his wariness when it came to making television appearances: in such instances the questions he would be asked would pertain to the quiz show matter instead of his literary achievements.[363]

In 1990 Van Doren met Julian Krainin, a documentary filmmaker, who told him that a production company was considering the idea of doing a television program about the quiz show scandal. Krainin, suggested they would want him to participate in the proposed broadcast. The production would originate with WGBH in Boston. Krainin had another proposal he wanted to present to Van Doren: "Have you ever thought of returning to television, Charles? I think you have a lot to offer." He cited a pair of public-TV series, James Burke's *Connections* and Jacob Bronowski's *The Ascent of Man*, suggesting that Van Doren might host a series as well.

Saying he knew something about the history of philosophy, Van Doren went on to outline a series about the subject: "Think of Plato, Aristotle, Cicero, Augustine, Aquinas, Bacon, Locke, Hume, Voltaire, Jefferson, Hegel, Marx, Nietzsche," he said. "That's thirteen right there." Krainin liked the idea. After he left, Van Doren and his wife Gerry went for a walk, then returned home.

"What do you think of that?" he asked her.

"I think you're being foolish."

Van Doren's proposed history of philosophy series never materialized. Van Doren felt it never had a chance. When "The Quiz Show Scandal," which was written and produced in part by Krainin as part of PBS's *American Experience* series, aired in 1992, it listed Van Doren's name among those cited in the end credits—even though Van Doren had in no way participated in the project.

---

[363] Halberstam, *The Fifties*, 665–666.

The next time Van Doren heard from Krainin was when the latter called to say that Robert Redford was planning a feature film on the quiz show scandal and that Redford wanted Van Doren's approval—"my 'guarantee of its truthfulness'" was how Van Doren phrased it. The filmmakers were willing to pay him $50,000 for his services; when Krainin forwarded him the contract, the filmmakers' fee had risen to a hundred thousand dollars. After discussing the matter with his family and his son's wife's father—a lawyer— Van Doren tore up the contract. Before Redford's film, *Quiz Show*, debuted in 1994, a car pulled up next to Van Doren's residence. The driver explained he was lost and asked for directions. Van Doren subsequently realized that the lost motorist was actor Ralph Fiennes, who played him in *Quiz Show*. "He told a reporter that he had driven by my house and had seen me looking 'sad.'"

Van Doren recalled that during the distressing six week period in 1959 encompassing his appearance before the Harris subcommittee and Christmas, he found strength in a gift he received from his father: a gyroscopic compass, "the kind you can start spinning and put on the edge of a glass, where it will stay upright till the spinning stops." A quotation accompanied the gift: "May this be for you the whirligig of time that brings in his revenges." The quotation originated with "Twelfth Night." "Feste, the mean-spirited clown, has been unmasked, but those are his last words, thrown over his shoulder. The play's audience knows that somehow he will survive and live to taunt some other master." For Van Doren, it was unnecessary to ask his father what he meant by this, "because I knew he was saying that I, too, would survive and somehow find a way back." One morning during a trip he and his wife were taking to Rome, a fiftieth-anniversary gift to one another, Van Doren placed the gyroscope on the edge of an orange-juice glass, and set it spinning. Looking at it, he said "'Thank you'—to it and to my father and mother and to all the other people who helped us to survive."[364]

---

[364] Charles Van Doren, "All the Answers: The Quiz-Show Scandals–and the Aftermath," www.newyorker.com/reporting/2008/07/28/080728fa_fact_vandoren?printable=true 5 December 2008.

9. Aftermath: The Expanding Credibility Gap

With the dawn of the 1960s, there was mounting evidence that the Silent Generation of the decade just ended was giving way to a more vocal, more activist crop of young people, belying the prophecy, articulated the year before, by Clark Kerr, president of the University of California that "the employers will love this generation. They are going to be easy to handle. There aren't going to be any riots." Events before Kerr's declaration had already discredited him. Students nationwide were becoming involved in campaigns against segregation, war, nuclear tests, and college ROTC programs. The year Kerr spoke, University of Chicago students founded the Student Peace Union, while students at Wisconsin began publishing *Studies on the Left*. The tempo of student activism increased in 1960. May of that year witnessed protests against the execution of Red Light Bandit Caryl Chessman at San Quentin and hearings of the House Un-American Activities Committee at San Francisco's City Hall. Earlier, on February 1, four black freshmen from North Carolina Agricultural and Technical State College in Greensboro, North Carolina, began a sit-in demonstration against segregation policies at the all-while lunch counter at downtown Greensboro's F. W. Woolworth store. From there, the sit-in protests spread to other North Carolina communities and elsewhere, eventually extending to segregated swimming pools, public libraries, motion picture theaters, hotels and motels, public parks, beaches, and other accommodations. By early summer, desegregated lunch counters were a reality in Greensboro and numerous additional Southern cities. By the end of 1960, over 50,000 mainly young people had taken part in sit-in demonstrations; of that number, some 3,600 had been incarcerated. Yet the effort had produced tangible results: desegregation had come to lunch counters and other public facilities in 126 Southern cities.

In the midst of the sit-in movement, approximately 200 students gathered at Raleigh, North Carolina's Shaw University to consider means of coordinating the sit-ins and other anti-segregation efforts. This conclave and a subsequent gathering in Atlanta sired the Student Nonviolent Coordinating Committee (SNCC). Though SNCC members dedicated themselves to the nonviolent philosophy advocated by Dr. Martin Luther King, Jr., they announced that "arrest will not deter us" and that "this is no fad. We're trying to eradicate the whole system of being inferior." While collaborating with other civil rights organizations under the direction of older black leaders, SNCC refused to be officially linked to them and would be a major participant in the civil rights struggles of the coming decade.[365]

The loss of innocence affecting young people in real life as the 1960s began was also evident in television during this period. In 1959, children were shocked at the news that George Reeves, the small-screen incarnation of Superman, had committed suicide—an act many believed had resulted from Reeves' typecasting in the role. For his young fans, Reeves' death made it clear that the make-believe world they witnessed on television was just that—a fabrication; not even Superman was immortal. Reeves' passing was followed, in March 1960, by the divorce of television's first family, Lucille Ball and Desi Arnaz. Then, in September 1960, *Howdy Doody*, a staple of children's television programming since the medium's birth, faded from view after 2,343 broadcasts. At the end of that final telecast, Clarabelle the clown, who had been mute since the show's beginning, looked into the camera and uttered his first words on-air: "Goodbye, kids."[366] 1960 also witnessed the final broadcast of what had come to represent television's Golden Age of the 1950s, *Playhouse 90*, and the debut of a series that denoted the restlessness of young people that would characterize the decade just beginning—*Route 66*.[367] Inspired by Jack Kerouac's *On the Road*, the series followed two free-spirited young men, as they roamed America in a 1960 Corvette, seeking not only adventure but purpose as well.[368] The most intriguing series of the era debuted on CBS Friday evening October 2, 1959. Breaking completely out of Fifties' normality, it transported audiences to "a fifth dimension beyond that which is known to man. This is the dimension of the imagination. It

---

[365] Oakley, *God's Country*, 403-406.

[366] Castleman and Podrazik, *Watching TV*, 138.

[367] Mary Ann Watson, *The Expanding Vista: American Television in the Kennedy Years* (New York: Oxford University Press, 1990), 36.

[368] John Patrick Diggins, *The Proud Decades: America in War and in Peace, 1941-1960* (New York: W. W. Norton and Company, 1988), 217; Michael McCall, *The Best of 60s TV* (New York: Mallard Press, 1992), 42; Watson, *The Expanding Vista*, 36.

is an area we call *The Twilight Zone*."369 Its creator, Rod Serling, was perhaps the best-known writer to emerge from the Golden Age of television drama. Because his stories tackled controversial subjects (union corruption, racial prejudice), Serling faced constant battles with the censors. "Before the script goes before the cameras," he observed, "the networks, the sponsors, the ad agency men censor it so that by the time it's seen on the home screen, all the message has been squeezed out of it." Because he "simply got tired of battling" the censors, Serling turned to fantasy, creating what ultimately became *The Twilight Zone*.370 Serling penned 89 of *Zone's* 151 episodes, the majority of them involving well-crafted, offbeat stories with moralistic twists.[371] For Serling, the series was an outlet for his social conscience, enabling him to comment on the issues of the day: prejudice, nuclear war, conformity, the trial of Adolph Eichmann for Nazi war crimes.[372]

On the surface, these events, coupled with the quiz show scandal and the U-2 incident, seemed to suggest that America had turned a corner, both culturally and politically. The "innocent" decade of the '50s had ended with revelations of deceit, while the start of the '60s indicated a wake-up call—the beginning of a new, grittier time—one where America would lose its nobility and seem less angelic, a notion that would spawn the "credibility gap" that came to color the American people's attitude toward its government and institutions and the "culture war" that raged between liberals and conservatives during the latter twentieth and into the early twenty-first centuries.

Such changes, however, were slow to emerge. Eisenhower, it will be recalled, remained popular with the American people despite the U-2 incident and its disastrous impact on the Paris Summit Conference. And, in the case of the quiz show scandal, though quiz show rigging was criminalized as a result, there didn't seem to be much else changed regarding television. Jack Gould noted:

> The scandal caused no lasting loss in income audience size, or general acceptability of the medium. . . . In many ways the peril of TV is greater since the scandal. An industry that so simply survived a storm of such huge proportions is going to be less inclined than ever to see merit in proposed changes. The status quo has been undeniably hardened.

369 Sander, *Serling*, 151; Joel Engel, *Rod Serling: The Dreams and Nightmares of Life in The Twilight Zone* (Chicago: Contemporary Books, 1989), 186; Michael McCall, *The Best of 50s TV* (New York: Mallard Press, 1992), 78.

370 Gary Gerani with Paul H. Schulman, *Fantastic Television* (New York: Harmony Books, 1977), 35-37.

371 McCall, *The Best of 50s TV*, 78.

372 Sander, *Serling*, 151, 152, 153, 154-155, 169-170, 181-182.

The problem of television entertainment remains precisely what it was before the contestants showed up: how to make a practical case for higher standards in programming when the public will look at whatever it receives free of charge rather than turn off a set. To the solution of that dilemma of the video age the quiz scandal and its aftermath appear to have contributed nothing.[373]

The public's indifference to quiz show riggings, not the fact that the programs themselves were rigged, was the true source of concern among most social pundits. Lacking any large demand that television be reformed, the American people were content to watch another decade of run-of-the-mill offerings on the small-screen. Such indifference, though, didn't extend to other areas of national life—as demonstrated by the public's responsiveness to John F. Kennedy's call for a renewed political activism. Kent Anderson believed that the quiz scandal signified the low point of an era in American history when the apathy of the American people regarding the disreputable conduct of their leaders in various national realms suggested both the public's willingness to overlook the quiz show deception and a sense of powerlessness to correct such misconduct. Particularly infuriating was the fact that each individual punished in connection with the scandal wasn't an employee of the quiz shows but a contestant. "The image of the system protecting the powerful while prosecuting the weak was reinforced by the several perjury convictions of contestants."[374]

Meanwhile NBC's contribution to the television documentary genre, *White Paper,* began with "The U-2 Affair,"[375], the latter airing in late November 1960 so as to avoid accusations it was influencing the outcome of that year's presidential election, and a broadcast which incurred the displeasure of the President of the United States. The broadcast presented every public aspect of the U-2 incident. Among those interviewed, presidential press secretary Jim Hagerty was asked what lesson could be learned from the affair, to which Hagerty simply replied, "Don't get caught." Concluding the broadcast, NBC News correspondent Chet Huntley noted that when the same query was put to Christian Herter, the latter replied, "Not to have accidents," after which Huntley observed:

> We leave it to the American public to decide whether "Don't get caught" and "Not to have accidents" are the only lessons to be learned from the U-2. . . . This is not a matter for the history books but vitally

[373] Anderson, Television Fraud, 180.

[374] Anderson, *Television Fraud,* 180-182.

[375] Edward Bliss, Jr., *Now the News: The Story of Broadcast Journalism* (New York: Columbia University Press, 1991), 404, 392-393, 404, 405.

affects our ability to survive as a nation. In the world as it is today, we cannot afford another U-2 affair. Good night.[376]

Upon seeing the telecast, an enraged Eisenhower protested to NBC founder and chairman David Sarnoff, who said he had no prior knowledge of the report before it was broadcast; further, his son, NBC's president, would be summoned to explain the program. The elder Sarnoff would do everything he could "to correct any unpleasantness or embarrassment." As a final gesture of appeasement, NBC News would be directed to air a televised tribute to Eisenhower before his exit from the Presidency.[377]

The generation gap; the credibility gap. The cracks had already appeared—the deceits regarding the quiz shows and the U-2—but hadn't quite widened into deep fissures. The Cold War consensus that America was a shining light in a world imperiled by the Communist threat. That notion that such a supposed menace gave it a license to take whatever actions—morally repugnant though the latter might be—to uphold freedom still prevailed. Proof of this was the spy craze that swept American popular culture in the mid-1960s—a mania the U-2 incident helped start and one that became as characteristic of the '60s as television westerns were to the '50s.

Because of the U-2, Americans first became aware that there was such an organization as the CIA and that their government practiced espionage.[378] The Eisenhower Administration had conducted foreign policy on the basis that the world was divided between two camps—one good, the other evil. By the early 1960s printed stories about CIA activities were emerging. The publication of former CIA chief Allen Dulles' *The Craft of Intelligence* furnished confirmation of these stories. Dulles' work was followed by Haynes Johnson's *The Bay of Pigs* and David Wise's and Thomas B. Ross's *The Invisible Government*—the latter publications furnishing the public a greater view of CIA activities. For Americans, who found these revelations unsettling, the best way to accept them was to justify them as being necessitated by urgent circumstances.

But both the spy fun and the people's trust in their government was about to end. The cracks in the image of '50s America that began with the quiz show scandal and the U-2 incident soon widened: first there was the Kennedy assassination, which gave life to accusations of a conspiracy to kill JFK, followed by nearly weekly, erroneous reports of "success" in Vietnam, and finally, Watergate and Richard Nixon's disgrace.[379] And this was only

[376] Beschloss, Mayday, 342.

[377] Beschloss, *Mayday*, 342.

[378] Beschloss, *Mayday*, 395.

[379] Steven B. Stark, *Glued to the Set: The 60 Television Shows and Events That Made Us Who We Are Today* (New York: The Free Press, 1997), 74.

the beginning. Soon after he had taken over the Presidency from Nixon, Gerald Ford naively admitted that the CIA had participated in the ouster of the Allende government in Chile in 1973. There quickly followed another revelation—this time from *New York Times* correspondent Seymour Hersh: the CIA, in violation of its statutory authority and the American people's constitutional rights, had engaged in domestic spying, involving the use of wiretapping, burglary, surveillance, and mail intercepts.

Given the prevalence of conspiracy thinking in relation to significant events in history, it should come as no surprise that such theories came up regarding Francis Gary Powers' doomed U-2 flight of May 1, 1960. That same month, CIA officials quietly hinted to journalists that Khrushchev had been ambiguous when asserting that Powers had been knocked out of the sky by a Soviet missile at over 65,000 feet. The truth of the matter was, according to the Agency functionaries, that most likely a flameout or other malfunction had forced Powers to a lower altitude, putting him within range of Soviet military defenses.

In seeking to convince the American people that this was the truth behind the May Day incident, the American government was motivated by the fact that the main mode of delivering American nuclear weapons to an enemy in 1960, the manned bomber, lacked the capability of attaining altitudes anywhere near 65,000 feet. If the American people knew that the Russians could bring down aircraft at that altitude, they might have assumed that the U.S.S.R. could defend itself against nuclear attack. The hysteria such knowledge would generate might have been greater than that incited by *Sputnik* and almost certainly have sown up that year's presidential election for the Democrats. Moreover, when senators were examining the CIA's involvement in the U-2 incident and threatening stricter control of the Agency, the safest course might have been to shift the onus for the disaster from the CIA's failure to divine that the Soviets possessed the kind of missile capable of downing the U-2 to just plain bad luck.

Fifteen years after the May Day incident, when revelations of CIA dirty tricks were coming to light, an article by James Nathan of the University of Delaware appeared in *Military Affairs*, hinting that someone in the U.S. government, the CIA possibly, may have intentionally employed the U-2 as a means of destroying detente:

> The anomalies in the Powers case suggest that the U-2 incident may have been staged. There was the timing of his trip, the unusually long route chosen to overfly the Soviet Union, his undisguised American origins, his retrieval by and continued association with the CIA, the reluctance of Congressional committees charged with the over-

sight of such matters to ask any searching questions, and other indications that Powers had done essentially what he had been told. . . .

> The cover story was preposterous and unserious. There was the unwillingness to affix responsibility for the flight below the level of the White House . . . the loudly-repeated claim that the violation of Soviet airspace was necessary for American security and might be resumed . . . and the last-minute nuclear alert. All these "administrative failures" indicate that even if the weird flight and strange behavior of Powers was fortuitous, the U-2 presented an opportunity which may not have been unwelcomed.[380]

Would it have been in Allen Dulles' interests to undo Eisenhower's quest for detente with the Soviet Union? Even if Dulles wanted to frustrate his commander-in-chief's desire for improved Soviet–American relations, it is unlikely that the course of action he might have chosen to achieve such an objective would have brought such calamity to his Agency and lead to scrutiny of the CIA on the part of Congress. Eisenhower, for his part, could have avoided the Paris conclave by means less injurious to his and America's interests than the U-2 overflight on May Day.

Appearing on a 1975 television documentary, Selmer Nilsen, a Norwegian fisherman and convicted Soviet spy, asserted that the reason for the U-2's downing was a bomb placed in the aircraft's tail by a Soviet agent prior to the U-2's departure from Peshawar. According to Nilsen, he had surveyed the Bodo installation for Soviet intelligence and had learned about the bomb from a KGB officer in Moscow at a May 1960 party celebrating Powers' downing.

All during the U-2 program, American counterintelligence had apparently questioned Turkish broom sweepers and others working at U-2 facilities on the notion that they were spying or were seeking to sabotage the aircraft. Soviet intelligence may have played a part in downing Powers' plane through their efforts of obtaining data regarding the pilots, planes, installations and ground arrangements. Errors in American security may also have contributed to the Soviets' efforts: a supposed malfunction in sending coded radio messages to Adana on May 1, 1960, prompted a CIA man in Germany to dispatch clearance for Powers' flight via an open telephone the Russians might have been tapping, informing Moscow ahead of time when Powers was flying into Russian airspace. "But," Michael Beschloss has written, "how much that would have helped the Russians to down the plane is questionable." Given the fact that Khrushchev praised the Russian armed forces for

---

[380] Beschloss, Mayday, 357-358.

shooting down the U-2, it wasn't beyond the realm of possibility that a KGB operative would seek to bring glory to his organization by claiming that Soviet intelligence had been responsible for the downing—an idea Powers and Bissell both dismissed.[381]

The theory the Russians had advance knowledge of Powers' flight cites Lee Harvey Oswald who, as a seventeen-year-old Marine private, was assigned for a time to the U.S. naval air station at Atsugi, Japan, which was serving as a U-2 base. In October 1959, just after being released from the Marine Corps, Oswald went to the Soviet Union, where he doubtless revealed his knowledge about radar, his specialty in the service, and Atsugi. While it is true that Atsugi was a staging area for U-2 missions, the U-2 section there was off-limits to those in no way involved with the program, and Oswald most likely never breached U-2 security at the base. After studying an Oswald connection to the U-2, American intelligence reached the conclusion that he couldn't have compromised the May Day flight. Additionally, the U-2s stationed at Atsugi didn't fly over Soviet territory.

Victor Sheymov, a Soviet KGB communications expert who defected to the United States in 1980, contended a friend, a weapons specialist for the Soviet Air Force, was designated to bring down a U-2. This individual, in Sheymov's account, declared that the Soviets "knew the exact flight plan of every U-2 invading Soviet airspace several days in advance." Sheymov's friend added:

> We figured that the Soviet source leaking the flight information not only knew the flight plan but was also able to influence them. On the occasion the source fixed things so that one of the flights, scheduled for a major Soviet holiday, required the pilot to fly within reach of the ground-to-air missiles and execute a turn—banking left at precisely the necessary point. A perfect setup.[382]

Neither in his book, in which he made this declaration, or in conversations with Norman Polmar, who wrote a history of the U-2, did Sheymov provide additional information as to the identity of the one who made this assertion. Polmar was skeptical of Sheymov's story: "It is highly unlikely that the Soviets could have had a highly placed intelligence source able to provide virtually last-minute details of U-2 flights. Knowledge of other Soviets in the U.S. intelligence community - John A. Walker and his spy ring and National Security Agency (NSA) traitor Ronald Pelton, indicate that such spies conveying virtually real-time intelligence to Moscow was almost impossible."

---

[381] Beschloss, *Mayday*, 355-359.
[382] Polmar, Spyplane, 147.

The most probable "source," in Polmar's view, was Soviet communications intercepts, perhaps rooted in information related to U-2 operations passed to Soviet intelligence by a pair of Americans—William Martin and Benson Mitchell. Cryptography specialists with the NSA, Martin and Mitchell traveled to Cuba in December 1959; there, in violation of NSA regulations, the pair likely met with Soviet officials. This raises the question: did they give the Soviets information concerning the method by which last-minute orders and other data were transmitted to U-2 installations, thus allowing the Soviets to intercept the spy flights? "Unlikely," Polmar feels, "but not beyond the realm of possibility." Though the NSA has never disclosed the magnitude of Martin and Mitchell's involvement with the U-2, there remains, in Polmar's view, a remote possibility that they might have given communications intercept secrets to the Soviets during their time in Cuba.

Another source of information concerning prior Soviet knowledge of U-2 flights, this time furnishing some information as to where this knowledge originated, was Colonel Alexander Orlov, a former Soviet air defense officer, who wrote that in the aftermath of the failure to down the April 9, 1960, U-2 incursion:

> The Soviet leadership appointed a commission . . . to investigate the reasons for the failure of the Air Defense forces to move successfully against the aircraft that had violated Soviet airspace for so many hours. The investigation uncovered serious shortcomings in air combat training and in command and control of Air Defense and Air Force personnel and weapons systems. Many omissions were discovered in the operation of advanced radio equipment. In particular, information related to this reconnaissance activity had been acquired by Soviet communications interception facilities ... but the information was not reported to the command elements because of a number of chance happenings.[383]

Whatever the reason Francis Gary Powers' U-2 fell onto Soviet territory in 1960, the truth may never be known.[384] Simultaneous with the loss of trust in government and institutions as a result of the Credibility Gap was the growing disdain for authority. Accompanying this growing sense of skepticism about the fidelity of various American institutions was a burgeoning culture of scandal—one that arguably traced back to the quiz show frauds of the '50s and had multiplied in the ensuing years to the point where the majority of Americans—and the media—now take it for granted that lying and dishonesty are a standard fact of life.

---

[383] Polmar, Spyplane, 148.
[384] Beschloss, Mayday, 363.

In this modern scandal culture, shame doesn't carry the same stigma it used to. Looking back on the quiz show scandal, John Leo noted: "What really makes this period seem distant isn't innocence, but the moral outrage that all this lying provoked. Charles Van Doren may not have been our most egregious public sinner, but he was certainly the last one to lead a long life of shame and ignominy for what he did."[385] This is a far-cry from modern culture: today someone like Charles Van Doren might be celebrated—and do quite well as a result. He would become a celebrity precisely because he did something infamous without being penalized for it.[386]

Many factors explain this. Since Vietnam and Watergate, people have come to take for granted that every aspect of our society and institutions are corrupt and that dishonesty is the norm: public officials act in perfidious ways because that's how the system works and nothing can be done to change it for the better. Secondly, we live in a culture that idolizes scandal. If a public figure or a celebrity commits a foul deed, the public eagerly latches onto it. Part of this certainly has to do with the ambivalence the masses feel toward their idols. We like to hoist them to heights of greatness, then delight in knocking them off their pedestals—just a reminder that we still envy and resent the successful for their achievements. It can make "the little people" feel better about their ordinary lot in life.

There is also the role of the media. The fact that several high-level correspondents were aware of the U-2's existence and its purpose before the Francis Gary Powers' episode made it public knowledge indicates the degree of credibility journalists gave the federal government during the 1950s and their willingness to believe what the government told them. Patriotism may have been a factor here as well—this was during the Cold War: the Russians were the enemy and any course of action we did to defeat their communist aims was necessary and all for the good. The deceptions arising from Vietnam and Watergate led to a more skeptical press corps, one which not only distrusted the government's version of events but no longer respected the privacy of Presidents and other political figures.

This sense of skepticism came to full flower after Vietnam and Watergate but its roots lay earlier in the quiz show scandal and the U-2 incident. It was the beginning of America's loss of innocence—the consequences of which we still have yet to recover from more than half a century later.

---

[385] Quoted in James B. Twitchell, *For Shame: The Loss of Common Decency in American Culture* (New York: St. Martin's Press, 1997), 94.
[386] *Ibid.*, 94-95.

Bibliography

Primary Sources

ABC News, American Broadcasting Companies, Inc., 1985.

Aldrich, David. "Are TV Quiz Shows Fixed?" *Look* 20 August 1957. 45-47.

The American Experience: "The Quiz Show Scandal," www.pbs.org/wgbh/amex/ Quizshow/filmmore/transcript/index.html. 5 January 2007.

The American Experience: "The Quiz Show Scandal"/www.pbs.org/wgbh/amex/ Quizshow/peopleevents/pande05.html 5 November 2007.

"The Big Fix," http://www.time.com/time/magazine/article 10,9171,869307,00. Html 18 February 2008.

"The Big Money," www.time.com/time/printout/0,8816,82434700.html 17 February 2008.

CIA: Hollywood Spyteck, Discovery Communications, Inc., 2000.

"Fort Knox or Bust?" www.time.com/time/printout/0,8816,807567,00.html 17 February 2008.

"How It Was Done," www.time.com/time/magazine/article/0,9171,811467,00. Html 18 February 2008.

"Human Almanac," www.time.com/time/printout/0,8816,809214,00. Html 18 February 2008.

"'A Make-Believe World': Contestants Testify to Deceptive Quiz Show Practices." http://historymatters.gmw.edu/d/6555 30 October 2007.

"Moderation," www.time.com/time/printout/0,8816,891543.00 html 6 April 2008.

The 9/11 Conspiracies: Fact or Fiction, The History Channel, January 6, 2008.

"Semper Chow," www.time.com/time/printout/0,8816,807608,00.html 2 February 2008.

"The $60 Million Question," www.time.com/time/magazine/article/0,9171, 824828,00.html 18 February 2008.

"'A Sop to the Public at Large': Contestant Herbert Stempel Exposes Contrivances In a 1950s Television Quiz Show," historymatters.gmu.edu/d/6565 30 October 2007.

"'The Truth Is the Only Thing with Which a Man Can Live': Quiz Show Contestant Charles Van Doren Publicly Confesses to Deceiving His Television Audience," Historymatters.gmu.edu/d/6566 30 October 2007.

Van Doren, Charles. "All the Answers: The Quiz-Show Scandals—and the Aftermath," www.newyorker.com/reporting /2008/07/28/080728 fa_fact_ vandoren?printable=true 5 December 2008. "The Wizard of Quiz," February 11, 1957, www.time.com/printout/0,8816,809055, 00.html 18 February 2008.

"Van Doren & Beyond," www.time.com/time/magazine/article/0,9171, 811467,00.Html 18 February 2008.

www.pbs.org/wgbh/amex/quizshow/peopleevents/pande 04. Html.

www.pbs.org/wgbh/amex/quizshow/peoplevents/pande 01.html 5 November 2007.

Books

Altschuler, Glenn C. *All Shook Up: How Rock'n'Roll Changed America* New York: Oxford University Press, 2003.

Ambrose, Stephen E., with Richard H. Immerman. *Ike's Spies: Eisenhower and the Espionage Establishment* Garden City, New York: Doubleday & Company, Inc., 1981.

_____, *Eisenhower. Volume II: The President* New York: Simon and Schuster, 1984.

_____, *Nixon: The Education of a Politician 1913-1962* New York: Simon and Schuster, 1987.

Anderson, Kent. *Television Fraud: The History and Implications of the Quiz Show Scandals* Westport, Connecticut: Greenwood Press, 1978.

Andrew, Christopher. *For the President's Eyes Only: Secret Intelligence and the American Presidency from Washington to Bush* New York: HarperCollins Publishers, 1995.

Barnouw, Erik. *The Image Empire: A History of Broadcasting in the United States From 1953* New York: Oxford University Press, 1970.

Bergreen, Lawrence. *Look Now, Pay Later: The Rise of Network Broadcasting* Doubleday & Company, Inc., 1980.

Beschloss, Michael R. *Mayday: Eisenhower, Khrushchev and the U-2 Affair* New York: Harper & Row, Publishers. 1986.

_____, *The Crisis Years: Kennedy and Khrushchev 1960-1963* New York: HarperCollins Publishers. 1991.

Bliss, Edward, Jr. *Now the News: The Story of Broadcast Journalism* New York: Columbia University Press, 1991.

Brodie, Fawn M. *Richard Nixon: The Shaping of His Character* New York: W. W. Norton & Company, 1981.

Brugioni, Dino A. *Eyeball to Eyeball: The Inside Story of the Cuban Missile Crisis* New York: Random House, 1990, 1991.

Brzezinski, Matthew. *Red Moon Rising: Sputnik and the Hidden Rivalries that Ignited the Space Age* New York: Time Books, 2007.

Carlson, Peter. *K Blows Top: A Cold War Comic Interlude Starring Nikita Khrushchev, America's Most Unlikely Tourist* New York: PublicAffairs, 2009.

Carroll, Peter N. *It Seemed Like Nothing Happened: The Tragedy and Promise Of America in the 1970s* New York: Holt, Rinehart and Winston, 1984.

Castleman, Harry and Walter J. Podrazik. *Watching TV: Four Decades of American Television* New York: McGraw-Hill Book Company, 1982.

Clark, Dick and Richard Robinson. *Rock, Roll & Remember* (New York: Thomas Y. Crowell Company, 1976.

Clarke, Arthur C. and the Editors of Time-Life Books. *Life Science Library: Man And Space* New York: Time-Life Books, 1968.

Croker, Richard. *The Boomer Century, 1946-2046. How America's Most Influential Generation Changed Everything* New York: Springboard Press, 2007.

D'Antonio, Michael. *A Ball, A Dog and a Monkey. 1957—The Space Race Begins* New York: Simon & Schuster, 2007.

Diggins, John Patrick. *The Proud Decades: American in War and in Peace 1941-1960* New York: W. W. Norton & Company, 1988.

The Editors of Time-Life Books. *This Fabulous Century. Volume VI: 1950-1960* New York: Time, Inc., 1970.

Eisenhower, Dwight D. *The White House Years. Mandate for Change, 1953-1956* Garden City, New York: Doubleday & Company, Inc., 1963.

_____, *Waging Peace—The White House Years, A Personal Account 1956-1961* Garden City, New York: Doubleday & Company, Inc. 1965.

Engel, Joel. *Rod Serling: The Dreams and Nightmares of Life in The Twilight Zone* Chicago: Contemporary Books, 1989.

Friendly, Fred W. *Due to Circumstances Beyond Our Control* New York: Random House, 1967.

Fursenko, Aleksandr and Timothy Naftali. *Khrushchev's Cold War: The Inside Story of an American Adversary* New York: W.W. Norton and Company, 2006.

Gates, Gary Paul. *Air Time: The Inside Story of CBS News* (New York: Harper & Row, Publishers, 1978.

Gerani, Gary with Paul H. Schulman. *Fantastic Television* New York: Harmony Books, 1977.

Goldman, Eric F. *The Crucial Decade—And After. America, 1945-1960* New York: Vintage Books, 1956, 1960.

Goodwin, Richard N. *Remembering America: A Voice from the Sixties* Boston: Little, Brown and Company, 1988.

Halberstam, David. *The Fifties* New York: Villard Books, 1993.

Hitchcock, William I. *The Age of Eisenhower: America and the World in the 1950s* New York: Simon & Schuster, 2018

Hoerschelmann. Olaf. *Rules of the Game: Quiz Shows and American Culture* Albany, New York: State University of New York Press, 2000.

Isaacs, Jeremy and Taylor Downing. *Cold War: An Illustrated History, 1945-1991* Boston: Little, Brown and Company, 1998.

Khrushchev, Nikita. *Khrushchev Remembers: The Last Testament* Translated and Edited by Strobe Talbott Boston: Little, Brown and Company, 1974.

Kisseloff, Jeff. *The Box: An Oral History of Television, 1920-1961* New York: Viking, 1995.

LaFeber, Walter. *The American Age: United States Foreign Policy at Home and Abroad since 1750* New York: W. W. Norton & Company, 1989.

Leuchtenburg, William E. and the Editors of Time-Life Books, *The Life History of The United States. Volume 12: From 1945. The Age of Change* Alexandria, Virginia: Time-Life Books, 1977, 1974, 1964.

Lytle, Mark Hamilton. *America's Uncivil Wars: The Sixties Era from Elvis to the Fall of Richard Nixon* New York: Oxford University Press, 2006.

McCall, Michael. *The Best of 50s TV* New York: Mallard Press, 1992. *The Best of 60s TV* New York: Mallard Press, 1992.

MacDonald, J. Fred. *Television and the Red Menace: The Video Road to Vietnam* New York: Praeger Publishers, 1985

_____, *Who Shot the Sheriff? The Rise and Fall of the Television Western* New York: Praeger Publishers, 1987.

_____, *One Nation Under Television: The Rise and Decline of Network TV* New York: Pantheon Books, 1990.

McDougall, Walter A. ...*The Heavens and the Earth: A Political History of the Space Age* (New York: Basic Books, Inc., 1985.

Manchester, William. *The Glory and the Dream: A Narrative History of America, 1932-1972* New York: Bantam Press, 1975.

Mansfield, John M. *Man on the Moon* New York: Stein and Day, 1969.

Marling, Karal Ann. *As Seen on TV: The Visual Culture of Everyday Life in the 1950s* Cambridge, Massachusetts: Harvard University Press, 1994.

Metz, Robert. *CBS: Reflections in a Blood-shot Eye* Chicago: Playboy Press, 1975.

Miller, Douglas T. and Marion Nowak. *The Fifties: The Way We Really Were* Garden City, New York: Doubleday & Company, Inc., 1975, 1977.

Nixon, Richard M. *Six Crises* Garden City, New York: Doubleday & Company, Inc., 1962.

_____, *RN: The Memoirs of Richard Nixon* New York: Grosset & Dunlap, 1978.

O'Neill, William L. *American High: The Years of Confidence, 1945-1960* New York: The Free Press, 1986.

O'Toole, G.J.A. *Honorable Treachery: A History of U.S. Intelligence, Espionage, And Covert Action from the American Revolution to the CIA* New York: The Atlantic Monthly Press, 1991.

Oakley, J. Ronald. *God's Country: America in the Fifties* New York: Dembner Books, 1986.

Pach, Chester J. Jr. and Elmo Richardson. *The Presidency of Dwight D. Eisenhower, Revised Edition* Lawrence, Kansas: The University Press of Kansas, 1991.

Parmet, Herbert S. *Eisenhower and the American Crusades* (New York: The Macmillan Company, 1972.

Patterson, James T. *Grand Expectations: The United States, 1945-1974* New York: Oxford University Press, 1996.

_____, *Restless Giant: The United States from Watergate to Bush v. Gore* New York: Oxford University Press, 2005.

Persico, Joseph E. *Edward R. Murrow: An American Original* New York: McGraw-Hill Publishing Company, 1988.

Perret, Geoffrey. *Eisenhower* New York: Random House, 1999.

Polmar, Norman. *Spyplane: The U-2 History Declassified* Osceola, WI: MBI Publishing Company, 2001.

Powers, Francis Gary, with Curt Gentry. *Operation Overflight* New York: Holt, Rinehart and Winston, 1970.

Rich, Ben R. and Leo Janos. *Skunk Works: A Personal Memoir of My Years at Lockheed* Boston: Little, Brown and Company, 1994.

Sander, Gordon F. *Serling: The Rise and Twilight of Television's Last Angry Man* New York: Dutton, 1992.

Sann, Paul. *Fads, Follies and Delusions of the American People* New York: Bonanza Books, 1967.

Sayre, Nora. *Running Time: Films of the Cold War* New York: The Dial Press, 1982.

Sharnik, John. *Inside the Cold War: An Oral History* New York: Arbor House, 1987.

Solberg, Carl. *Riding High: America in the Cold War* New York: Mason & Lipscomb Publishers, 1973.

Stark, Steven B. *Glued to the Set: The 60 Television Shows and Events That Made Us Who We Are Today* New York: The Free Press, 1997.

Stone, Joseph and Tim Yohn. *Prime Time and Misdemeanors: Investigating the 1950s TV Quiz Scandal—The D.A.'S Account* New Brunswick, New Jersey: Rutgers University Press, 1992.

Szatmary, David P. *Rockin' In Time: A Social History of Rock-and-Roll Second Edition* Englewood Cliffs, New Jersey: Prentice Hall, 1991, 1987.

Taubman, Philip. *Secret Empire: Eisenhower, the CIA, and the Hidden History of America's Space Espionage* New York: Simon & Schuster, 2003.

Tedlow, Richard S. *Giants of Enterprise: Seven Business Innovators and the Empires They Built* New York: Harper Business, 2001.

Tobler, John and Pete Frame. *Rock'n'Roll: The First 25 Years* New York: Exeter Books, 1980.

Twitchell, James B. *For Shame: The Loss of Common Decency in American Culture* New York: St. Martin's Press, 1997.

Walker, Martin. *The Cold War: A History* New York: Henry Holt and Company, 1994.

Wallmann, Jeffrey. *The Western: Parables of the American Dream* Lubbock, Texas: Texas Tech University Press, 1999.

Watson, Mary Ann. *The Expanding Vista: American Television in the Kennedy Years* New York: Oxford University Press, 1990.

Weisberger, Bernard A. *Cold War, Cold Peace: The United States and Russia since 1945* New York: American Heritage Publishing Co., Inc., 1984.

Whitfield, Stephen J. *The Culture of the Cold War* Baltimore: The Johns Hopkins University Press, 1991.

Wise, David. *The Politics of Lying: Government Deception, Secrecy, and Power* New York: Random House, 1973.

INDEX

68, 98, 142, 164, 168, 171, 178, 179, 195, 197
Dulles, John Foster, 26, 40, 42, 70, 89, 96

E

Eden, Anthony, 34
Eisenhower, Dwight D., 1, 15, 16, 25-27, 69, 87-90, 140, 153, 159, 163, 166, 203, 205
Eisenhower, stroke (1957), 75
Enright, Daniel, 45, 48
Entertainment Productions, Incorporated (EPI), 10
Ericson, Bob, 143
Evans, Bergen, 9
Explorer I, 77

F

Fadiman, Clifton, 6, 7, 53, 54
Falke, Kirsten, 117, 118
Federal Communications Commission (FCC), 6, 124
Felsher, Howard Davis, 117
Fox, Sonny, 11
Franklin, Art, 110, 114
Freed, Alan, 136
Freedman, Albert, 52, 54, 115, 116, 118, 121, 132
Friendly, Fred, 10, 204
Fulbright, J. William, 164

G

Gardner, Trevor, 23, 24
Garroway, Dave, 111, 130
Garst, Roswell, 105
Gelman, Dave, 58
Geneva, "spirit of", 29, 37, 108
Geneva Summit (1955), 15, 26, 29, 108
Goodpaster, Andrew, 144
Goodwin, Richard N., 124, 125, 204
Gould, Jack, 9, 109, 193
Gromyko, Andrei, 89, 163
Gunsmoke, 5

H

Hagerty, James, 75, 77, 166, 194

Halberstam, David, 8, 10, 13, 32, 47, 51, 52, 54, 56, 57, 59, 61, 71, 75-77, 126, 143, 145, 173, 189, 204
Harris, Oren, 123, 124, 126-128, 132-136, 182, 183, 185, 187, 190
Herter, Christian, 153, 164, 194
Hilgemeier, Ed, 112, 115
Hillman, Antoinette Dubarry, 126
Hitchcock, William I., 80, 204
Hogan, Frank S., 113, 182
Howdy Doody, 192
Hughes, Emmet, 18

I

I Love Lucy, 12, 57
Information, Please, 6, 7
Intercontinental ballistic missile (ICBM), 20
Intermediate range ballistic missile (IRBM), 20
International Geophysical Year (IGY), 68

J

Jackson, C.D., 18, 26
Jackson, Reverend Charles E. (Stoney) Jr., 111
Johnny Carson Show, 5
Johnson, Kelly, 23, 143, 178
Johnson, Lyndon B., 79
Joiner, Ernie L., 30
Juvenile Jury, 46

K

Kapustin Yar, 22, 23, 42
Kennan, George F., 82, 164
Khrushchev, Nikita, 1, 15, 37, 74, 85, 104, 106, 172, 203, 204
Killian, James F., 20
"Killian Report", 20
Kintner, E. Robert, 129
Kistiakowsky, George, 144
Knutson, Marty, 37
Koplin, Mert, 133
Koplin, Merton, 9, 11, 187
Korolyov, Sergei, 72
Kozlov, Frol, 90
Krainin, Julian, 189
Kyser, Kay, 7

Printed in the United States
By Bookmasters